Temporary Agency Work in the European Union and the United States

BULLETIN OF COMPARATIVE LABOUR RELATIONS – 82

Temporary Agency Work in the European Union and the United States

Editor

Roger Blanpain

Guest Editor

Frank Hendrickx

Contributors

Chris Engels
Alvin Goldman
Frank Hendrickx
Mijke Houwerzijl
Fons Leroy
Alan Neal
Birgitta Nyström
Andrzej Marian Świątkowski
Piet Van den Bergh
Manfred Weiss
Marcin Wujczyk

Published by:
Kluwer Law International
PO Box 316
2400 AH Alphen aan den Rijn
The Netherlands
Website: www.kluwerlaw.com

Sold and distributed in North, Central and South America by:
Aspen Publishers, Inc.
7201 McKinney Circle
Frederick, MD 21704
United States of America
Email: customer.service@aspenpublishers.com

Sold and distributed in all other countries by:
Turpin Distribution Services Ltd
Stratton Business Park
Pegasus Drive, Biggleswade
Bedfordshire SG18 8TQ
United Kingdom
Email: kluwerlaw@turpin-distribution.com

Printed on acid-free paper.

ISBN 978-90-411-4769-1

© 2013 Kluwer Law International BV, The Netherlands

DISCLAIMER: The material in this publication is in the nature of general comment only. It is not offered as advice on any particular matter and should not be taken as such. The authors expressly disclaim all liability to any person with regard to anything done or omitted to be done, and with respect to the consequences of anything done or omitted to be done wholly or partly in reliance on the basis of any matter contained in this volume without first obtaining professional advice regarding the particular facts and circumstances at issue. Any and all opinions expressed herein are those of the particular author, they are not necessarily those of the publisher of this volume and they do not reflect the views of any institution or organization.

All rights reserved. No part of this publication may be reproduced, stored in a retrieval system, or transmitted in any form or by any means, electronic, mechanical, photocopying, recording, or otherwise, without written permission from the publisher.

Permission to use this content must be obtained from the copyright owner. Please apply to: Permissions Department, Wolters Kluwer Legal, 76 Ninth Avenue, 7th Floor, New York, NY 10011-5201, USA. Email: permissions@kluwerlaw.com

Printed and Bound by CPI Group (UK) Ltd, Croydon, CR0 4YY.

Summary of Contents

Notes on Contributors	xv
Preface	xvii
CHAPTER 1 Regulating Temporary Work in the European Union: The Agency Directive *Chris Engels*	1
CHAPTER 2 Regulating Temporary Work: Protection of the National Labour Market or the Individual Worker? *Andrzej Marian Świątkowski*	29
CHAPTER 3 Regulating Temporary Work in the United States *Alvin Goldman*	51
CHAPTER 4 Public-Private Partnerships on Temporary Work: The Case of Flanders *Fons Leroy*	79
CHAPTER 5 Regulating Temporary Work in Belgium *Frank Hendrickx & Piet Van den Bergh*	91
CHAPTER 6 Regulating Temporary Work in Germany *Manfred Weiss*	113
CHAPTER 7 Regulating Temporary Work in the Netherlands *Mijke Houwerzijl*	125

CHAPTER 8
Regulating Temporary Work in Poland
Andrzej Marian Świątkowski & Marcin Wujczyk   145

CHAPTER 9
Regulating Temporary Work in Sweden
Birgitta Nyström   159

CHAPTER 10
Regulating Temporary Work in the United Kingdom
Alan Neal   179

Table of Contents

Notes on Contributors   xv

Preface   xvii

CHAPTER 1
Regulating Temporary Work in the European Union: The Agency Directive
Chris Engels   1

§1.01	General Introduction			1
§1.02	Directive 91/383/EEC of 25 June 1991: Safety and Health at Work			1
	[A]	Introduction		1
	[B]	Definition: Scope		2
		[1]	Kind of Working Relationship	2
		[2]	Possible Restriction of Scope of the Work to Be Performed	2
	[C]	Rights of the Temporary Worker		3
		[1]	Equal Treatment with Respect to Health and Safety	3
		[2]	Right to the Appropriate Job Preparation: Information and Training	3
	[D]	Provision of Information by the User to the Temporary Work Agency		4
§1.03	Directive 2008/104/EC of 19 November 2008: Temporary Agency Work			4
	[A]	Introduction		4
	[B]	Scope		5
		[1]	Kind of Working Relationship: Parties Involved	5
			[a] Employment Contract or Relationship	5
			[b] Worker	6
			[c] Temporary Work Agency as Employer	7
			[d] User Undertaking, Including Public Undertaking	8
		[2]	Potential Exclusion from the Scope	10
		[3]	Territorial Scope: Internal National Situation	10

	[C]	Restrictions or Prohibitions on the Use of Temporary Agency Work			11
		[1]	Principle of Acceptable Restrictions and Prohibitions		11
		[2]	Evaluation: Abolition of Restrictions		12
			[a]	Evaluation Process	12
			[b]	Duty to Abolish Unjustified Restriction	13
	[D]	Rights of Temporary Work Agency Workers			14
		[1]	Equal Treatment with Respect to Basic Working and Employment Conditions		14
			[a]	Principle	14
			[b]	Possible Derogations	16
				[i] Pay Derogation	16
				[ii] Derogation by the Social Partners Respecting the Overall Protection of Temporary Agency Workers	16
				[iii] Derogation by the Member States Respecting an *Adequate* Level of Protection of the Temporary Agency Worker	17
				[iv] Prevention of Misuse	18
		[2]	Access to Employment, Collective Facilities and Vocational Training		19
			[a]	Access to Employment	19
				[i] Information Access	19
				[ii] Restrictive Clauses	19
				[iii] Fees	20
			[b]	Access to Collective Facilities	20
				[i] At the User Undertaking	20
				[ii] At the Temporary Work Agency	21
				[iii] Access to Training	21
		[3]	The Right to Be Taken into Account for Determining Threshold Levels for Employee Representative Bodies		21
			[a]	At the Temporary Work Agency	21
			[b]	At the User Undertaking	22
		[4]	Rights of the User Undertaking Workers		22
			[a]	Right to Count in the Temporary Workers	22
			[b]	Information to Workers' Representatives	22
§1.04	Other Provisions				23
	[A]	No State Monopolies			23
	[B]	Freedom of Services			24
		[1]	Posting Directive		24
		[2]	Services Directive		24
		[3]	Freedom to Provide Services		24

Table of Contents

	[C]	Acquired Rights Directive	25
		[1] Transfer of a Temporary Work Agency or Part of It: Application of the Transfer Directive	25
		[2] Transfer of the User Undertaking or Part of It: Protection of the Temporary Agency Worker Working at the User Undertaking or Part of It	26
§1.05		Concluding Remarks	27

CHAPTER 2
Regulating Temporary Work: Protection of the National Labour Market or the Individual Worker?
Andrzej Marian Świątkowski   29

§2.01	Introduction	29
§2.02	Social and Economic Context of EU Laws on Temporary Work	36
§2.03	Compliance of National Labour Laws on Employment with the Standards Established by Directive 2008/104/EC	45
§2.04	Final Conclusions	48

CHAPTER 3
Regulating Temporary Work in the United States
Alvin Goldman   51

§3.01	Law		56
	[A]	Collective Bargaining and Collective Representation	57
	[B]	Minimum Wage and Overtime Pay Law	61
	[C]	Migrant and Seasonal Farm Labourers	63
	[D]	Employment Discrimination	64
	[E]	Pension, Disability and Health Care Insurance	64
	[F]	Family and Medical Leave Act	66
	[G]	Occupational Safety and Health	67
	[H]	Workers Compensation	68
	[I]	Unemployment Insurance	71
	[J]	Worker Adjustment and Retraining Act	74
	[K]	Regulation of Temporary Hiring Agents and Agencies	74
	[L]	Other Laws	75
§3.02	Conclusions		76

CHAPTER 4
Public-Private Partnerships on Temporary Work: The Case of Flanders
Fons Leroy   79

§4.01	Regionalization in 1980	79
§4.02	'Weer Werk' (Back to Work)	80

§4.03	Forerunners of the ILO Convention		80
§4.04	New Impulse		81
§4.05	Independence for T-interim		81
§4.06	Instant A		82
§4.07	Building Bridges		83
§4.08	Temporary Agencies as a Commercial Sector in Their Own Right		83
§4.09	Service Vouchers		83
§4.10	Temp Agencies Going Strong		84
§4.11	Collaboration between VDAB and Temp Agencies: A New Lease of Life		84
§4.12	Zooming in on a Diverse Collaboration		85
§4.13	CERTO		85
§4.14	Youth Work Plan		86
§4.15	Sea Ports		86
§4.16	Training for Temp Workers		87
§4.17	In-House Temp Agency at the VDAB Competency Centre		87
§4.18	Interregional Mobility		87
§4.19	High-Profile Jobseekers		87
§4.20	Meet & Greet, Hands On, Learning Exchange		88
§4.21	Temp Agencies and the VDAB: Every Day Life		88
§4.22	Conclusion		89

CHAPTER 5
Regulating Temporary Work in Belgium
Frank Hendrickx & Piet Van den Bergh   91

§5.01	General Introduction			91
§5.02	Temporary Work			93
	[A]	Notion		93
	[B]	Cases in Which Temporary Work Is Allowed		93
		[1]	Replacement of a Permanent Employee	93
			[a] Temporary Work Without Interference of a Temporary Work Agency	94
			[i] Procedure	94
			[ii] Duration	95
			[b] Temporary Work Through a Temporary Work Agency	95
			[i] Procedure	95
			[ii] Duration	96
		[2]	Temporary Increase of the Workload	96
			[a] Temporary Work Without Interference of a Temporary Work Agency	97
			[b] Temporary Work Through a Temporary Work Agency	97
		[3]	Exceptional Work	97

		[4] Recruitment	98
	[C]	Cases in Which Temporary Work Is Prohibited	100
§5.03	The Temporary Worker		100
	[A]	Legal Qualification Relationship Worker-Agency	100
		[1] Object and Nature of the Employment Contract	101
		[2] Form of the Employment Contract	101
		[3] Trial Clause	101
		[4] Contents of the Employment Contract	102
	[B]	Remuneration, Seniority and Social Advantages	102
	[C]	Termination of the Contract	103
	[D]	Employment with the User	104
§5.04	The Temporary Work Agency		104
	[A]	Licensing	105
		[1] Flemish Region	105
		[2] Walloon Region	107
		[3] Brussels Region	107
	[B]	The Agency as an Employer	108
§5.05	The User		108
	[A]	The Relationship User: Temporary Work Agency	108
	[B]	The Relationship User: Temporary Worker	109
		[1] Labour Protection and Collective Facilities	109
		[2] Temporary Nature of the Relationship	110
		[3] Representation of Temporary Agency Workers	110
§5.06	Collective Labour Relations Aspects		111
§5.07	The Role of the Government		111
§5.08	Directive 2008/104 and Conclusion		112

CHAPTER 6
Regulating Temporary Work in Germany
Manfred Weiss 113

§6.01	Introduction		113
§6.02	The Situation before the Transposition of the Directive		114
	[A]	The Situation between 1972 until the End of 2002	114
		[1] Licensing	114
		[2] The Employment Relationship	116
		[3] The Relationship to the User	116
	[B]	The Situation since 2003 Up to the Transposition of the Directive	117
		[1] Deregulation	117
		[2] Equal Treatment	118
		[3] Collective Bargaining	118
§6.03	Innovations Introduced by the Transposition of the Directive		119
	[A]	Scope of Application	119

	[B]	Period of Assignment to a User Company	120
	[C]	Equal Treatment	120
	[D]	Minimum Wage	121
	[E]	Additional Information and Access to Collective Facilities	122
§6.04	Conclusion		122

CHAPTER 7
Regulating Temporary Work in the Netherlands
Mijke Houwerzijl 125

§7.01	Approach and Structure	125
§7.02	TAW as a Means of Achieving Flexicurity	125
§7.03	TAW in the Context of Cross-Border Service Provision within the EU	127
§7.04	The Evolution of Temporary Agency Work in the Netherlands	129
§7.05	Current Statutory Framework of TAW in the Netherlands	131
§7.06	Collective Labour Agreements in the TAW Sector	133
§7.07	Equal Treatment Clause in Law and Collective Agreements	135
§7.08	Cross-Border Supply of Agency Workers	137
§7.09	Enforcement of CLA and Legislation: Achilles Heel	138
§7.10	Final Remarks	141

CHAPTER 8
Regulating Temporary Work in Poland
Andrzej Marian Świątkowski & Marcin Wujczyk 145

§8.01	Introductory Note			145
§8.02	Temporary Work			147
	[A]	Notion of Temporary Work		147
	[B]	Temporary Work Through TAW		147
§8.03	The Temporary Worker (TW)			148
	[A]	Legal Qualifications Relationship Worker: Agency		148
		[1]	Object and Nature of the Employment Contract	149
		[2]	Form of the Employment Contract	149
		[3]	Contents of the Employment Contract	149
	[B]	Equal Treatment and Holiday Leave		150
	[C]	Termination of the Contract		152
	[D]	Employment with the User Employer		152
§8.04	The Temporary Agency Work (TAW)			152
	[A]	Establishing TAW		152
	[B]	Obligations of TAW as an Entrepreneur		153
	[C]	Removal from the Register		154
	[D]	The Agency as an Employer		154
§8.05	The User Employer			155

	[A]	The Relationship User Employer: TAW	155
	[B]	The Relationship User Employer: TW	156
§8.06	Collective Labour Relations Aspects		156
§8.07	The Role of the Government		157

CHAPTER 9
Regulating Temporary Work in Sweden
Birgitta Nyström 159

§9.01	Introduction		159
§9.02	Temporary Agency Work in Sweden		160
	[A]	Background	160
		[1] Temporary Agency Work: Illegal	160
		[2] Deregulation	161
	[B]	Agency Work in Practice	162
	[C]	The Legislative Framework	163
	[D]	The Social Partners and Collective Agreements	167
§9.03	The 2012 Agency Work Act		170
	[A]	The Equal Treatment Principle in Detail	172
	[B]	Posted Temporary Agency Workers	173
	[C]	Prohibitions and Restrictions	175
§9.04	Comments and Conclusions		176

CHAPTER 10
Regulating Temporary Work in the United Kingdom
Alan Neal 179

§10.01	The Nature of the Beast	179
§10.02	Attitudes to Temporary Agency Work	182
§10.03	Regulating the Labour Supplier Side	185
§10.04	Regulating the Commercial Relationship between Labour Supplier and End-User	190
§10.05	Safeguarding the Worker: In Search of 'the Employer'	192
§10.06	Impact of the EU Directive on Temporary Work	197
§10.07	Temporary Agency Working in Times of Economic Crisis	202

Notes on Contributors

Chris Engels, Professor of labour law at the Institute for Labour Law, University of Leuven (Belgium) and senior partner at *Claeys& Engels*.

Alvin Goldman, Professor Emeritus, University of Kentucky College of Law (United States).

Frank Hendrickx, Professor of labour law at the Institute for Labour Law, University of Leuven (Belgium) and part-time Professor of European labour law at ReflecT, Tilburg University (The Netherlands).

Mijke Houwerzijl, Professor of labour law at the Department of Social Law and Social Policy, Tilburg University en Professor of European and comparative labour law,University of Groningen (The Netherlands).

Fons Leroy, CEO of VDAB, the Flemish Public Employment Service (Belgium).

Alan Neal, Professor of Law in the University of Warwick (United Kingdom) and Convenor of the European Association of Labour Court Judges.

Birgitta Nyström, Professor of Private Law at the University of Lund (Sweden). At the moment she has the national chair in labour law, especially EU labour law and international labour law in the Swedish and Nordicperspectives.

Andrzej Świątkowski, Jean Monnet Professor of European labour law and social security. Head of Chair of Labour Law and Social Policy, Faculty of Law and Administration, Jagiellonian University, Krakow (Poland). He is Member and vice-president (2002-2012)of the European Committee of Social Rights of the Council of Europe in Strasbourg.

Piet Van den Bergh, Legal counsel at ACV/CSC, the Christian trade union (Belgium).

Manfred Weiss, Professor Emeritus of Civil Law and Labour Law at the Goethe University of Frankfurt (Germany).

Marcin Wujczyk, Assistant Professor, Chair of Labour Law and Social Security, Faculty of Law and Administration, Jagiellonian University, Krakow (Poland). He is Member of the European Committee of Social Rights of the Council of Europe in Strasbourg.

Preface

Since the very beginning, temporary agency work has been an accepted feature in the United States' labour market. Not so in the European Union. It took more than 30 years for the EU to agree on a Directive on Temporary Agency Work (2008/104/EC), which was promulgated on 19 November 2008. A European consensus was possible as the Directive left Member States many options, such as regarding the fundamental issue of equal treatment between the temporary agency worker and the comparable worker, employed by the user.

Indeed, according to Article 5,1 of the Directive 'The basic working and employment conditions of temporary agency workers shall be, for the duration of their assignment at a user undertaking, at least those that would apply if they had been recruited directly by that undertaking to occupy the same job. But the Directive leaves many options to member States, when implementing this principle. Member States may, as regards pay, provide an exemption where temporary agency workers who have a permanent contract of employment with a temporary work agency continue to be paid in the time between assignments (Article 5.2). Member States may uphold collective agreements which, while respecting the overall protection of temporary agency workers, may establish arrangements concerning the working and employment conditions of temporary agency workers which derogate from the non-discrimination principle (Article 5.3).

Member States may derogate from the non-discrimination principle and provide for arrangements concerning working and employment conditions, which may include a qualifying period for equal treatment (Article 5.4).

By 5 December 2011, Member States had, after consulting the social partners in accordance with national legislation, collective agreements and practices, to review any restrictions or prohibitions on the use of temporary agency work in order to verify whether they are justified. Prohibitions or restrictions on the use of temporary agency work are justified only on grounds of general interest relating in particular to the protection of temporary agency workers, the requirements of health and safety at work or the need to ensure that the labour market functions properly and abuses are prevented (Article 4).However, the Directive provides that it is without prejudice to national requirements with regard to registration, licensing, certification, financial guarantees or monitoring of temporary work agencies. Here Member States remain competent.

Member States, furthermore, have to provide for various rules and conditions, such as regarding information of agency workers of vacant posts in the user undertaking; clauses preventing temporary agency workers of concluding an employment contract with the user; allowing compensation for temporary workers agencies in case a worker is hired by the user; prohibition to charge fees to agency workers in arranging to be recruited by a user; access to amenities or collective facilities in the user undertaking; access to training (Article 6); information of workers representatives of the user undertaking on the use of temporary workers (Article 8).

The European Union Member States had to implement the Temporary Agency Work Directive by 5 December 2011. The time was thus appropriate to examine the way in which various issues have been transposed in the national legislation, collective agreements and practices of the Member States of the European Union. To give perspective to this analysis, it was found useful to make a comparison with the United States. Such examination and comparative analysis allows to make an assessment of the level of protection of temporary agency workers and gives insights into the regulation of this sector in the labour markets in the EU and the US.

The perspective has also been connected with the European Union rules and principles on free movement of services, which concerns one of the fundamental freedoms guaranteed by the Treaty on the Functioning of the European Union. Temporary work is closely connected with the posting of workers. We say that a worker is 'a posted worker' when she/he is employed in one EU Member State but sent by his employer on a temporary basis to carry out his work in another Member State. The Posting of Workers Directive (96/71/EC) regulates employees sent to another Member State in three situations, of which concerns the case where the employer, being a 'temporary employment undertaking or placement agency', hires out a worker to a user undertaking established or operating in another Member States. The question arises how this provision is applied in practice, especially as the system of temporary agency work across borders seems to trigger the issue of social dumping.

In doing this research, various authors were asked to write reports on the implementation of the EU directive in their national systems. We also included European Union law insights and legal perspectives from the United States. The reports were presented at a conference, organized in Brussels by the Institute for Labour Law (University of Leuven) on 10 November 2012, and which was kindly supported by the company Randstad, specialized in human resources services and the organization of temporary agency work. Most of the papers have described the legal situation up to the date of this conference, as only minor editorial changes could be made afterwards in the publication process.

We hope to have offered an interesting contribution to a central object of academic study in modern labour markets.

The Editors,
Roger Blanpain, General editor
Frank Hendrickx, Guest editor

CHAPTER 1
Regulating Temporary Work in the European Union: The Agency Directive

Chris Engels

§1.01 GENERAL INTRODUCTION

This report gives an overview of European Union (EU) legislative rules applicable to temporary agency work. It does not focus on transnational provision of temporary agency work. The latter topic is the subject of another report.

This focus of the report is not on the historical development of agency work rules and regulations either, but on its current status.

First, the 1991 Directive dealing with health and safety issues is discussed. The major part of the discussion, however, focuses on the 2008 Directive on Temporary Agency Work.

§1.02 DIRECTIVE 91/383/EEC OF 25 JUNE 1991: SAFETY AND HEALTH AT WORK

[A] Introduction

In 1989 the Framework Directive on the introduction of measures to encourage improvements in the safety and health of workers at work was passed.[1] It contained measures to improve health and safety of workers in general.

Council Directive 91/338 EEC of 25 June 1991 deals with the specific situation of fixed term and temporary employment relationships in the area of health and safety.[2]

---

1. Directive 89/391/EEC of 12 Jun. 1989 on the introduction of measures to encourage improvements in the safety and health of workers at work, OJ No L 183, 29 Jun. 1989.
2. Council Directive 91/383/EEC of 25 Jun. 1991 supplementing the measures to encourage improvements in the safety and health at work of workers with a fixed-duration employment

The Directive starts from the premise that in general workers with a fixed-duration employment relationship or a temporary employment relationship are, in certain sectors, more than other workers,[3] exposed to the risk of accidents at work and occupational diseases. The particular situation of these kinds of workers and the special nature of the risks they face in certain sectors, calls for special additional rules, particularly as regards the provision of information, training and medical surveillance.[4]

[B] Definition: Scope

[1] Kind of Working Relationship

The temporary employment relationship to which the Directive applies is defined as the employment relationship between a temporary employment business which is the employer of the worker who is assigned to work for and under the control of an undertaking and/or establishment making use of his services.[5]

The Directive equally defines what is to be understood as a fixed-duration contract of employment. In its definition it encompasses what is often referred to as fixed term contracts of employment and contracts of employment for a specific work or project.[6]

The Directive refers to temporary employment *relationships*, while with respect to fixed term engagements, it refers to *contracts*.

[2] Possible Restriction of Scope of the Work to Be Performed

Members States are allowed to exclude from the scope of temporary work (or fixed term work as defined in the Directive), work which the Member State considers to be particularly dangerous to the health and safety of workers, and in particular certain work requiring special medical surveillance.[7]

In case temporary workers are allowed to engage in work that requires special medical surveillance, they shall be provided with the *adequate* special medical surveillance.[8] This surveillance is therefore not entirely the same as the one provide to the regular worker. The reference to the term adequate seems to imply at the same time that it could be more or less, or even different, depending on the particular circumstances of the temporary work assignment.

---

relationship or a temporary employment relationship, OJ No L 206, 29 Jul. 1991, amended by Directive 2007/30/EC of the European Parliament and of the Council of 20 Jun. 2007 amending Council Directive 89/391/EEC, its individual Directives and Council Directives 83/477/EEC, 91/383/EEC, 92/29/EEC and 94/33/EC with a view to simplifying and rationalizing the reports on practical implementation, OJ No L 165, 27 Jun. 2007.
3. Consideration (4), Council Directive 91/383/EEC of 25 Jun. 1991.
4. Consideration (7), Council Directive 91/383/EEC of 25 Jun. 1991.
5. Article 1.2, Council Directive 91/383/EEC of 25 Jun. 1991.
6. Article 1.1, Council Directive 91/383/EEC of 25 Jun. 1991.
7. Article 5.1, Council Directive 91/383/EEC of 25 Jun. 1991.
8. Article 5.2, Council Directive 91/383/EEC of 25 Jun. 1991.

The Directive explicitly states that the Member States may provide that this appropriate medical surveillance may be extended beyond the end of employment relationship.[9]

[C] Rights of the Temporary Worker

[1] Equal Treatment with Respect to Health and Safety

The purpose of the Directive is to ensure that with respect to health and safety, the same level of protection is awarded as other workers receive in the undertaking or establishment.[10] The difference with a 'normal' employment relationship, does not justify any difference in treatment with respect to health and safety at work, in general and with respect to personal protective equipment in particular.[11]

The Framework Directive and the Individual Directives in furtherance of it are fully applicable to temporary workers.[12]

With respect to jobs requiring special medical surveillance, the Directive imposes that the temporary worker should receive adequate special medical surveillance, which does not necessarily mean the same.[13]

During the assignment it is the user undertaking or establishment that is responsible for the conditions governing the performance of the work, which means those conditions connected to safety, hygiene and health at work.[14] This of course does not detract from the temporary business' own responsibility.[15]

[2] Right to the Appropriate Job Preparation: Information and Training

The worker needs to be appropriately prepared to take up the temporary job with the user company. This requires the worker to be sufficiently informed and trained.

Prior to taking up the work, the temporary worker has to be informed by the user of his services, of the risk that he will face.[16] This information needs to cover:

- any special occupational qualifications or skills or special medical surveillance that is required (as defined under national law);
- any increased specific risk that the job may entail (again, as defined in national law).[17]

The worker then needs to receive *'sufficient training appropriate to the particular characteristics of the job, account being taken of his qualifications and experience'*.[18]

---

9. Article 5.3, Council Directive 91/383/EEC of 25 Jun. 1991.
10. Article 2.1, Council Directive 91/383/EEC of 25 Jun. 1991.
11. Article 2.2, Council Directive 91/383/EEC of 25 Jun. 1991.
12. Article 2.3, Council Directive 91/383/EEC of 25 Jun. 1991.
13. Article 5.3, Council Directive 91/383/EEC of 25 Jun. 1991.
14. Article 8, Council Directive 91/383/EEC of 25 Jun. 1991.
15. Article 8.1, Council Directive 91/383/EEC of 25 Jun. 1991.
16. Article 3.1, Council Directive 91/383/EEC of 25 Jun. 1991.
17. Article 3.2, Council Directive 91/383/EEC of 25 Jun. 1991.
18. Article 4, Council Directive 91/383/EEC of 25 Jun. 1991.

The internal or external person(s) or service designated by the user employer to carry out activities related to the protection and prevention of occupational risks in the undertaking or establishment,[19] needs to be informed of the assignment of temporary workers at the user, to the extent necessary for the workers, services or persons designated to be able to carry out adequately their protection and prevention activities for all the workers in the undertaking and/or establishment.[20]

[D]   Provision of Information by the User to the Temporary Work Agency

Besides providing the temporary worker directly with information on the risks that he or she will be facing, an additional duty rests upon the user undertaking or establishment to provide the temporary employment business, *inter alia*, the occupational qualifications required and the specific features of the job to be filled.[21]

All these facts have to be brought to the attention of the temporary workers.[22]

Member States can impose that the details of this information are contained in the assignment contract.[23]

§1.03   DIRECTIVE 2008/104/EC OF 19 NOVEMBER 2008: TEMPORARY AGENCY WORK

[A]   Introduction

The Agency Directive, as it stands, is the result of a long legislative negotiation process. Not only was it impossible for the European level social partners to negotiate an agreement with respect to agency work, but the legislative process was also quite long and complicated. Furthermore, the debate was not just a debate on the content of the Directive as such, but the discussion on the potential modification of the working time directive was thrown in at the same time. This long and complicated legal history has been the object of many reports and papers already.

The aim of the Agency Directive is explicitly reflected in its Article 2. It is geared at the improvement of the quality of temporary work and the protection of temporary workers, by ensuring equal treatment and by recognizing temporary work agencies as employers, besides establishing a suitable framework for the use of temporary work in an effort to contribute towards job creation and flexible forms of work.

Temporary work, so Consideration (11) to the Directive states, 'meets not only undertakings' needs for flexibility but also the need of employees to reconcile their working and private lives. It thus contributes to job creation and to participation and integration in the labour market'.

---

19. Article 7, Directive 89/391/EEC of 12 Jun. 1989 on the introduction of measures to encourage improvements in the safety and health of workers at work, OJ No L 183, 29 Jun. 1989.
20. Article 6, Council Directive 91/383/EEC of 25 Jun. 1991.
21. Article 7.1, Council Directive 91/383/EEC of 25 Jun. 1991.
22. Article 7.2, Council Directive 91/383/EEC of 25 Jun. 1991
23. Article 7.3, Council Directive 91/383/EEC of 25 Jun. 1991.

[B] Scope

[1] Kind of Working Relationship: Parties Involved

Article 1.1 of the Directive states that it is applicable 'to workers with a contract of employment or an employment relationship with a temporary agency who are assigned to user undertakings to work temporarily under their supervision and direction'.

[a] Employment Contract or Relationship

The Temporary Agency Directive refers to both employment relationships and contracts. It indicates that the user will make the worker work under its supervision and direction. The Health and Safety Directive 91/383/EEC (see *supra*) only referred to temporary employment contracts. The Expert Report 2011 indicates: 'The mention of an "employment relationship" is meant to encompass the situations where the distinctive features of an employment relationship are present, but no contract of employment has been concluded'.[24] It makes reference to the frame work agreement on part-time work in which this standard wording has also been used. Further reference could be made to the *Albron* case[25] in which the European Court of Justice made the correlation between the employment relationship and a non-contractual employer who in that capacity establishes working relationships as employer, even in the absence of a contractual relationship. The *Albron* case dealt with the Acquired Rights Directive.[26]

A typical work is not excluded from the scope of the Directive. Member States cannot exclude form the scope of the Directive works, contracts of employment or employment relationships merely because they are part-time, fixed term or with a temporary work agency.[27] The latter seems to be a rather strange observation.

The 91/383/EEC Directive defined the authority exercised by the user over the temporary worker differently, by merely referring to the control of the user under which the work would be performed. The Temporary Work Agency Directive refers to the supervision and direction of the user. Control, supervision and direction all seem to be expressions of employer authority being exercised by a user over a worker with respect to whom the user is not the employer. It is doubtful whether this change in terminology should be attributed any importance. Most likely not.

---

24. Expert Report 2011, 12
25. ECJ, 21 Oct. 2010, *Albron Catering BV v. FNV Bondgenoten, John Roest*, Case C-242/09.
26. Council Directive 2001/23/EC of 12 Mar. 2001 on the approximation of the laws of the Member States relating to the safeguarding of employees' rights in the event of transfers of undertakings, business or parts of undertakings or business, OJ No L 082, 22 Mar. 2001, hereinafter Acquired Rights Directive or Council Directive 2001/23/EC of 12 Mar. 2001.
27. Article 3.2, para. 2, Directive 2008/104/EC of the European Parliament and the Council of 19 Nov. 2008 on temporary agency work, OJ No L 327, 5 Dec. 2008.

[b]   Worker

The worker is defined as the person who in the Member State concerned, is protected as a worker under national employment law. While this definition of worker is not uncommon in employment law directives, it is not very clear what the concept 'protected under national employment law' really means. Is it intended to mean that national law civil servant who are not ruled by employment law, but for instance by national public or administrative law, for this reason alone are excluded from the scope of the Directive? What if the national civil servants are covered by part of the national employment law, for instance dealing with working time restrictions? Or does the reference to 'protection under national law' only refer to national employment dismissal law?

Similar language can be found back in the Acquired Rights Directive and the Frame Work Directive on information and consultation,[28] when they restrict their scope also to those protected as employees under national employment law.

Persons who are protected in the Member States concerned as workers under national labour law fall within the scope of the Acquired Rights Directive.[29] The Directive does not apply to persons who are not protected as employees under national employment law, regardless of the nature of the tasks these persons perform.[30] If workers are covered by public law (a matter always to be determined by national courts) and thus have public law status, and are not subject to employment law, then the protection of the Acquired Rights Directive does not kick in.[31]

Article 4.1, second paragraph of the Acquired Rights Directive contains a provision stating that *'Member States may provide that the first subparagraph shall not apply to certain specific categories of employees who are not covered by the laws or practice of the Member States in respect of protection against dismissal.'*[32] Reading this provision in combination with the definition of employee, as being the person who is protected under national employment law, clearly indicates that the protection required to fall within the concept of employee for the purposes of the Directive, has to be wider than dismissal protection. Otherwise, the potential to exclude certain employees from the scope of the prohibition to dismiss at the occasion of the transfer of a business would seem to be entirely superfluous.

---

28. Article 3 (1) Directive 2002/14/EC of the European Parliament and of the Council of 11 Mar. 2002 establishing a general framework for informing and consulting employees in the European Community, OJ No L 80, 23 Mar. 2002.
29. See: ECJ, 6 Sep. 2011, *Ivana Scattolon v. Ministerio dell' Instruzione, dell' Universita e della Ricerca*, Case C-108/10, n 39.
30. ECJ, 14 Sep. 2000, *Renato Collino and Luisella Chiappero v. Telecom Italia SpA*, Case C-343/98, n°38.
31. ECJ, 14 Sep. 2000, *Renato Collino and Luisella Chiappero v. Telecom Italia SpA*, Case C-343/98, n° 40.
32. Article 4.1, 2nd para. Council Directive 2001/23/EC of 12 Mar. 2001.

The EFTA[33] Court which interprets the transfer directive for the EFTA Member States (currently Iceland, Lichtenstein and Norway) seems to focus primarily on the question whether or not the national employment law *dismissal protection* applies or not.

> On the basis of the foregoing, the court finds that the Directive is only applicable in the present case if the Plaintiff was at the time of the transfer protected under national employment law. It also follows that the directive is not applicable to the situation in the main proceedings if the Plaintiff enjoyed, at the relevant point in time, the special protection against dismissal granted only to civil servants for reasons associated with the public law function or the character of their employment. This must apply regardless of the specific nature of the Plaintiff's task as a server of the Post and Telecommunications administration.[34]

[c]   *Temporary Work Agency as Employer*

The temporary work agency is defined in Article 3.1(b) as 'any natural or legal person who, in accordance with national law, concludes contracts of employment or employment relationships with temporary agency workers in order to assign them to user undertakings to work there temporarily under their supervision and direction'.

The Directive 91/383/EEC used the wording of temporary employment business. Directive 2008/104/EEC states as an introduction to its Article 3 that 'for the purposes of this directive . ....' This indicates that the definitions in it, are not supposed to hold for other directives. It is hard to see though how the notion of temporary work agency would be different from the notion defined in Directive 91/383/EEC.[35]

The Expert Report 2011 states that the notion of 'temporary employment undertaking or placement agency' as used in the posting directive[36] cannot be considered as having exactly the same meaning and scope as the notion 'temporary work agency in Directive 2008/104/EC given the fact that the two directives use different wordings'.[37]

It does not matter whether the temporary work agency is a public or private undertaking, as long as it is engaged in economic activities. Whether or not it is operating for gain is irrelevant.[38]

The 2011 Expert Report quotes from the discussions in the Social Questions Working Party to state that charities, the armed forces, trade unions and government departments that are not engaged in economic activities would be excluded from the

---

33. EFTA stands for European Free Trade Agreement.
34. EFTA Court, 22 Mar. 2002, Alda Viggosdottir and Islandspostur hf. 5Iceland Post Ltd, Case E-3/01, n° 29.
35. The same may not necessarily be true in the national context of for instance the United Kingdom. See: Nicola Countouris & Rachel Horton, *The temporary Agency work directive: Another Broken Promise?*, 38 Indus. L. J. 329, 330 (2009).
36. Directive 96/71/EC of the European Parliament and the Council of 16 Dec. 1996 concerning the posting of workers in the framework of the provision of services, OJ, No L 18, 21 Jan. 1997.
37. Expert Report 2011, 15.
38. Article 1.2, Directive 2008/104/EC of the European Parliament and the Council of 19 Nov. 2008.

scope.[39] It seems hard to understand why trade unions would be considered as not engaging in economic activities. They may not necessarily be in it for gain, but membership interest defence, bargaining, legal services provided by trade unions etc. seems to be economic activities.

Labour market intermediaries who just match supply and demand on the labour market are not covered by the Directive, since they will not have any employment contract or relationship with the worker that they place and who enters into the direct employment of the entity to which the services are delivered. In this case, the ultimate user will also itself be the employer. This situation differs from the temporary agency one, in which there is always a triangular relationship.

Any form of working relationship where there is not a transfer of any form of authority from the employer to the end beneficiary of the activities, is not covered by the Directive.[40]

[d]   User Undertaking, Including Public Undertaking

User undertakings are, in their turn, defined as 'any natural or legal person for whom and under the supervision and direction of whom a temporary agency worker works temporarily'.[41] The user undertaking could be any natural or legal person from whom and under the supervision and direction of whom, a temporary agency worker works temporarily.[42]

With respect to public sector (national public sector) user undertakings, the question will have to be asked whether they are engaging in any form of economic activity which would bring them into the scope of the Directive.

One could wonder if the question whether the public sector entity is engaged in any economic activity, needs to be raised with respect to each of the public undertakings concerned as such, rather than the activities in which they are engaged in separately. Or taking it a step further whether one should look at the kind of activity the individual worker is engaged in within the undertaking?

At the level of the public undertaking, this would mean that when the public undertaking itself is as such not engaged in economic activities, that as an undertaking, it would fall outside the scope of the Directive and this even with respect to for instance the cleaning and catering activities which are equally an integral part of that same undertaking.

It may be instructive to look at the language that is used in the Acquired Rights Directive with respect to its scope. Article 1.1(c) of the Acquired Rights Directive states:

---

39. Expert Report 2011, 7.
40. Expert Report 2011, 13.
41. Article 3.1 (d), Directive 2008/104/EC of the European Parliament and the Council of 19 November 2008.
42. Art. 3.1 (d), Directive 2008/104/EC of the European Parliament and the Council of 19 Nov. 2008.

> This Directive shall apply to public and private undertakings engaged in economic activities whether or not they are operating for gain.[43]

The wording is exactly the same as the wording used in the Agency Directive 2008/104. The latter Directive merely added that this applied to both the temporary agency and to the user undertaking.

The Acquired Rights Directive then continues to state – referring to prior case law of the European Court of Justice – that 'an administrative organization of public administrative authorities, or the transfer of administrative functions between public administrative authorities, is not a transfer within the meaning of this Directive'.[44] Activities that involve the exercise of public authority are excluded from the scope.[45]

Within the frame work of the Acquired Rights Directive, the European Court of Justice has already held in relation to outsourcing of cleaning activities by a municipal authority that 'it cannot be automatically excluded that Directive 2001/23 might apply in circumstances, where a municipal authority unilaterally decides to terminate a contract with a private undertaking and to carry out itself the cleaning work it used to contract out to that undertaking'.[46] This clearly seems to indicate that at least for the Acquired Rights Directive one should not look at the public undertaking as such, but at the different entities that may compose the public undertaking. The fact, that the text of the Agency Directive, like the text of the Acquired Rights Directive refers to the term activities in plural, instead of the term activity in singular, may be seen as an indication that the different components of the public undertaking have to be looked at separately.

This would mean that within the catering service of a municipal entity which on the whole is occupied with administrative functions in the exercise of public authority, nevertheless agency work should be allowed (unless there would be an authorized and justified prohibition or restriction). Self-evidently the protection of the Agency Directive and its implementing legislation would kick in only for those protected under national employment law.

When administrative functions of several municipalities were grouped together in order to enhance the performance of these municipalities' administrative tasks, this related, so it was held, to activities involving the exercise of public authority, even if it

---

43. Article 1.1 (c), Council Directive 2001/23/EC of 12 Mar. 2001 on the approximation of the laws of the Member States relating to the safeguarding of employees' rights in the event of transfers of undertakings, businesses or parts of undertakings or businesses, OJ No L 82, 22 Mar. 2001, hereinafter Council Directive 2001/23/EC of 12 Mar. 2001.
44. Article 1.1 (c), Council Directive 2001/23/EC of 12 Mar. 2001.
45. ECJ, 14 Sep. 2000, *Renato Collino and Luisella Chiappero v. Telecom Italia SpA*, Case C-343/98, n° 31; ECJ, 10 Dec. 1998, *Francisca Sanchez Hidalgo and Others v. Asociacion de Servicios Aser and Sociedad Cooperativa Minerva* (C-173/96), and *Horst Ziemann v. Ziemann Sicherheit GmbH and Horst Bohn Sicherheitsdienst* (C-247/96), Joined Cases C-173/96 and C-247/96, n° 24; ECJ, 25 Jan. 2001, Oy Liikenne Ab and Pekka Liskojärvi, Pentti Juntnen, Case C-172/99, n° 19.
46. ECJ, 20 Jan. 2011, *Clece SA v. Maria Socorro Martin Valor, Ayuntamiento de Cobisa*, Case C-463/09, n° 32.

is assumed that those activities had aspects of an economic nature.[47] Since the entity was not covered by the Transfer Directive or better to say, its national implementing legislation, the secretary working for the entity – even though engaged in an economic activity as a secretary – could not count on the protection of the Acquired Rights Directive.

It remains to be seen whether the European Court of Justice would apply the same approach with respect to the Agency Directive as it applied in the framework of the Acquired Rights Directive. It certainly would be the logical thing to do.

[2] Potential Exclusion from the Scope

Member States may provide that the Directive does not apply to employment contracts or relations concluded under a specific public or publicly supported vocational training, integration or retraining programme.[48] In order to provide such exclusion, the Member State concerned first has to consult with the social partners on it.

It seems that Article 1.3 of the Directive also:

> covers the situation of charities which operate as temporary-work agencies by putting vulnerable people such as handicapped persons or former detainees at the disposal of user undertakings in order, whenever possible, to allow them to progressively readapt themselves to normal working conditions. Such charities are obviously not operating for gain and are often financed by religious communities, trade unions, employers' organizations and humanitarian NGOs.[49]

[3] Territorial Scope: Internal National Situation

The Commission explained that the Directive 2008/104/EC in principle covers national situations, whereas the Posting Directive provides a mechanism for cross-border situations.[50] The latter directive remains unaffected by Directive 2008/104/EC.[51]

As the explanatory memorandum to the draft directive stated:

> The proposal for a directive is intended to clarify and harmonize the conditions for posting workers at a national level. At the same time, it can be seen as an extension of arrangements already in force for transnational posting of temporary workers. In a proper internal market, it is only logical for the rules posting temporary workers to be aligned with each other, irrespective of whether a posting is national or transnational.[52]

The Directive does not mention anything with respect to its territorial scope.

---

47. ECJ, 15 Oct. 1996, Annette Henke and Gemeinde Schierke, Verwaltungsgemeinschaft 'Brocken', Case C-298/94, n° 16-17.
48. Article 1.3, Directive 2008/104/EC of the European Parliament and the Council of 19 November 2008.
49. Expert Report 2011, 10.
50. Expert Report 2011, 21.
51. Consideration (22) Directive 2008/104/EC of the European Parliament and the Council of 19 Nov. 2008.
52. Explanatory Memorandum to Proposal for a Directive of the European Parliament and the Council on working conditions for temporary workers COM(2002) 149 final, 10.

The Report of the Expert Group 'Transposition of directive 2008/104/EC on Temporary agency work'[53] stresses that the mere fact that the actual work would have to be carried out outside the EU territory, does not necessarily prevent the applicability of the Directive. In the same way, the fact that the work is performed for an agency established outside of the EU territory does not prevent the applicability. To the contrary, there would be no reason to exclude its applicability.[54]

Whether or not the Directive applies to Seafarers occupied on vessels that do not just navigate inland waters seems to be a complex matter to be determined on a case-by-case basis.[55] Formally, they are certainly not excluded from the scope of Directive 2008/104/EC.

[C] Restrictions or Prohibitions on the Use of Temporary Agency Work

[1] Principle of Acceptable Restrictions and Prohibitions

If temporary agency work is restricted or even prohibited, the restrictions or prohibitions can be justified on grounds of general interest relating in particular to:

- the protection of temporary agency workers;
- the requirements of health and safety at work; or
- the need to ensure that the labour market functions properly; and
- the prevention of abuses.[56]

According to the Expert Report, it cannot be excluded, on the basis of a comparison of the linguistic versions of the Directive that other justifications than the above three may be invoked.[57] However, all justifications have to be of general interest.

It seems that the justification grounds should not be interpreted broadly, but rather restrictively, given the fact that they are exceptions to a general rule.

In light of Article 4.1 of Directive 2008/104/EC, it seems very hard to justify national legal systems that install blanket prohibitions as acceptable restrictions on temporary agency work. Excluding all public undertakings, including those engaged in true economic activities, from using temporary agency work seems not warranted. The same holds in case a legal system would only allow temporary work, for instance when dealing with replacement of sick workers or workers who have been dismissed, unless of course there is a clear and established relationship with one of the justification grounds mentioned above. The 2011 Expert Report refers to a list of potential prohibitions or restrictions, by way of example:

---

53. Report of the Expert Group 'Transposition of directive 2008/104/EC on Temporary agency work, August 2011, Social Europe (hereinafter Expert Report 2011), 43pp.
54. Expert Report 2011, 5.
55. Expert Report 2011, 6.
56. Article 4.1, Directive 2008/104/EC of the European Parliament and the Council of 19 Nov. 2008.
57. Expert Report 2011, 31.

- prohibition to use temporary agency work in sectors of activity which are considered as dangerous;
- prohibition to offer contracts of indefinite duration to temporary agency workers;
- existence of limitative list of permissible reasons for using temporary agency work (e.g. to cover temporary and exceptional peaks of work, to replace an absent employee …);
- limitation of the number of possible renewals of temporary agency workers' contracts of employment;
- limitation of the number or proportion of agency workers that may work in user companies;
    Furthermore these imply equally matters such as
- obligations to carry out exclusively the activity of temporary-work provider; or
- obligations to have a specific legal form.[58]

'The improvement in working conditions of agency workers, in particular through the recognition of the principle of equal treatment would make many restrictions obsolete.'[59]

Restrictions in the name of the general interest will of course have to pass the test normally applied by the European Court of Justice and implying a check on the necessity of the measure and the proportionality to the aim of the measure.[60]

[2] Evaluation: Abolition of Restrictions

[a] Evaluation Process

By 5 December 2011 Member States needed to review the restrictions or prohibitions on the use of temporary work in order to verify whether these were justified on the ground of general interest described above.[61] The text of the Directive no longer contains a *periodic* review of these restrictions and prohibitions.

The kind of measure these restrictions were part of, is not important. They could be part of national legislation, collective agreements or even practices. Regulations or administrative provisions will also have to be scrutinized.[62] It does not matter whether the regulations of any kind are national, regional or local. They all have to be the subject of the review.[63]

As far as the process of consultation is concerned, the Directive requires the Member States to consult with the social partners prior to reporting on the restrictions and prohibitions to the Commission.[64] If the restrictions are contained in collective

---

58. Expert(Report 2011, 29.
59. Expert Report 2011, 29.
60. Explanatory Memorandum to Proposal for a Directive of the European Parliament and the Council on working conditions for temporary workers COM(2002) 149 final, 13.
61. Article 4.1, Directive 2008/104/EC of the European Parliament and the Council of 19 Nov. 2008.
62. Expert Report 2011, 29.
63. Expert Report 2011, 29.
64. Article 4.2, Directive 2008/104/EC of the European Parliament and the Council of 19 Nov. 2008.

agreements, the Member States may leave it up to the social partners to undertake the review process.[65]

It is reported, that the Commission is of the opinion that the review should deal with any kind of restrictive or prohibited measures, even beyond the scope of the Directive.[66] Given the absence of any specific indication in the text of the Directive, that the review process should have a wider scope than the Directive itself, the reporting obligation should logically, however, not extend beyond its scope.

Article 4.4 of the Directive indicates national requirements with regard to registration, licensing, certification, financial guarantees or monitoring of temporary agencies are not disturbed by the provisions of Article 4 of the Directive. It is understood as implying that there is no obligation resting on the Member States to also review this kind of limitation.[67] The Commission does favour also reporting on these requirements though.[68]

While such requirements are therefore not targeted by Article 4.1 of the Directive, it is clear that any such restrictions are to respect the rules of the fundamental freedom of establishment and the freedom of services. Consideration (22) of the Directive indicates that the Directive should be implemented in compliance with the provisions of the Treaty regarding the freedom to provide services and the freedom of establishment.

The provisions of the Directive on restrictions or prohibitions on temporary agency work are without prejudice to national legislation or practices that prohibit workers on strike being replaced by temporary agency workers.[69] The Directive itself, however, does not contain any positive obligation for the Member States to prohibit temporary work agencies to make workers available to a user in case of strike at the user undertaking.[70]

[b]   Duty to Abolish Unjustified Restriction

In the prior version of the text that would finally lead to the Directive, it was indicated that a periodic review of restrictions and prohibitions should take place and that unjustified restrictions or prohibitions should be discontinued.[71]

The final text of the Directive 2008/104/EC no longer contains an explicit duty to discontinue restrictions or prohibitions that cannot or can no longer by justified on the basis of the grounds mentioned in Article 4.1 of the same Directive. However, Article

---

65. Article 4.3, Directive 2008/104/EC of the European Parliament and the Council of 19 Nov. 2008.
66. Expert Report 2011, 31.
67. Expert Report 2011, 33.
68. Expert Report 2011, 34.
69. Consideration (20), Directive 2008/104/EC of the European Parliament and the Council of 19 Nov. 2008.
70. Nicola Countouris & Rachel Horton, *The Temporary Agency Work Directive: Another Broken Promise?*, 38 Indus. L. J. 329, 336 (2009).
71. See Amended proposal for a Directive of the European Parliament and the council on working conditions for temporary workers (presented by the Commission in accordance with Art. 250(2) of the EC Treaty), Brussels, 28 Nov. 2002, COM(2002)701 final.

4.1 of the Directive seems to be clear enough. Restrictions and prohibitions can only be justified on the basis of general interests grounds mentioned in it. If unjustified, the restrictions and prohibitions would violate the provisions of the Directive and would hence have to be set aside. Otherwise, the dictate of Article 4.1 of the Directive would have no effect. This provision cannot be read as just an invitation to do away with unwarranted restrictions or prohibitions. It is an obligation to do so.

[D] Rights of Temporary Work Agency Workers

[1] Equal Treatment with Respect to Basic Working and Employment Conditions

[a] Principle

During the assignment[72] at a user undertaking, the temporary agency worker shall at least benefit from the basic working conditions and employment conditions that he or she would have received if he or she would have been directly recruited by the user to perform that same job.[73]

The comparison to be made is one with a hypothetical worker, hereby avoiding the discussion whether the comparison had to be made with a comparable worker at the user undertaking or at the temporary work agency. Most likely, the existence of an actual employee broadly doing similar work at the user undertaking could be treated as useful evidence in this respect.[74]

The Directive refers the worker directly hired by the user undertaking, leaving it open whether one is dealing with permanent or fixed term hiring by the user.

Basic working and employment conditions are defined in Article 3.1(f) of the Directive 2008/104/EC as:

> any working and employment conditions laid down by legislation, regulation, administrative provisions, collective agreements and/or other binding general provisions in force in the user undertaking relating to:
>
> (i) The duration of working time, overtime, breaks, rest periods, night work, holidays and public holidays;
> (ii) Pay.

For the purposes of the principle of equal treatment established in the Directive, the rules in force in the undertaking relating to the protection of pregnant women and nursing mothers and the protection of children and young people, as well as the rules on equal treatment for men and women and any action to combat any discrimination

---

72. Assignment is defined in Art. 3.1 (c) as follows: 'means the period during which the temporary agency worker is placed at the user undertaking to work temporarily under its supervision and direction'.
73. Article 5.1, Directive 2008/104/EC of the European Parliament and the Council of 19 Nov. 2008.
74. Nicola Countouris & Rachel Horton, *The Temporary Agency Work Directive: Another Broken Promise?*, 38 Indus. L. J. 329, 333 (2009).

based on sex, race, ethnic origin, religion, beliefs, disabilities, age or sexual orientation must be complied with, as established by legislation, regulations, administrative provisions, collective bargaining agreements and/or any other general provision.[75]

The temporary agency worker should receive all the above benefits to which the worker directly hired by the user would be entitled on the basis of any form of binding and general rule in force at the user's undertaking. If no such entitlement would exist for this worker, the agency worker would not be able to claim any entitlement either.

Given the fact that the definition includes a reference to the fact that the rules do not only have to be general, but also binding, it seems that voluntarily and unilaterally granted benefits by the employer, would not qualify. One seems to have to deal with binding rules that are also general and not just applicable to one or a few persons. Business Europe seemed to stress 'binding provisions should be taken into account, but not voluntary or incidental ones'.[76]

With respect to bonuses, it was observed in the Expert Report that they are most of the time not determined in employment contracts and not have a binding character. The Commission nevertheless indicated that the bonuses which would have been paid to a worker recruited directly for the same duration should, in principle, be taken into account when applying equal treatment, without prejudice to possible derogations.[77] This conclusion is questionable since the Directive refers to both binding and general rules in its definition of basic working and employment conditions.

With respect to the concept of pay, the Directive states that it is without prejudice to national law.[78] The Expert Report notes 'Nevertheless, should the European Court of Justice have to interpret the concept of pay, it cannot be excluded that it would use Article 157 of the Treaty on the Functioning of the European Union, which defines equal pay for male and female workers, as a source of interpretation.'[79]

However, in this case the Directive explicitly refers to national law with respect to the definition of pay.[80] Furthermore, the provision in Article 5.4. of the Directive in which it is stated that certain derogations from the principle of equal treatment for basic working employment conditions are allowed, requires Member States to specify whether occupational social security schemes including pension, sick pay of financial participation schemes are included in the basic working and employment conditions. This seems to underline the national character of the pay provision in this Directive.

---

75. Article 5.1, Directive 2008/104/EC of the European Parliament and the Council of 19 Nov. 2008.
76. Expert Report 2011, 19.
77. Expert Report 2011, 20.
78. Article 3.2, Directive 2008/104/EC of the European Parliament and the Council of 19 Nov. 2008.
79. Expert Report 2011, 19.
80. See also Art. 5.4, para. 2, Directive 2008/104/EC of the European Parliament and the Council of 19 Nov. 2008.

[b]   Possible Derogations

   [i]   Pay Derogation

Article 5.2 of the Directive 2008/104/EC concerns pay only and does not address the rest of the basic working and employment conditions.

A potential of a derogation of the principle of equal pay is provided for temporary agency workers who have a permanent contract of employment with the temporary work agency and who continue to be paid in the period of time between assignments. On the basis of Consideration (15) to the Directive one could state that the Directive refers to a permanent contract of employment as a contract of employment for an indefinite duration, which it still considers to be the 'general form of employment relationship'.[81] Because such a permanent contract of employment offers special protection, exemptions from the rules applicable in the user undertaking should be permitted.[82] One can wonder whether fixed term contracts of contracts of employment quite often do not provide for at least a similar level of protection, especially if the contracts are of a long term duration. However, during the entire legislative process the Commission seems to have been adamant in defending the position that only permanent or indefinite contracts of employment should be taken into account in order to prevent the risk of circumventing the Directive.[83]

Member States themselves have to provide for this derogation in their legislation and following consultation of the social partners.

There is no indication in the Directive as to the level of pay that should be provided to the temporary agency worker and certainly not for the period of time in-between assignments. The level of pay to be provided has to be determined at national level. If there are national collective agreements that are applicable or minimum pay provisions that are applicable to this kind of contracts, they will have to be respected by the temporary work agency.[84]

   [ii]   Derogation by the Social Partners Respecting the Overall Protection of Temporary Agency Workers

The second derogation allows the Member States, following consultation with the social partners, to give these social partners the opportunity to uphold or conclude collective bargaining agreements in which they deviate from the principle of equal treatment with respect to basic working and employment conditions as guaranteed by Article 5.1 of the Directive. When determining what the potential scope of these

---

81. Consideration (15), Directive 2008/104/EC of the European Parliament and the Council of 19 Nov. 2008.
82. Consideration (15), Directive 2008/104/EC of the European Parliament and the Council of 19 Nov. 2008.
83. Expert Report 2011, 23.
84. Expert Report 2011, 23.

collective bargaining agreements would be, it is indicated that the collective agreements may relate to not only *basic* working and employment conditions, but to *all* working and employment conditions.

One basic condition that is imposed, is that the overall protection of temporary workers is respected.[85] It is not indicated how to determine whether the overall level of protection of temporary workers is respected. It will most likely lead to difficult weighing exercises where the lower level of pay in-between assignments may for instance be off-set against additional training rights.[86]

This derogation requires the social partners to 'legislate'. Reference is made to the social partners at the appropriate level, which is not necessarily the same as the national level.[87]

[iii]   Derogation by the Member States Respecting an *Adequate* Level of Protection of the Temporary Agency Worker

This derogation does not refer to an overall level of protection for the temporary workers, but merely refers to an adequate level of protection.

This derogation is only available to Member States in which either there is no system in law for declaring collective agreements universally applicable or no system in law or practice for extending provisions to similar undertakings in a certain sector or geographical area.[88]

Following consultation with the social partners at national level (whether appropriate or not) and on the basis of an agreement reached between the national social partners, Member States are allowed to deviate from the principle of equal treatment with respect to basic working and employment conditions.

It is explicitly mentioned that these deviating arrangements 'may include a qualifying period for equal treatment'.[89] The question can be raised whether the length of the qualifying period could have an impact on the evaluation of the adequacy of the protection that the Member State is supposed to providing. If for instance a twelve-week qualifying period would exclude more than half of the agency workers in a given Member State, would the protection still be considered adequate?[90] Or should the adequacy only be considered for those to whom the measures implementing the Directive effectively apply?

A question the Directive does not answer is whether a qualifying period could be applied for each separate assignment that a temporary agency worker is working with

---

85. Consideration (16), Directive 2008/104/EC of the European Parliament and the Council of 19 Nov. 2008.
86. Expert Report 2011, 24.
87. Article 5.3, Directive 2008/104/EC of the European Parliament and the Council of 19 Nov. 2008.
88. Article 5.4, para. 1, Directive 2008/104/EC of the European Parliament and the Council of 19 Nov. 2008.
89. Article 5.4, para. 1, last sentence Directive 2008/104/EC of the European Parliament and the Council of 19 Nov. 2008.
90. See: Nicola Countouris & Rachel Horton, *The Temporary Agency Work Directive: Another Broken Promise?*, 38 Indus. L. J. 329, 333 (2009).

the same user undertaking, but while working a different kind of (often unskilled) job. Could a new qualifying period be imposed, with or without even an interruption? Most likely an argument can be advanced that the identity of the user undertaking should not be determinative for allowing or prohibiting a new qualifying period being imposed, given the fact that the qualifying period is one that precedes the period before the agency worker will be entitled (hopefully) to equal basic working conditions as the one he or she would have obtained if he or she were directly hired as a permanent worker. Since the equality of working conditions is attached to performance of a particular kind of job, it would seem logical that the qualifying period if and when foreseen in national rules, is equally attached to the nature of the specific job or work performed and not to the sole identity of the user undertaking.

Member States also need to specify whether occupational social security schemes, including pension, sick pay or financial participation schemes are part of the basic working and employment conditions for which normally equal treatment should be guaranteed.[91]

Any such arrangements need to be drafted in such way that sectors and firms are able to comply with the obligations resulting from them. They therefore need to be sufficiently clear and accessible.[92]

There is no specification as to the length of the qualifying period that could be foreseen.

[iv]   Prevention of Misuse

Member States need to take the appropriate measures in order to prevent misuse in applying the derogations. Particular attention needs to be paid to prevent successive assignments designed to circumvent the provisions of the Directive. Member States need to inform the Commission of such measures.[93]

While this anti-abuse provision aims at the entire spectrum of derogations provided for in Article 5.5 of the Directive, particular attention needs to be paid to systems allowing a qualifying period before equal treatment rights kick in.[94] Even though the Directive does not foresee a maximum duration of the qualifying period, it is not totally unthinkable that allowing qualifying periods that are too long, could be seen as an abuse of Article 5 of the Directive.

---

91. Article 5.4, para. 2 Directive 2008/104/EC of the European Parliament and the Council of 19 Nov. 2008.
92. Article 5.4, para. 2, Directive 2008/104/EC of the European Parliament and the Council of 19 Nov. 2008.
93. Article 5.5, Directive 2008/104/EC of the European Parliament and the Council of 19 Nov. 2008.
94. Expert Report 2011, 25.

[2] Access to Employment, Collective Facilities and Vocational Training

[a] Access to Employment

While bringing agency work closer to mainstream employment, it is clear that the point of departure of the Directive 2008/104/EC is still a permanent contract of employment for an indefinite period of time.[95] The Directive therefore aims to stimulate temporary workers' access to permanent employment at the user undertaking.

[i] Information Access

Temporary agency workers shall be informed of any vacancies at the user so as to give them the same opportunity as other workers at the user, to find permanent employment.[96] However, the duty to inform the agency workers of vacant posts exist independently and is not linked to the provision of information to the user undertaking's own workers.

Since the temporary agency workers have to be informed of *any* vacant position, there is no link between the information the temporary worker needs to receive and the job actually being performed by the same worker, or the qualifications required to perform it.[97]

It is possible that the information is provided by a general announcement in a suitable place at the user undertaking. Intranet sites or hall ways of companies seem to qualify as areas where such information can be made available.[98]

[ii] Restrictive Clauses

Any clauses that prohibit or have the effect of preventing the conclusion of an employment contract or relationship between the temporary worker and the user following his or her assignment at the user undertaking, should be considered null and void or may be declared null and void. The same holds for clauses having the same effect.[99]

Contract clauses in the contracts between the temporary agency and the user undertaking in which it is foreseen that the user can only offer employment to the temporary agency worker, following the end of the assignment if and when the user undertaking pays a penalty (equal to x-days of pay for instance) are to become ineffective. There should not be any obstacles for the temporary agency worker to

---

95. Consideration (15), Directive 2008/104/EC of the European Parliament and the Council of 19 Nov. 2008.
96. Article 6.1, Directive 2008/104/EC of the European Parliament and the Council of 19 Nov. 2008.
97. Expert Report 2011, 39.
98. Expert Report 2011, 39.
99. Article 6.2, para. 1, Directive 2008/104/EC of the European Parliament and the Council of 19 Nov. 2008.

conclude a permanent contract with the user undertaking once their posting has ended.[100]

However, the Directive recognizes that temporary agencies work may require the payment of reasonable level of recompense for services rendered to user undertakings for the assignment, recruitment and training of the temporary agency workers.[101] It seems reasonable though that this fee or recompense is established and charged independently of the user undertaking permanently hiring the temporary worker or not.

[iii] Fees

The temporary work agencies cannot charge the temporary workers any fee in exchange for arranging for them to be recruited by a user undertaking or for concluding a contract of employment following the assignment.[102]

The temporary agency can thus not charge any kind of placement fee to the temporary worker in order to broker an employment contract with the user undertaking.

[b] Access to Collective Facilities

[i] At the User Undertaking

Temporary agency workers shall be given access to the amenities or collective facilities in the user undertaking, in particular any canteen, child-care facilities and transport services, under the same conditions as the workers directly employed by the user undertaking.[103] A difference in treatment between the temporary agency workers and the permanent workers of the user undertaking may be made though, inasmuch as the difference in treatment is justified by objective reasons.[104]

Equality of access is the rule; inequality the exception.[105] In this respect the Expert Report refers to the Commission's position explaining that for some amenities, it will be difficult, if not impossible to objectively justify the denial of access:

> For instance, no objective reason could justify not granting agency workers access to company canteens, regardless of the duration of the assignment, provided that they are accessible to all categories of directly employed workers. As regard

---

100. Explanatory Memorandum to Proposal for a Directive of the European Parliament and the Council on working conditions for temporary workers COM(2002) 149 final, 14.
101. Article 6.2, para. 2, Directive 2008/104/EC of the European Parliament and the Council of 19 Nov. 2008.
102. Article 6.3, Directive 2008/104/EC of the European Parliament and the Council of 19 Nov. 2008.
103. Article 6.4, Directive 2008/104/EC of the European Parliament and the Council of 19 Nov. 2008.
104. Article 6.4, Directive 2008/104/EC of the European Parliament and the Council of 19 Nov. 2008.
105. Expert Report 2011, 39.

transport services, a difference in treatment may be justifiable only where a certain category of workers does benefit from these services. In the case of child-care facilities, where there is only a limited number of places available and it is insufficient to meet the needs of the own staff of the undertaking, this could possibly justify restrictions on the access of agency workers to this service.[106]

Economic reasons as such could never be considered an objective reason justifying the difference of treatment in the opinion of the Commission.[107]

The list of collective facilities or amenities provided for in the text of the Directive is considered by the Commission not to be a limitative one. It is therefore suggested that transposition measures should be general.[108]

[ii]   At the Temporary Work Agency

The Directive holds that Member States shall take suitable measures or shall promote social dialogue between the social partners in order to improve the access of temporary workers to child-care facilities in the temporary work agencies, even in periods between their assignments.[109]

[iii]   Access to Training

The Directive indicates that the Member States should take suitable measure or promote social dialogue in order to improve the agency workers' access to training both at the temporary work agency and at the user undertaking, for training for user undertakings' workers.[110]

The Directive does not seem to impose any given result to be reached. Nevertheless, agency workers, so the Expert Report states, should in principle not be denied access to training in the user undertaking.[111] The big question is also when this training should take place.

[3]   The Right to Be Taken into Account for Determining Threshold Levels for Employee Representative Bodies

[a]   At the Temporary Work Agency

While Member States can determine the conditions under which this is to occur, the temporary agency workers shall be taken into account in order to determine whether

---

106. Expert Report 2011, 39.
107. Expert Report 2011, 39.
108. Expert Report 2011, 40.
109. Article 6.5.5 a), Directive 2008/104/EC of the European Parliament and the Council of 19 Nov. 2008.
110. Article 6.5.5 a) and b), Directive 2008/104/EC of the European Parliament and the Council of 19 Nov. 2008.
111. Expert Report 2011, 40.

the threshold levels are reached as from which employee representative bodies have to be established at the temporary work agency.[112]

[b]   At the User Undertaking

As an alternative of taking the temporary agency workers into account for determining threshold levels for employee representative bodies at the temporary work agency, Member States may provide that they are counted for in the user undertaking, in the same way as if they were workers employed directly for the same period of time by the user undertaking.[113]

If a Member State opts for this option, it is not obliged to also have the temporary workers be taken into account for the determining whether the threshold levels are reached at the temporary work agency.[114]

Nothing seems to prevent a Member State from taking the agency workers into account for the threshold levels, both at the temporary work agency, and at the user undertaking.

[4]   Rights of the User Undertaking Workers

[a]   Right to Count in the Temporary Workers

In case the Member State has not opted for the option in which the temporary workers are taken into account in order to determine whether the threshold levels for employee representative bodies at the temporary work agency are reached, these workers should be taken into account for the same purposes, but then at the user undertaking.[115]

Member States may also opt to take the agency workers into account for threshold determination both at the temporary work agency, and at the user undertaking.[116]

[b]   Information to Workers' Representatives

The user undertaking must provide suitable information on the use of temporary workers when providing information on the employment situation in the undertaking, to bodies representing workers and which have been set up in accordance with national and Community law.[117]

The information that is provided to the bodies representing workers must be substantial, so the Expert Report states and must ensure the effectiveness of Article 8 of the Directive.[118]

---

112. Article 7.1 Directive 2008/104/EC of the European Parliament and the Council of 19 Nov. 2008.
113. Article 7.2 Directive 2008/104/EC of the European Parliament and the Council of 19 Nov. 2008.
114. Article 7.3 Directive 2008/104/EC of the European Parliament and the Council of 19 Nov. 2008.
115. Article 7.2 Directive 2008/104/EC of the European Parliament and the Council of 19 Nov. 2008.
116. Article 7.3 Directive 2008/104/EC of the European Parliament and the Council of 19 Nov. 2008.
117. Article 8 Directive 2008/104/EC of the European Parliament and the Council of 19 Nov. 2008.
118. Expert Report 2011, 42.

§1.04 OTHER PROVISIONS

[A] No State Monopolies

The European Court of Justice made it clear that state monopolies in the area of employment intermediaries would most likely run against European law.

After dealing with a German case on headhunting monopolies[119] the Court was asked to address the Italian state monopoly as an employment intermediary.[120] Job Centre Coop. arl or JCC was being set up as a limited liability company. In its company statutes it declared that it wanted its business to include, in particular serving as an intermediary between supply and demand on the employment market and providing temporary staff to third parties.[121] It claimed the right to act as an intermediary between supply and demand on the employment market and to provide temporary staff.[122] The then Italian law prohibited acting as an employment intermediary, whether as an employment agency or as an employment business.[123] The prohibition did not hold for public employment agencies.

The Court held that within the context of competition law, the concept of undertaking encompasses every entity engaged in an economic activity, regardless of its status and the way in which it is financed and second, that the placement of employees is an economic activity.[124]

The European Court of Justice continued:

> A Member State which prohibits any activity as an intermediary between supply and demand on the employment market, whether as an employment agency or as an employment business, unless carried on by those offices, is in breach of Article 90(1) of the Treaty where it creates a situation in which those offices cannot avoid infringing Article 86 of the Treaty. That is the case, in particular, in the following circumstances:
>
> - The public placement offices are manifestly unable to satisfy demand on the market for all types of activity; and
> - The actual placement of employees by private companies is rendered impossible by the maintenance in force of statutory provisions under which such activities are prohibited and non-observance of that prohibition gives rise to penal and administrative sanctions; and
> - The placement activities in question could extend to the nationals or to the territory of other Member States.[125]

---

119. ECJ, 23 Apr. 1991, *Klaus Höfner and Fritz Elser v. Macretron GmbH*, Case C-41/90.
120. ECJ, 11 Dec. 1997, *Job Centre Coop. Arl*, Case C-55/96.
121. ECJ, 11 Dec. 1997, *Job Centre Coop. Arl*, Case C-55/96, n° 3.
122. ECJ, 11 Dec. 1997, *Job Centre Coop. Arl*, Case C-55/96, n 12.
123. ECJ, 11 Dec. 1997, *Job Centre Coop. Arl*, Case C-55/96, n° 5.
124. ECJ, 11 Dec. 1997, *Job Centre Coop. Arl*, Case C-55/96, n° 21
125. ECJ, 11 Dec. 1997, *Job Centre Coop. Arl*, Case C-55/96, n° 38.

[B] Freedom of Services

[1] Posting Directive[126]

In Article 1 of the Posting Directive, a clear reference is made to agency work:

> This Directive shall apply to the extent that the undertakings referred to in paragraph 1 take one of the following transnational measures:
>
> (a) ...
> (b) ...
> (c) *Being a temporary employment undertaking or placement agency, hire out a worker to a user undertaking established or operating in the territory of a Member State, provided there is an employment relationship between the temporary employment undertaking or placement agency and the worker during the period of posting.*[127]

The relationship between the Posting Directive and the Agency Directive is not within the scope of the present paper.

[2] Services Directive[128]

The Services Directive is clear in excluding from its scope 'services of temporary work agencies'.[129]

[3] Freedom to Provide Services

The Treaty principles on the freedom to provide services are applicable to services of an economic nature, such as temporary agency work, when the services are being provided transnationally.

Since the transnational provision of agency services is not part of the present discussion, the restrictions that Member States try to impose on foreign temporary agencies providing temporary services in their territory will not be covered in the present paper.[130]

---

126. Directive 96/71/EC of the European Parliament and of the Council of 16 Dec. 1996 concerning the posting of workers in the framework of the provision of services, OJ No L 18, 21 Jan. 1997.
127. Article 1.3 (c) Directive 96/71/EC of the European Parliament and of the Council of 16 Dec. 1996 concerning the posting of workers in the framework of the provision of services, OJ No L 18, 21 Jan. 1997.
128. Directive 2006/123/EC of the European Parliament and of the Council of 12 Dec. 2006 on services in the internal market, OJ No L 376, 27 Dec. 2006. See also Tineke Vaes & Tom Vandenbrande, *Implementing the new Temporary Agency Work Directive* 17 (KULeuven, ww.jhiva.be 2009).
129. Article 2.2 (e) Directive 2006/123/EC of the European Parliament and of the Council of 12 Dec. 2006 on services in the internal market, OJ No L 376, 27 Dec. 2006.
130. For a general discussion, see: Roger Blanpain, *European Labour Law* 367–422 (12th ed., Wolters Kluwer Law & Business 2010).

[C] Acquired Rights Directive

[1] Transfer of a Temporary Work Agency or Part of It: Application of the Transfer Directive

Like a number of other labour and employment law directives, the Transfer Directive now explicitly indicates that:

> Member States shall not exclude from the scope of the directive contracts of employment or employment relationships solely because ... they are temporary employment relationships within the meaning of Article 1(2) of Directive 91/383/EEC and the undertaking, business or part of the undertaking or business transferred is, or is part of, the temporary employment business which is the employer.[131]

Temporary employment relationships such as the employment contracts of temporary workers with the agency they work for, are therefore protected by the Acquired Rights Directive if and when the temporary work agency as such or a part of it, is being transferred. The European Court of Justice already dealt with a situation in which part of a temporary work agency was being transferred. In the *Jouini* case[132] the European Court of Justice applied the provisions of the Directive, taking into account the particularities of an interim agency as a business. After stating that the economic entity to be transferred does not need to have significant tangible or intangible assets, the Court continued:

> That applies with even more force to temporary employment businesses in the light of Article 2(2) of directive 2001/23. If follows from this provision that temporary employment relationships with such businesses fall, in principle under directive 2001/23, implying that their special characteristics must be taken into account when analysing the taking over of such relationships. Such businesses are characterised, in general, as pointed out in the order for reference, by the lack of a suitable business structure from which it is possible to identity, within such a business, various economic entities which can be detached on the basis of the transferor's organisational arrangements.
> As a result, in the absence of an identifiable organisational structure of the temporary employment business, an analysis should take account of its special characteristics rather than aim to establish whether an economic entity exists at the level of the organisational structure. In that context, the assessment of the existence of an economic entity for the purposes of Article 1(1) of directive 2001/23 requires an assessment whether the assets transferred by the transferor constituted for its purposes an operational grouping sufficient in itself to provide services characterising the business's economic activity, without recourse to other significant assets or to other parts of the business.
> In that regard it must be pointed out that the activity of temporary employment businesses is characterised by temporary assignments of employees to user undertaking in order that they may carry out a diverse range of tasks according to the needs and instructions of those undertaking. The pursuit of such an activity

---

131. Article 2, 2 Acquired Rights Directive.
132. ECJ, 13 Sep. 2007, *Mohamed Jouini and others v. Princess Personal Services GmbH* PPs°, Case C-458/05.

requires inter alia, expertise, an administrative structure capable of organising that assignment of employees and a grouping of temporary workers who are capable of integrating in the user undertaking and of carrying out the tasks required of them. On the other hand, other significant assets are not indispensable for the pursuit of the economic activity in question.

As pointed out by the referring court, the fact that the workers assigned on a temporary basis are integrated in the organisational structure of the client to whom they are assigned is not capable, as such, of precluding a finding that an economic entity has been transferred. Those workers are nevertheless essential assets, without which the temporary employment business would, by definition, not be capable of performing its economic activity. Moreover, the fact that, in terms of point 2 of Article 1 of Directive 91/383, which is referred to in Article 2. (2)(c) of directive 2001/23, they are linked to the transferor by a working relationship and are remunerated by him directly, serves to confirm their connection to the transferor's business and furthermore their contribution to the existence of an economic entity within it.[133]

[2] Transfer of the User Undertaking or Part of It: Protection of the Temporary Agency Worker Working at the User Undertaking or Part of It

The question could be raised whether the temporary agency worker who is performing a temporary assignment at the user undertaking could invoke any form of protection from the Acquired Rights Directive if and when the part of the user's business to which he or she is assigned is being transferred.

While it seemed that temporary agency workers would not be covered by the Transfer Directive, unless there was a transfer of a temporary work agency or part of it, a 2010 Order of the European Court of Justice casts doubt on this.[134] The *Briot* case deals with the restaurant services for the Council of the European Union. Mr Briot was a temporary agency worker, in the service of Randstad. From 1 January 2003, the Council entrusted the management of the restaurant to a single subcontractor, Sodexho. Mr Briot's contract of employment was one for a fixed period of time, coming to an end on 20 December 2002. In first instance the labour tribunal of Brussels had refused to consider there to be a transfer of rights and obligations with respect to Mr Briot, in the absence of a contract of employment between the Council and Mr Briot.

The European Court of Justice rephrases a preliminary question raised by the Brussels Appeals Court:

> By its second question,... the national court asks, in essence whether the non-renewal of the fixed-term contracts of employment of the temporary workers attributable to the transfer of the activity to which they were assigned disregards the prohibition laid down in Article 4 (1) of Directive 2001/23 in such a way that

---

133. ECJ, 13 Sep. 2007, *Mohamed Jouini and others v. Princess Personal Services GmbH* (PPs), Case C-458/05, nos 33–36.
134. Order ECJ, 15 Sep. 2010, *Johnny Briot v. Randstad Interim*, Sodexho SA, Council of the European Union, Case C-386/09.

those temporary workers must be regarded as still being available to the user business on the date of the transfer.[135]

Instead of an outright rejection of the claim by stating that the temporary workers do not have an employment contract or relationship with the transferor, the Court went about it in an entirely different way. It basically held that in line with the existing case law, the protection of the Acquired Rights Directive is available only to those in employment at the time of the transfer. Since Mr Briot's contract came to an end around ten days before the potential transfer, he was not protected. It furthermore held that non-renewal of a fixed term contract cannot be equated to a dismissal as referred to in Article 4 of the Acquired Rights Directive.

In light of the Court's reasoning it is not unlikely that the Court may extend the protection of the Acquired Rights Directive and its national implementing legislation to those temporary workers whose employment contract or relationship is still up and running at the time of the transfer.

§1.05 CONCLUDING REMARKS

The Agency Directive is unlikely to establish equality of treatment between agency workers on the one hand and workers on a permanent contract of employment at the user, on the other. It does not require a direct comparison to be made between the comparable worker at the user enterprise and the agency worker.

Moreover, the equality of treatment principle is limited only to basic working and employment conditions as defined in a restrictive way in the Directive itself.

The Directive, furthermore, leaves ample room for derogations even from its core principle by Member States and or the social partners, combined with vague undefined levels of overall or adequate protection.

Self-evidently Member States do not have to use the derogations the Directive allows. However, given the political compromises that were made in order to get the current text of the Directive approved, it is very likely that derogations will be used to their fullest extent.

But even against such pessimistic background, it is clear that the Directive will certainly help to get a number of restrictions on agency work lifted, as not justified on grounds of general interest. If Member States are not very willing to live up to their obligation to review and eradicate such unjustified restrictions, hopefully the European Court of Justice will step in.

---

135. Order ECJ, 15 Sep. 2010, *Johnny Briot v. Randstad Interim*, Sodexho SA, Council of the European Union, Case C-386/09, n. 23.

CHAPTER 2
Regulating Temporary Work: Protection of the National Labour Market or the Individual Worker?

Andrzej Marian Świątkowski

§2.01 INTRODUCTION

On 19 November 2008 the European Parliament and the Council adopted Directive 2008/104/EC on temporary agency work. Adoption of this Directive concluded the almost thirty-year period of debates within international organizations, predecessors of the present European Union (EU). Participants in these debates were the Union institutions, Member States and social partners operating in the European space. The standpoints presented by the participants in the debates depended on the last thirty years of changing views concerning social policy within the common market presented by the Union authorities and authorities of the European Economic Community as well as the Member States of the European Union.

    The EU and its predecessor regional organizations were established to ensure free movement, within the common market, of capital, goods, services and workers, as well as persons engaged in an activity in a self-employed capacity and entrepreneurs, as well as family members of the mentioned categories of vocationally active persons. A legislative activity of the Union institutions in the field of labour consists in setting out uniform legal standards to guarantee harmonization of separate regulations in force in particular Member States. The purpose of the directives adopted in the field of labour is harmonization of the national labour law systems in the Member States of the EU. The Open Method of Coordination of the labour law systems of particular Member States aims at achieving uniform objectives, desired from the EU point of view. It should be considered whether Directive 2008/104/EC on temporary agency work is able to lead to harmonization of the national laws on the temporary agency work in the Member States. Further, it should be considered what are the reasons behind the actions taken by the EU institutions with a view to harmonizing the national labour law systems. In the EU labour law doctrine, there are two hypotheses. The first one states that the tendency to harmonize the laws on the temporary agency work is aimed at limiting and further eliminating the unlawful competition among the entrepreneurs operating on the common market.[1]

Directive 2008/104/WE includes cross-border norms functioning on the common market of the EU, international regional organization within which administrative territorial divisions exist – delineated by the borders of the Member States – and where national labour markets are protected by state and administrative authorities of the Member States. The entrepreneurs' freedom to provide services and the freedom of movement of workers and persons engaging in professional activity within the common market allows to admitting to the labour markets of the Members States, within the common market, the temporary agency workers. This form of employment, common in the EU, brings certain advantages to entrepreneurs – users of temporary agency workers. All the public duties imposed on employers (taxes, insurance contributions) are paid by the temporary work agencies which employ temporary agency workers and assigned to work for the user undertaking, therefore the lack of harmonization of the national labour laws under which the authorities of particular Member States specify the obligations of employers hiring agency workers directly contributes to differentiation of employment costs incurred by user employers.[2] According to the second hypothesis, the validity of which I want to verify in this study from a perspective of the Polish Act on employment of temporary agency workers of 9 July 2003,[3] in its version which came into force as of 24 January 2010, the harmonization of laws on temporary agency work on the EU level is explained as willingness to guarantee to the temporary agency workers a uniform and comparable legal protection. Considering the intention of the EU employer who endeavours to guarantee to temporary agency workers the conditions of employment and remuneration which are identical, similar or at least approximate to those guaranteed in the labour laws of particular Member States to full-time workers employed under contracts of employment of indefinite duration, an argument may be raised that the Directive 2008/104/EC aims at blurring any distinctions between workers who perform the same work within employment based on different types of employment contracts. Therefore, one may want to reason that the Directive 2008/104/EC, as a cross-border legal act laid down by Union institutions competent to regulate the common market within the EU, is aimed at unification of labour laws and practices of their application by authorities of particular EU Member States in matters relating to the legal situation of the temporary

---

1. B. Bercusson, *Introduction: Transnational Labour Regulation: Process and Substance*, in *Transnational Labour Regulation. A Case Study of Temporary Agency Work* 15, 321 ff. (K. Ahlberg et al. eds.., P.I.E. Peter Lang, Bruxelles, Bern, Berlin, Frankfurt am Mein, New York, Oxford, Wien 2008).
2. General Report: Temporary agency work in the European Union, The European Foundation for the Improvement of Living and Working Conditions, Dublin 2002, http://www.eurofound.eu.int/publications/files/EFO247EN.pdf; R. Blanpain & R. Graham, *Temporary Agency Work and the Information Society*, Bulletin of Comparative Labour Relations, No. 50 (2004).
3. Polish Journal of Laws Dz.U. No. 166, item 1608.

agency workers. In this study I will try to consider what is the key objective of the Directive 2008/104/EC: regulation of the temporary agency work or unification, in the labour law systems of the EU Member States, of the legal situation of the workers performing such work – temporary agency workers. A comparison of the titles of the EU and national legal acts, for example the Polish Act of 9 July 2003, regulating various matters concerning employment where temporary agency workers perform temporary work, shows significant discrepancies between EU laws which put an emphasis on regulating the temporary agency work and the Polish laws which accentuate the necessity to regulate the legal situation of temporary agency workers. Therefore, it should be considered whether it is possible to bring the Polish laws on employment of the temporary agency workers in line with the standards applicable in the EU which specify the temporary agency work in the categories and terms of the labour law. However, first it is necessary to answer the first question put in the introduction to the analyses concerning the supranational (EU) and national aspects of the temporary agency work: whether Directive 2008/104/EC contains provisions which provide for obligations of the authorities of particular Member States, obligations of employers who have employment relationships with temporary agency workers and user employers hiring temporary agency workers and for rights of temporary agency workers who have employment relationships with temporary work agencies and user employers. It is because EU directives may contain provisions called *soft* labour laws. In such situation the provisions of the EU labour law are considered guidelines addressed exclusively to the authorities of the Member States from which no rights and obligations of the parties to individual employment relationships can be derived. This, in turn, makes it impossible for the national judicial authorities to settle disputes between the parties to the employment relationships in accordance with the provisions of the directives.

Having regard to the ambitions of the EU in the field regulated by labour laws: protection of human rights regulated by individual and collective labour laws, improvement of working conditions, compliance with the principle of equal treatment and prohibition of discrimination in work relations based on forbidden criteria of differentiation of a legal situation of workers, promotion of social partnership and encouraging the parties to the collective labour relations to take up and pursue the social dialogue, it can be expected that Directive 2008/104/EC, like other labour law directives, contains clear and well-defined regulations which, upon their implementation by the authorities of the Member States into the national labour law systems, will lead to harmonization of laws which specify the terms and conditions of performance of temporary agency work and the legal situation of the temporary agency workers.

Directive 2008/104/EC is another EU legal act of the series of laws enacted in order to regulate atypical employment: work performed under fixed-term employment contracts, part-time employment and temporary agency work. According to statistical data published by Union institutions for fifteen years between 1990 and 2005, there was a 100% increase in employment (from 20% to 40%) of workers based on atypical forms of employment, other than full-time employment based on employment contracts of indefinite duration.[4] The EU institutions which endeavour to guarantee equal treatment in employment for workers in typical (full-time workers with employment contracts of indefinite duration) and atypical (part-time workers or workers with employment contracts other than contracts of indefinite duration) employment relationships, have defined eight determinants used to compare the legal situation of workers in typical and atypical employment relationships. These include: access to trainings, determination of the number of workers for the purposes connected with appointment of worker representative bodies in the work establishment; provision of information by the employer to the representative bodies on matters relating to atypical workers and on the actions planned by the employer to be taken towards these workers; provision of information on the causes of any legal actions planned by the employer to be taken towards the atypical workers; provision of information to atypical workers on the employer's plans of hiring workers for indefinite period; right of atypical workers to benefit from social aid; access of atypical workers to social facilities in the work establishment. The seventh indicator was applicable to temporary agency workers only. The last indicator defined by the Union institutions is the legal situation of the temporary agency workers in work establishments to which they were assigned by their employers – temporary work agencies.[5] The EU institutions had shown their interest in the legal status of the temporary agency workers in connection with preparation of Directive 96/71/WE concerning the posted workers. The Union institutions did not attempt to regulate the work relationships of atypical workers – despite the similarity with the legal situation of part-time workers or workers with employment contracts other than contracts of indefinite duration and the social and economic differences which characterize the situation of these workers in comparison with typical workers – but they merely used their efforts to regulate work under fixed-term employment contracts, to determine the legal situation of workers seconded by employers to work in other Member States of the EU and to regulate temporary agency employment due to formal and legal requirements stipulated in the Union primary law for directives regulating conditions of employment, protection of common market against unfair competition and safety and hygiene at work and protection of health and life of workers. The attempts for regulation of the temporary agency work within the framework of one of the three above mentioned legal bases specified in the primary Union law required unanimous decision of the EU Council of Ministers on matters concerning regulation of conditions of employment (Article 94, ex Article 100 TEC) or a qualified majority in the Council of Ministers in other two categories of matters (Article 95, ex Article 100A TFEU – unfair competition; Article 137(1a), ex Article 118A

---

4. *A Social Portrait of Europe* 62, 64 (Luxemburg 1991); Commission Green Paper of 2006 'Modernizing Labour Law to Meet the Challenges of the 21st Century', COM (2006)708 final, Brussels 2006, 7.
5. Explanatory Memorandum to the Proposal for a Council Directive concerning the hosting of Workers in the framework of the provision of services, COM(91)230 final –SYN 346, Brussels 1, 1 Aug. 1991F, § 48.

TFEU – safety and hygiene at work).[6] The qualified majority was obtained in voting in the EU Council of Ministers only on the matter concerning guarantee of safe and hygienic work conditions for workers with a fixed-duration employment relationship or a temporary employment relationship. On 25 June 1991, the EU Council adopted Directive 91/383/EEC supplementing the measures to encourage improvements in the safety and health at work of workers with a fixed-duration employment relationship or a temporary employment relationship.[7] The Union institutions were interested in regulating the temporary employment relationship and in specifying uniform legal requirements to regulate the legal situation of temporary agency workers on the common market. Studies on the legal situation of the temporary agency workers in the EU Member States have shown that the authorities in these states applied one of two methods of control of the spreading temporary agency employment:

(1) They undertook actions to limit employment based on agreements between user employers and temporary work agencies for assignment of temporary agency workers to work. They did not endeavour to guarantee to temporary agency workers the rights comparable to those guaranteed to full-time workers employed under typical contracts of employment of indefinite duration.[8] This method is applied by the Polish legislature in the Act of 9 July 2003 on Employment of Temporary Agency Workers.[9] It prevents the user employers from hiring, as temporary agency workers, those workers who have employment relationships with such employers, regardless of the type of the employment contract and the number of working hours (Article 4). An entrepreneur may not, in relation to the same workers, act in the social role of an employer and a user employer. The above prohibition is a consequence of the specific character of the legal relationships which form the basis and framework for the performance of temporary agency work. An entrepreneur – a beneficiary of a contract concluded with a temporary work agency, acting as a user employer – uses the work performed by workers assigned by the

---

6. Article 94 (ex Art. 100) TFEU authorized the Council to unanimously issue directives for the approximation of such laws, regulations or administrative provisions of the Member States as **directly** affecting the establishment or functioning of the common market. By way of derogation from Art. 94 TFEU the Council shall, acting in accordance with the procedure referred to in Art. 251 (ex Art. 189b) TFEU adopt the measures for the approximation of the provisions laid down by law, regulation or administrative action in Member States which have as their object the establishment and functioning of the internal market. Art. 251(2) TFEU requires qualified majority in the Council to adopt the amendments or a proposed act or to adopt a common position to communicate it to the European Parliament. The Lisbon Treaty amending the Treaty on European Union and the Treaty Establishing the European Union, drawn up in Lisbon on 13 December 2007 (Polish Journal of Laws Dz.U. of 2009, No. 203, item 1569) changed the sequence of Art. 94 and Art. 95. Art. 94 was numbered Art. 95, and Art. 95 was numbered Art. 94 (point 80). The contents of Art. 251(1) TFEU remained unchanged in the part relating to the requirement of qualified majority for Council resolutions on the adoption of legal acts (point 239).
7. OJ 1991 L 206/19.
8. L. Zappala, *Legislative and Judicial Approach to Temporary Agency Work In EU Law – An Historical Overview*, in *Transnational Labour Regulation, supra*, 158.
9. Polish Journal of Laws Dz.U. No. 166, item 1608 as amended.

temporary work agency where such agency is the employer – within the meaning of the generally applicable laws – for such workers. The prohibition stipulated in Article 4 of the Employment of Temporary Agency Workers Act is a consequence of a relationship, characteristic for temporary agency work, between two private economic law and labour law entities: employer of temporary agency workers (temporary work agency), user worker and temporary agency workers performing work for the user employer at the time when they are in employment relationship with other employer for whom they do not perform any work. Since in the legal relationships one and the same entity cannot enter into legal relationship 'with oneself', therefore the temporary work agency cannot act at the same time as a user employer and enter 'with oneself' into an agreement for employment of temporary agency workers whom it would assign to itself as an intermediate body in employment. However, Article 4 of the Employment of Temporary Agency Workers Act in my opinion does not apply to such workers with whom the user employer has an employment relationship and who will be assigned by the temporary work agency to perform temporary work other than the work which they have previously performed for this employer. In my opinion, the Polish Labour Code does not create a legal obstacle for the same entities to remain in one or more legal relationships at the same time. Therefore, there are no obstacles which would prevent the employer from being the user employer in relation to the workers whom he/she hires, provided that the work performed as a temporary agency work by workers hired by the user employer is different from the work that they perform for the employer.

Other prohibitions and restrictions on employment of temporary agency workers set out in the above Act relate to particularly dangerous works defined in the laws enacted under Article 237[15] of the Polish Labour Code, to work positions held by workers on strike, to filling the posts held – for the past three months preceding the date of hiring the temporary agency workers – by workers dismissed for reasons not related to the individual workers concerned (Article 8 points 1–3).

The restriction on employment of temporary agency workers is pursued also by the maximum, eighteen-month period of employment of such workers by the same employer, falling within thirty-six consecutive months, as stipulated in Article 20(1) of the Employment of Temporary Agency Workers Act. By way of an exception, Article 20(2) of the said Act authorizes a single employer to hire a temporary agency worker for a period of thirty-six months, if such worker performs work for the user employer which involves duties which are normally performed by an absent worker who is in an employment relationship with the user employer. The temporary agency worker may be re-assigned to work for the user employer not earlier than after thirty-six months from the last temporary agency employment (Article 20(3)).

(2) They made efforts to guarantee to the temporary agency workers such protection which would be identical or comparable to protection ensured

under generally applicable labour laws in the Member State to full-time workers employed under contracts of employment of indefinite duration. Pursuant to these national labour law systems, hiring temporary agency workers is accepted by the employer provided that the legal situation of the temporary agency workers, in particular their worker and social rights, dependent on the length of service with the user employer, do not differ from the rights guaranteed to workers by the employer with whom they have work relationship. Because of the legal obstacles connected with award of worker and social rights which can be exercised by workers hired by an employer, the above regime is more seldom applied by the authorities of the Member States of the EU to the temporary agency workers for whom the employer is the temporary work agency – a legal entity which is not subject to laws applicable in the industry of the user employer. Therefore, most frequently the obligation imposed on the user employer to guarantee to the temporary agency workers the status equal to that enjoyed by the workers for whom the entrepreneur – acting towards the temporary agency workers as a user employer is limited to the obligation of temporary agency workers, to pay them similar or comparable remuneration for the equal work or work of equal value and awarding them the rights to use the social facilities which exist in the work establishment in which they temporarily perform work.

Protection of worker and social rights in the EU labour law was not – and still is not – treated by the Union institutions as a condition precedent for exercising the basic right of free movement of workers to enter the common labour market. The freedom of movement within the EU covers all job seekers. The above freedom does not depend on the form and type of employment. Therefore it covers workers performing work within typical and atypical forms of employment. The European labour law literature explicitly states that EU laws which relate to cross-border standards of employment of temporary agency workers cannot be considered an obstacle for exercising the right to take up employment in other Member States of the EU by persons assigned to work in these Member States by the temporary work agencies registered in the territory of other EU Member States.[10] Entrepreneurs also exercise the right to provide services freely within the EU. Placement services provided by the temporary work agencies are one of the types of services protected under primary European law.

The temporary agency employment existed also in the European states which accessed the EU on 1 May 2004 – ten years prior to their accession.[11] The laws applicable in the EU and relating to temporary agency work are subject to labour law expert studies in other industrialized countries. I share

---

10. B. Bercusson, *supra*, 24–25; L. Zappalà, *supra*, 155–156.
11. In Poland, in 1994, the first temporary work agency assigned twenty-one workers to work for user employer. In 2004 the temporary work agencies employed 167,000 workers – 0.4% of the population of vocationally active people. See K. Ahlberg, *The New Member States: Regulating a New Phenomenon*, in *Transnational Labour Regulation, supra*, 146–147.

the views presented in the European labour law literature that the EU and its supranational labour law – as regards regulation of temporary agency work – plays a pioneering role on a global scale.[12] When describing the results of the legislative activity of EU institutions, European Parliament and Council, in matters relating to regulation of temporary work in the context of the Union institutions' approach to the social policy in the field of employment and social security of temporary agency workers – I analyse the legal nature of the legal provisions included in the Directive 2008/104/EC and the legal consequences of the above mentioned directive for the systems of individual and collective labour laws and the social security law in the Member States of the EU. This study includes three substantial parts. In the first part, I present the social and economic context of a supranational – EU legislative process, preceding the adoption of cross-border provisions on temporary work. In the second part, I analyse the legal situation of the participants in legal relations which are the basis for temporary agency employment and I describe their rights and obligations. In the third part, I analyse the scope of the amendments which will need to be entered, by 5 December 2011, to the Act of 9 July 2003 on employment of temporary agency workers, currently in force in Poland. There is a reason to fear that Directive 2008/104/EC on temporary agency work established 'soft' standards which allow the Member States of the EU to inform the Commission of applicable provisions necessary to fulfil the obligation specified in Article 11(1) of the above directive: to adopt and publish the laws, regulations and administrative provisions necessary to comply with this directive. Considering the previous Polish experience relating to the implementation of some labour law directives, there is a reason to fear that amendment of the provisions of the Act of 9 July 2003 on employment of temporary agency workers will be limited to fulfilment of formal obligations specified in Article 11(2) of Directive 2008/104/EC, namely to inclusion in the mentioned act of the provisions including a reference to Directive 2008/104/EC. The purpose of this study is the analysis of cross-border (European) and national (Polish) laws on temporary work and/or temporary agency workers in order to determine the obligations of the Member States of the EU.

§2.02   SOCIAL AND ECONOMIC CONTEXT OF EU LAWS ON TEMPORARY WORK

By the end of 2002, the EU institutions initiated legislative works aimed at preparation and adoption of a directive which would protect the part of the common labour market in the Member States of an 'old' EU against competition from entrepreneurs who exercise their freedom of movement within the Union to provide services. The

---

12. *International Regulatory Competition and Coordination: Perspectives on Economic Regulation in Europe and the United States* 4 (W. Bratton, J. McCahery, S. Picciotto & C. Scott eds., Clarendon Press 1996).

placement services were considered service. Provision by temporary work agencies of workers from the 'new' Member States of the EU to entrepreneurs established in the Member States of the 'old' Union who conduct business activity in those states would disturb the rules of competition due to the difference in remuneration for work of the workers performing work within typical and atypical work relations.

At first, the vigorously developing atypical forms of employment and the temporary work were subject to legal regulation in the Member States in which the authorities found that exercising the freedom of movement by entrepreneurs from less developed countries poses a threat to fair competition on the local labour markets since the employers who post workers to perform work in wealthier EU Member States or who acted as agents in provision of workers from the less developed EU Member States to work for the user employers in the more industrialized Member States benefited from lower costs of business activity. Legal or administrative prohibitions and restrictions on employment of temporary agency workers established by the authorities in particular EU Member States posed a threat to the functioning of the common internal market within the EU. They were contrary to the freedom of services and freedom of movement of people guaranteed in the European primary laws. The first attempts to adopt directives – according to the drafts which aimed at elimination or restriction of unfair competition among entrepreneurs where some of them had access to cheaper workforce and thus were able to conduct more cost-effective and competitive activity – were not successful. Having evaluated the temporary employment in a long-term perspective, the authorities of the Member States and the EU institutions concluded that the new form of employment of workers, including the temporary work, cannot be considered an alternative for the traditional employment policy. After years of experiments in the field of social policy with measures which were to ensure more flexibility to employers when taking decision on dismissal of redundant worker, after attempts made to liberalize the too restrictive (in the employers' opinion) protective labour laws, inability to guarantee the full social security to dismissed workers resulting from difficulties in coordination of activities undertaken to enable the unemployed persons to acquire new qualifications (at the earliest opportunity) which would enable them to undertake attractive, full-time work based on contract of indefinite duration – the EU institutions found that the atypical form of employment, including the temporary work, are not per se a sufficiently effective remedy for problems in economy and employment within the internal EU market.

In March 2005, the Council considered it vital for the social policy of the EU to relaunch the Lisbon Strategy and to refocus its priorities on growth of employment on the common market. The Council, taking all the activities to pursue this objective, considered it useful to promote flexibility combined with employment security within the common market. A condition precedent for achievement of this last objective is to reduce the disparities on the national labour markets functioning within the common market. In subparagraph eight of the preamble to Directive 2008/104/EC the European Parliament and the Council emphasized the necessity to include the social partners in the process of 'reduction of labour market segmentation'. They referred to the previous positive experience which resulted in conclusion on 18 March 1999 of a framework agreement on fixed-term work. The signatories of this agreement indicated their intention to consider the need for a similar agreement on temporary agency work. Therefore, they decided to exclude the temporary agency workers from the scope of the Council Directive no. 99/70/EC of 28 June 1999 concerning the framework agreement on fixed-term work concluded by the Union of Industrial and Employers' Confederations of Europe (UNICE), the European Centre of Enterprises with Public Participation (CEEP) and the European Trade Union Confederation (ETUC).[13] The social partners acknowledged that their negotiations on temporary agency work had not produced any agreement. For that reason the EU institutions returned to their shelved proposals of Directive on temporary agency work. In March 2005 the Commission developed an agenda of legislative works on the social matters in a period until 2010. Having approved the above agenda, the EU Council considered that the new, atypical form of employment and a greater diversity of contractual arrangements for workers and employers, would better contribute to adaptability than the traditional contracts of employment under which workers perform work directly for their employer, if they better combined employment flexibility and social security than the traditional contracts. In December 2007 the Council endorsed the agreed common principles of flexicurity, which strike a balance between flexibility and security in the labour market and help both workers and employers to seize the opportunities offered by globalization. On the basis of the arrangements and conclusions presented in a report prepared by the Commission chaired by W. Kok, former prime minister of the Netherlands, the European Parliament and the Council decided to adopt the Directive on temporary agency work since they considered that temporary agency work meets not only undertakings' needs for flexibility but also the need of employees to reconcile their working and private lives. It thus contributes to job creation and to participation and integration in the labour market. Since there are considerable differences in the temporary agency work laws, in the use of temporary agency work and in the legal situation, status and working conditions of temporary agency workers in the Member States of the EU, therefore the Directive 2008/104/EC establishes a common legal framework for legal standards applicable in the EU Member States in matters relating to regulation of temporary agency work and the legal status of temporary agency workers. The above directive does not harmonize the labour laws regulating temporary agency work in the Member States of the EU. Subparagraph twelve of the preamble to the Directive 2008/104/EC defines the intentions of the EU legislator who endeavoured to regulate the most important aspects of the temporary agency work and the legal status of the temporary agency workers in the most transparent way, in accordance with the principle of proportionality, thus without unreasonable interference in matters less important in terms of temporary agency work and the situation of the temporary agency workers. When establishing the legal framework for the temporary agency work, the EU legislator aimed to respect the specifics of different national labour markets and the industrial relations in the Member States of the EU. The above justifies the question raised in the first part of this study concerning the purpose of adoption of

---

13. OJ L 175, 10.07.1999, 49; OJ L 244, 16.09.1999, 64. See L. Mitrus, *Stosunek pracy* 119 (Universitas 2005).

the Directive 2008/104/EC. The main purpose of the Directive 2008/104/EC is protection of temporary agency workers against discrimination in labour and employment relations.

The basic working and employment conditions applicable in the Member States to temporary agency workers should be at least those which would apply to such workers if they were recruited by the user undertaking to occupy the same job as the job performed on the temporary agency basis. The prohibition of discrimination of the temporary agency workers formulated in subparagraph twelve of the preamble of Directive 2008/104/EC was presented in subparagraph fourteen of the preamble to the analysed directive as an obligation to ensure to temporary agency workers the working conditions identical to those which were ensured to workers employed under employment contract of an indefinite duration. The above mentioned contract, concluded by workers with an employer for whom the workers perform work, is a criterion which enables to distinguish between a typical employment and temporary agency employment. However, it does not mean that the temporary agency workers who have typical employment relationship based on permanent contract with their temporary work agency should enjoy identical treatment by the user employer as the employees with whom he concluded permanent employment contracts. Subparagraph fifteen of the preamble to the Directive 2008/104/EC permits the Member States to provide in the national labour laws for differences in treatment of temporary agency workers performing a specific work under permanent contract with the temporary work agency for the user employer who employs for the similar work the employees with whom he concluded permanent contracts. Therefore the prohibition of discrimination of temporary agency workers by the user employers applies only to temporary agency workers who have fixed-term employment contracts with the temporary work agencies. While it allows the Member States of the EU to differentiate between the legal situation of temporary workers who have permanent contract with their temporary work agency and the legal situation of the workers who have employment contract with the user employer, the Directive 2008/104/EC does not consider the position held or the type of work the only reference point for comparison of situation of the temporary agency workers with other workers employed directly by the user employer. Equally important criterion for comparison of the legal situation of the two categories of workers is the type of employment contract. However, the entities with which employment contracts of indefinite duration are concluded are not important for the above comparisons. Temporary agency workers employed by the temporary work agency under fixed-term employment contract should be treated by the user employer – as regards employee and social rights – equally to the workers employed directly by the said employer under permanent employment contracts if they perform work similar to work entrusted to such workers. The analysed subparagraphs of the preamble to the Directive 2008/104/EC do not mention the necessity of equal treatment and prohibition on differentiating between the right of temporary agency workers and other workers (employed directly by the user employer) in a situation where both types of workers are employed under similar, fixed-term employment contracts by different employers.

Subparagraph sixteen of the preamble to the analysed directive provides for the possibility to make further exceptions to the principle of equal treatment and obligation to refrain from discrimination of temporary agency workers who have fixed-term employment contracts with the temporary work agencies and who perform similar work to work performed by workers employed under permanent contracts concluded directly with the user employers. In order to cope in a flexible way with the diversity of labour markets and industrial relations, the EU institutions authorize the authorities in the particular Member States to allow the social partners to define working and employment conditions, provided that the overall level of protection for temporary agency workers formulated in subparagraph fourteen of the preamble, is respected.

Directive 2008/104/EC was adopted to regulate the conditions of temporary agency work. It seems useless to authorize the authorities in the Member States to delegate to social partners the right to define the social policy and labour relations within the administrative limits of particular Member States of the EU. Directive 2008/104/EC is not intended to harmonize the social policy within the common market. The name of the directive suggests that it was adopted to regulate the temporary agency work. However, from the principles formulated in the preamble to the above mentioned directive it can be concluded that its main objective is to regulate the principle of equal treatment in work relations involving temporary agency workers. The prohibition of discrimination of these workers is valid, regardless of the methods of regulation of national labour markets and industrial relations by the authorities of the Member States. Additional stipulation introduced in subparagraph sixteen of the preamble to Directive 2008/104/EC should be considered only an additional guideline from EU institution to the authorities of the Member States concerning the importance of the principle of equal treatment of temporary agency workers formulated in subparagraph fourteen of the preamble to the analysed directive. Subparagraph sixteen of the above mentioned preamble emphasizes the importance of the overall level of protection of temporary agency workers. After comparison of the provisions of subparagraph fourteen and sixteen of the preamble to the said directive it might be concluded that the legal protection and prohibition of discrimination of temporary agency workers formulated in a specific way in subparagraph fourteen of the preamble define the overall level of protection of this category of workers. The protection allows no exceptions to be made, neither by Member States nor by social partners. I used a conditional mood because in the next, seventeenth subparagraph of the preamble to the Directive 2008/104/EC the EU institutions authorized the social policy makers in the EU Member States which have powers to influence the local labour markets and regulate the national industrial relations, to cooperate – in certain limited matters – relating to setting out the limited exemptions from the principle of equal treatment of temporary agency workers. An exception to the principle of equal treatment of temporary agency workers formulated in subparagraph fourteen of the preamble to the analysed directive, confirmed in subparagraph sixteen of the said preamble, is allowed under subparagraph seventeen of the preamble to the Directive 2008/104/EC. The wording of the provisions of subparagraph seventeen of the preamble to the above mentioned directive on one hand reflects the intent of the European legislator willing to ensure to temporary agency workers who have fixed-term contracts with a temporary work agency the legal situation similar to that ensured to workers employed under contracts of unspecified duration by the user employer. The said subparagraph formulates three requirements which must be met so that the state authorities and social partners are able, 'in certain limited circumstances', to derogate from the above principle of equal treatment of the temporary agency workers. The first requirement relates to exceptional situations. The second one requires conclusion of a tripartite agreement on the national level by the authorities of a Member State with the representatives of workers and employers. The third one obligates the entities competent to conclude such agreement – who decide to derogate from the general principle of equal treatment – to provide an adequate level of protection of the rights of temporary agency workers. The problem is that the provisions of two out of the three requirements listed in subparagraph seventeen of the preamble to the Directive 2008/104/EC, the first and the third one, include vague concepts. The expression 'certain limited circumstances' may only be considered an announcement that situations will be specified, in which – in compliance with the tripartite principle – competent entities will be able to conclude an agreement providing for derogation from the principle of equal treatment in work relations involving temporary agency workers. Neither subparagraph seventeen nor any other provision of the said directive names an institution competent to indicate the 'certain limited circumstances' which justify derogation from the principle of equal treatment of temporary agency workers. Logically it might seem that the above competences were reserved for EU institutions. However, the restraint declared by the EU as regards issuance of a directive which would harmonize the labour laws regulating the temporary agency work and the situation of the temporary agency workers does not substantiate the above assumption. Respect for the diversity of labour markets and industrial relations as declared in the previously presented legal provisions included in subparagraph twelve and fourteen of the preamble to the Directive 2008/104/EC indicates that such competence should be granted to the Member States concerned. In my opinion, the tripartite principle stipulated in subparagraph seventeen of the preamble to the analysed directive does not preclude the authorities of a Member State from being granted competences to independently define, in compliance with the requirements set out in this provision, the exceptions to the general principle of equal treatment of temporary agency workers. The legal norm included in the above mentioned subparagraph seventeen of the preamble allows to distinguish two separate competences. The first one – to strictly specify the circumstances in which derogation from the principle of equal treatment of temporary agency workers is possible. There are no legal obstacles which would preclude the authorities of a Member State concerned from being granted a right to exercise the above competence. The second one – which results from exercising the right to strictly regulate the circumstances in which the authorities of a Member State are entitled to allow other entities to make a decision on derogation from the principle of equal treatment of temporary agency workers in labour relations. The resolution on the above matter is reserved to the competence of a tripartite committee composed of representatives of authorities of the Member State concerned and the social partners authorized under the national labour laws of a given Member State to participate in legal transactions in this state on the national level. The social partners were entitled by Directive 2008/104/EC to control the rationale of the activities undertaken by the authorities of the Member States of the EU. The absence of consent of a representative of employees or employers prevents introduction of limited derogations from the principle of equal treatment of temporary agency workers. The systematic interpretation of the subparagraph seventeen of the preamble to the Directive 2008/104/EC supports the proposed interpretation presented above. The cited provision also does not name an entity competent to issue legal acts applicable in the Member State pursuant to which the principle of equal treatment of workers could be partially limited. There is no such tradition in the Member States of the EU to determine the labour laws in compliance with tripartite principle. Under a resolution made by the tripartite committee which confirms that a relevant agreement has been concluded by authorized entities – authorities competent to determine applicable labour laws in particular Member States adopt applicable laws. Since the limitation of the right of equal treatment of a specific category of workers is considered interference of the state authorities in the fundamental human rights protected by labour laws, therefore the right to exercise the above mentioned competence is usually reserved for a legislative body – a parliament.

Subparagraph seventeen of the preamble to Directive 2008/104/EC suggests to the Member States that they should exercise the competence to grant exceptions to the principle of equal treatment of temporary agency workers reasonably and knowingly and only to the limited extent – when it is necessary to protect certain, important interests of the local labour market or the national labour relations in a given Member State of the EU.

The most difficult is the interpretation of the provision which allows for derogations from the principle of equal treatment of temporary agency workers provided that an 'adequate' level of protection is provided. The term 'adequate' is a synonym to 'suitable', 'appropriate', 'proper'. Since the adequate level of protection is a condition precedent for derogation from the principle of equal treatment of temporary agency workers, it should be considered what will be the standards for determination of the level of rights of such workers so as to satisfy the EU institutions which order to guarantee to the temporary agency workers who do not have permanent employment contracts with the temporary work agency such conditions of employment and remuneration as were guaranteed to workers who perform identical or similar work and who are employed under contracts of indefinite duration with other workers who remain in an employment relationship with user employers. It is even more difficult because of the fact that the provisions of the preamble to the analysed directive formulate two uncomparable levels of legal protection of the temporary agency workers: 'overall' and 'adequate'. The overall level of legal protection of temporary agency workers is mentioned in subparagraph sixteen of the preamble which formulates the principle of equal treatment. The term 'overall' is a term applied to specify the personal scope of this category of workers who should have the guarantee of legal protection. All temporary agency workers employed by the temporary work agencies under fixed-term employment contracts should be treated by the user employers equal to the employees who have employment contracts of indefinite duration with those employers. There are no exceptions to the above rule. In particular, the legal norm formulated in subparagraph seventeen may not constitute the basis for such exception. Since the term 'overall level of protection' cannot be used directly to determine the level of the legal protection which should be guaranteed to the temporary agency workers, then it should be considered whether it is possible to apply the guideline included in this norm when considering the personal scope of the reduced, however still suitable (adequate) level of legal protection. I think that the expression 'overall level of protection' may be used as a supporting element in the process of evaluation of the level of the protection guaranteed to the temporary agency workers if the right to derogate from the principle of equal treatment of these workers is exercised, as the above expression makes a reference to the principle included in subparagraph fourteen of the preamble to the analysed directive. The basic conditions of employment, namely the standards relating to working hours, overtime, breaks, period of rest, work at night, vacation, holidays and remuneration of these workers guaranteed by their temporary work agencies should be at least those which would be ensured to such workers if they were employed by the user undertakings as 'permanent' workers, i.e., employed under contract of employment of indefinite duration. However, the consequence of the common labour law principle of equal treatment of workers and prohibition of discrimination of workers who perform similar or comparable work is the obligation of similar treatment of workers. The 'adequate' level of protection which should be guaranteed in case of exceptions made under the agrements between the authorities of a Member State and social partners may deviate, in certain limited circumstances, from the standards listed in subparagraph fourteen of the preamble to the Directive 2008/104/EC. In exceptional situations, reasonably justified to maintain the flexibility of the local market and a specific, distinct nature of the industrial relations in particular Member States, the authorities in these Member States are entitled, in certain limited circumstances, to grant exceptions from the principle of equal treatment of temporary agency workers, that the temporary work agencies and user employers can apply.

Regulation of the legal situation of the temporary agency workers in labour relations should – according to the provisions of Directive 2008/104/EC – follow a dual approach. The improvement of the minimum protection for temporary agency workers should be accompanied by review and verification of any restrictions and prohibitions on application of this legal form of atypical employment in the Member States. The above obligation is imposed on the Member States of the EU by the provisions of subparagraph eighteen of the preamble to the described directive. This provision is not mandatory. The second sentence of this provision provides for an exception to the principle established in the first sentence, namely the restrictions and prohibitions on employment of temporary agency workers may be justified only on grounds of the 'general interest'. The above expression, which is a general clause, is followed by exemplary requirements listed in subparagraph eighteen of the preamble: protection of workers, the requirements of safety and health at work and the need to ensure that the labour market functions properly and that abuses are prevented. The cited subparagraph of the preamble specifies the reasons for which the EU institutions authorize the Member States to maintain the restrictions and prohibitions on temporary work for the need to ensure protection to the temporary agency workers and the local labour markets. However, it is difficult to agree with the reasoning of the EU institutions which based their decision to allow the authorities of the Member States to maintain the restrictions or prohibitions on employment of temporary agency workers on ground of protection of their employee and social rights, including in particular the right to work in safe and healthy conditions and protection of their health. The key objective formulated in Directive 2008/104/WE – of equal treatment of temporary agency workers – in my opinion prevents establishment of lawful excuses constituting legal norms which create restrictions or prohibitions on employment of such atypical employees. The work which is to be performed by temporary agency workers should be performed in such conditions which allow for employment of any worker, both typical and atypical. The above rule is the direct consequence of the principle of equal treatment of workers in work relations and of the prohibition of discrimination of temporary agency workers.

The next, nineteenth subparagraph of the preamble to the Directive 2008/104/EC includes a statement that regulation of the temporary agency employment on the European Level and guarantee of equal treatment in employment and in labour relations to temporary agency workers does not affect the autonomy of the social partners nor should it affect legal, social and economic relations between the social partners. In particular, the Directive 2008/104/EC has no legal effect in relations between such partners in the area which is partly regulated by collective labour laws concerning the right to negotiate and conclude collective agreements. As a foreword to the contents presented in the next, third part of this study, it must be held that Directive 2008/104/EC deals very little with the regulation of the temporary agency work in the context of legal issues subject to the collective labour laws in the EU Member States. Perhaps such restraint on the part of the EU institutions results from a limited personal scope of the European Labour law with regard to matters governed by the collective labour law. The European social laws (European labour and social security laws) have very developed part of the individual labour law which consists of primary and secondary legislation adopted for harmonization of legal institutions: freedom of movement within the EU to undertake employment, equal treatment of workers and prohibition of discrimination, information on the conditions of employment, atypical labour relations (part-time work, fixed-term employment, workers seconded to work in other EU Member State), protection of workers in case of restructuring the work establishments (acquisition by other employer, collective redundancies, insolvency of an employer), working time and vacation, protection of maternity, parental leaves, protection of minor workers, safety and hygiene at work. Also the provisions for coordination of national security systems are developed. However, the section: 'Collective labour law of the European Union' is limited to legal provisions which enable the workers employed in enterprises having the legal status of European establishments, to participate in the process of decision making by the employers in a form of information or consultations or via the European Works Council. The Directive 2008/104/EC follows this pattern. It obligates the authorities in the Member States to order the employers who conduct business activity within the common market to count – under conditions established by competent authorities of the Member States – the temporary agency workers for the purposes of calculating the threshold above which bodies representing workers provided for under Union and national law are to be formed at the temporary work agency or the user employer (Article 7(1) and (2)). Those Member States which decide to count the temporary agency workers to the total number of workers employed by the user employers for the purposes of calculating the threshold above which bodies representing all workers: employed and performing work for the user employer are to be formed in the user undertaking, shall not be obliged to adopt provisions which provide for an obligation to form the bodies representing workers in the temporary work agencies (Article 7(3)). Those employers which decide to choose an option provided in Article 7(2) are relieved from the obligation to imply the rule established by Article 7(1). The Member States which choose option provided for in Article 7(2) shall not be obliged to implement provisions of Article 7(1). The above doubt whether the states which choose option stipulated in Article 7(1) are not obliged to implement Article 7(2) is justified. It seems that the only intention of the EU legislator was to grant to the temporary agency workers the right to participate in the procedure which aims at formation in the respective establishments of bodies representing the workers. Because of a specific, double legal and organizational relation between the temporary agency workers and their employers with whom they have employment relations and employers for whom they perform work, it is justified to consider both norms of Article 7 of Directive 2008/104/EC as alternative solutions. I come to such a conclusion because I think that it is not possible to present arguments which would prove the higher value – in case of temporary agency workers – of the right of formation of and participation in the bodies representing the workers in the work establishment managed by the employer with whom they have employment relations (temporary work agency) or the employer for whom they perform work (user employer).

§2.03 COMPLIANCE OF NATIONAL LABOUR LAWS ON EMPLOYMENT WITH THE STANDARDS ESTABLISHED BY DIRECTIVE 2008/104/EC

The Act of 9 July 2003 on employment of temporary agency workers entered into force as of 1 January 2004. After six years of functioning of the Act in Poland it might be possible to make comparisons between the national and supranational labour laws if not for the different assumptions of legislators, underlying the compared measures.

Directive 2008/104/EC is without prejudice to the Member States' right to apply or introduce legislative, regulatory or administrative provisions which are more favourable to workers or to promote or permit collective agreements concluded between the social partners which are more favourable to workers (Article 9(1)). Because of the fact that the analysed directive contains only three types of legal norms which regulate the rights of temporary agency workers: right to equal treatment (Article 5), access to employment, collective facilities and vocational training (Article 6), participation in the bodies representing the workers – it should be analysed whether the provisions of the Polish Employment of Temporary Agency Workers Act are more favourable than the standards specifying the minimum level of rights of the temporary agency workers.

Article 15(1) of the Act obligates the user employer to treat the temporary agency workers – in terms of work conditions and other conditions of employment – at least the same way as he treats his own employees, employed in identical or similar position.

All conditions of work and employment of temporary agency workers, and not only the basic conditions, should comply with the minimum standards applied by the user employer towards other workers performing identical or comparable work, employed by such employer. The material scope of the obligation of equal treatment of temporary agency workers is wider in the Act, thus more favourable than the minimum standard established in the Directive 2008/104/EC. However, the Polish Employment of the Temporary Agency Workers regulates differently the point of reference for comparison of legal situation of the temporary agency workers and the situation of other workers employed on a permanent basis by the employer who acts towards the temporary agency workers as the user employer. In my opinion, the measures applied in Article 15(1) of the Polish Act are, for some of these workers, less favourable than the minimum standard specified in Article 5(1) of the Directive 2008/104/EC. The current Polish laws order the user employer to treat the temporary agency worker the same way as he treats the worker already employed by such employer. It means that in relations with the temporary agency worker the only decisive criterion as regards conditions of work and employment is the position held or the type of the work performed. Leaving aside other, legally acceptable criteria for differentiation of the legal situation of employed workers: the amount, quality of work, scope of responsibility, care and diligence, compliance with work discipline, a situation may occur when temporary agency workers who have outstanding results in comparison to all the other workers employed on a permanent basis by the employer will not be recognized by the user employer. Formally, the conduct of the user employer will have to be considered lawful even if in practice the outstanding temporary agency workers would be entitled, under Article 5(1) of the Directive 2008/104/EC to raise a claim of discrimination. Despite the fact that the deviation of the Polish laws from the standards of the directive will work for the benefit of the temporary agency workers who do not have better work results than the workers employed by such employer to occupy the same job, you cannot balance the profits and losses resulting from the differences in the national labour laws in the provisions regulating the obligation of equal treatment of temporary agency workers. The right of the temporary agency worker to receive equal treatment in labour relations is of personal nature. As it constitutes a subjective right, it cannot be compared with rights of other entitled persons. Moreover, it cannot be counterbalanced with more favourable treatment by the user employer of other entitled persons.

However, definitely more favourable is the regulation of the principle of equal treatment provided for in Article 15(1) of the Polish Employment of the Temporary Agency Workers Act, as it does not permit – contrary to the provisions of Article 5(2) and (4) of Directive 2008/104/EC – an exemption to the above principle in the national labour laws. As I have already mentioned, the Act of 9 July 2003 entered into force on 1 January 2004, several months prior to accession of Poland to the EU, with no possibility to apply transitional period connected with the EU membership.

The situation is different in case of comparison of the legal measures adopted in the Directive 2008/104/EC with the Polish regulations concerning access to employment, collective facilities and vocational training. In the beginning it should be underlined that Article 6(1) of the analysed directive is a legal norm which should be treated as a legal condition for the obligation of the user employer to enable the temporary agency workers to apply for employment with such employer. Article 4 of the Polish Employment of Temporary Agency Workers Act provides solely for the prohibition imposed on temporary agency workers to remain in labour relations in a period during which they perform for this employer, acting as the user employer, the temporary agency work. Introduction in Article 12 of the Act of 9 July 2003 of a sanction of absolute nullity of an agreement concluded by the temporary work agency with the user employer according to which the user employer should refrain from conclusion of employment contracts with temporary agency workers after termination of performance of the temporary work proves the compliance of the Polish laws with the EU standards.

Temporary agency workers in Poland have the right of access to social facilities of the user employer guaranteed in accordance with the principles stipulated for the permanent workers employed by such employer (Article 22 of the Act). It seems that the Polish regime fully complies with the EU standard established in Article 6(4) of the analysed directive. This provision imposes an obligation to ensure to the workers an access to the amenities or collective facilities in the user undertaking, and not only social facilities as provided for in Article 22 of the Polish Act.

However, the Act does not contain a provision which would be equivalent to Article 7 of Directive 2008/104/EC, which obligates the user employers or temporary work agencies to treat the temporary agency workers in the same way as if they were workers employed directly by this employer for the purposes of calculating the number of persons employed required to form the body representing the workers.

However, a significant difference exists between the directive and the Polish legal measures in terms of temporary work. Contrary to the Directive 2008/104/EC – which was issued to protect the labour market and fulfils this role by imposing on the Member States an obligation of equal treatment of temporary agency workers which will prevent admission to the local labour markets of the Member States of the EU of cheaper workforce – the purpose of the Polish Employment of Temporary Agency Workers Act is to regulate the legal situation of the temporary agency workers. The provisions of the Polish Act specify more precisely the obligations of the employers who have legal relations with temporary agency workers. Analysis of the provisions of this act from such perspective allows breaking down the legal norms into three categories. The first includes provisions which impose obligations on the temporary work agencies. These are: Article 7 (employment contract), Article 13 (characteristics of employment contract), Article 16 (compensation for unequal treatment by the user employer), Article 17(3) (allowance in lieu of holiday leave), Article 18a and Article 18b (certificate of employment), Article 20 (assignment to temporary work), Article 21 (exclusion of Article 25^1 of the Labour Code), Article 24 (determination of competent labour court). The second category includes the provisions which impose obligations on the user employer. These are: Article 8 (prohibition on entrusting specific tasks), Article 9(2) (obligation to inform the temporary work agency of certain conditions of work and employment), Article 10(2) (vacation), Article 14 (rights and obligations of the employer), Article 15 (obligation to provide equal treatment), Article 17(1) and (2) (vacation), Article 22 (access to social facilities), Article 23 (provision of information to unions). The third category includes the provisions which impose obligations on both employers who enter into legal relations with temporary agency workers. These are the norms which obligate the temporary work agency and the user employer to cooperate in matters relating to: arrangements on conditions of work and employment (Article 9(1) and (3)), vacation (Article 10(1)), notification of the worker of the arrangements made (Article 11), legal consequences of the arrangements contrary to the provisions of the act (Article 12).

A distribution of rights and obligations of the employers having legal relations with temporary agency workers between the temporary work agency and the user employer stipulated in the Polish law does not conflict with the legal measures introduced by the Directive 2008/104/EC. Protection of the labour market with legal measures which aim at regulation of the work relationship of the temporary agency workers so that it comes closest to the concept of obligatory work relationship applicable in the Member State seems effective method of protection of the local labour market. Its advantage is promotion by the authorities of the Member States the temporary work as one of atypical forms of employment and regulation of the legal status of the temporary agency workers. The Polish Act of 9 July 2003 on the employment of temporary agency workers stipulates that the temporary work is regulated by obligatory labour laws. Because of involvement of two employers on the part of the employing entity, the legislator distributed the rights and obligations on the part of the employers. Such solution obligated the Polish legislator to regulate in the labour laws the legal relations of the employers: the temporary work agency and the user employer. Considering the fact that the temporary work agency is solely liable to the temporary agency worker for non-fulfilment of the basic obligation to provide equal treatment imposed on the employer and is liable to the user employer for damage caused by the temporary agency worker, it must be held that in the labour relation entered into by the temporary work agency with the temporary agency worker, in which the user employer participates – the key entity out of the two employing entities is the temporary work agency which both under European and national (Polish) law acts as a formal employer.

§2.04 FINAL CONCLUSIONS

The method of presentation of the temporary work in the Directive 2008/104/WE – which considers the compliance by the Members States with the obligation of equal treatment of temporary agency workers in labour relations a key method of protection of the common labour market – guarantees to the authorities of particular Member States of the EU the wide freedom in implementation of provisions of the above directive in the national labour laws. In promoting the temporary work as an atypical form of employment, the EU institutions take advantage of the diversity of the national labour markets and local industrial relations for the purpose of protection of the common market. Additionally, they create a chance of permanent employment for the temporary agency workers to whom the performance of the temporary agency is a chance to enter into legal relations regulated by labour laws with their employers. In such case the temporary work agencies which conclude employment contracts with workers assigned to work for the user employers may additionally fulfil useful functions in the field of work placement.

Despite the fact that Directive 2008/104/EC does not regulate the work relationships of the temporary agency workers, it does not specify in detail the rights and obligations of the employers (temporary work agency and user employers) who remain in legal relations with the said workers, the above directive has serious chances to lead to harmonization of the labour laws of the EU Member States in matters relating to protection of local labour markets against provision by placement agencies on the common market of a cheaper workforce, formally employed by entrepreneurs from less industrialized, less developed and thus cheaper EU Member States. Directive 2008/104/EC adapts the labour law provisions of the EU Member States to the common model according to which the temporary work on the common market, as a form of atypical employment is acceptable, and the obligation of authorities of particular Member States is to abolish all the restrictions and prohibitions on employment of such workers. The legal status of the temporary agency workers in labour relations in the Member States in which they perform work for the user employers should be identical to the status they would benefit from under the labour laws in force in a given Member State if – by reason of employment relationship with the employer for whom they perform work – they were subject to labour laws in this state. The most significant advantage of the legal measures stipulated in the Directive 2008/104/EC is the possibility of the Member States to apply various legal regulations, all of which – because of the legal construction used in the said directive, characteristic for the 'Open Coordination Method' – will be in compliance with the model presented in the said directive, if they comply with the concept of equal treatment provided for by this directive.

The authorities of the Member States are obliged to apply effective, proportionate and deterring measures against the user employers who violate the principle of equal treatment of temporary agency workers and thus disturb the balance on the labour market. The Member States are obliged to inform the Commission on adaptation of the national labour laws to the standards established by Directive 2008/104/EC not later than by 5 December 2011. During the first two years of application of the directive in the EU Member States, not later than by 5 December 2013, the Commission – after consultation with the authorities of the Member States and the social partners operating in the European social space – will review the application of the said directive so as to be able to present, in appropriate circumstances, to the European employer – Parliament and the Council – the proposal for adoption of necessary amendments.

CHAPTER 3
Regulating Temporary Work in the United States

Alvin Goldman

In studying temporary work in the US it is necessary to understand that the government plays a minor role in job placement. Although state unemployment offices offer job referral services and some government welfare agencies provide such services, job placement in the US primarily is the domain of private entities. These include businesses devoted to providing job referral services, 'hiring halls' operated by labour organizations, work force recruitment conducted by employers that advertise their needs for new workers, and by placement offices provided by colleges and universities (public and private) and apprenticeship programmes that assist students and graduates in obtaining employment.

When the term 'temporary' employment is used in the US it is contrasted with the terms 'regular' or 'traditional' employment. The latter refer to employment that is expected to be of long duration regardless of whether for a specified extended length of time or for an indefinite period that both employer and worker expect to endure for the foreseeable future or until the worker retires or the enterprise closes. Nevertheless, in most states in the US 'regular' employment is 'at will'; as a general rule it may be terminated at the election of either party at any time unless, in the case of government employees, the right to terminate is restricted by statutory requirements of proven cause, or in the case of private sector employees, the right to terminate is restricted by a contract, such as a collectively bargained agreement or a grant of academic tenure, that explicitly limits dismissal to proven just cause.[1]

---

1. The 'at will' concept is no longer as rigidly adhered to as it was 35 years ago. See generally, A. Goldman & R. Corrada, *United States*, in *International Encyclopaedia of Labour Law* ¶¶ 148–165 (Wolters Kluwer, 2009) describing the basic principle and various common law and statutory exceptions.

Temporary work most often is of a contingent nature; the entire risk of short-term slowed or changed business activity is born by the employee or the duration of the relationship is tied to tasks that are expected to be completed within a period of days, weeks or a few months, or the employment engagement is to fill-in for an absent regular employee. Usually, temporary work is distinguished from other types of contingent work including being on-call, being leased by one's normal employer to do the work of another employer, or working for short durations as an individual contractor.

Generally, in the US, no specific form of contract is required for a temporary work or other contingent employment engagements, and arrangements for temporary or other contingent work are varied. There are a few situations, however, where mandated contractual instruments are used such as when migrant farm labour is obtained through a contracting agent,[2] the engagement of seafarers,[3] and the engagement of apprentices.[4]

The U.S. Bureau of Labor Statistics (BLS) uses several definitions in compiling data for those in contingent work arrangements. The narrowest of its measures excludes independent contractors, self-employed persons, and workers referred by temporary help agencies. (Temporary help agencies are defined as businesses that refer the worker to an employer. The latter hires, compensates and directs the worker.)[5] Another BLS measure of the contingent workforce combines those referred by temporary help agencies and leased employees who are expected to be assigned for less than a year. (Leased employees are in the regular employ of the lessor. Sometimes leased arrangements include providing supervisors to direct the other leased workers.) A third measure of contingent work further adds to the previous two groups those who are self-employed as well as those who do not expect their employment to continue for more than a year.

In 2005, the percentage of the workforce when measured by the BLS's narrowest contingent workforce category represented 1.8% of the total US workforce. Adding those referred by temporary help agencies and those leased for less than a year increased the portion of the contingent workforce to 2.3% of the total, and using the most inclusive definition raised the portion to 4.1%. From 1995 to 2001 there was a steady decline in each category of the portion in the contingent workforce. The portion of those in the contingent workforce thereafter began to increase.[6]

The Bureau of Labor Statistics uses an additional relevant data collection category. It measures 'alternative employment arrangements' and adds independent contractors and on-call workers to those counted in the contingent workforce. Using

---

2. 29 Code Fed. Reg. § 500.72.
3. 46 Code Fed. Reg. §§ 14.201-.209. The contract is called 'shipping articles'.
4. 29 U.S. Code § 50; 29 Code Fed. Reg. 29.4 et seq.
5. T. Luo, A. Mann & R. Holden, *The Expanding Role of Temporary Help Services from 1990 to 2008*, Mthly. Lab. Rev. 3 (Aug. 2010).
   'In the United States, temporary staffing services ... have existed since at least World War II and currently supply a large bulk of the temporary workforce' A. Valenzuela Jr., *Day Labor Work*, 29 Annual Rev. Sociology 307, 313 (2003).
6. C. von Hippel et al., *Operationalizing the Shadow Workforce*, in *The Shadow Workforce* 29, 31–33 (S. Gleason ed., Upjohn Inst. Press 2006).

Chapter 3: Regulating Temporary Work in the United States

this measure, in 2005 the portion of the workforce in alternative arrangements was 10.9%, an increase from 9.3% in 1995.[7]

The most recent data surveying those employed through temporary help agencies indicates that the current recession that began in 2007 in the US resulted in a reduction in the numbers of those who found temporary employment through such entities.[8] The decline in temporary help agency referred jobs actually began about twelve months before the start of the recession and declined by 19% while total employment declined 2.3%, suggesting that this form of employment may be a bell-weather for predicting a decline in prospective business activities.[9] During recoveries, gains in total non farm employment have begun 'just 3 or 4 months after those in the temporary industry.'[10] Similarly, it has been found that 'manufacturing plants tend to choose temporary workers over permanent workers when they expect output to fall, allowing them to avoid the costs of laying off permanent workers [and that] ... higher levels of uncertainty regarding output are associated with greater use of temporary workers'.[11] If employment referred by temporary help agencies is a bell-weather of impending work force changes, the most recent data is encouraging inasmuch as employment of workers referred by temporary help agencies experienced an almost steady increase since the start of 2010, though it was fairly level for the third calendar quarter of 2012.[12]

However, overall there has been considerable longer term growth in temporary help services over the past two decades. This trend may be a structural change reflecting the perception of American employers that a competitive edge is gained by enhanced flexibility resulting from favouring temporary employees over expanding the regular work force.[13]

---

7. C. von Hippel et al., *Operationalizing the Shadow Workforce*, in *The Shadow Workforce* 29, 34 (S. Gleason ed. 2006).
8. BLS, Employment, Hours, and Earnings from the Current Employment Statistics survey (National). In December 2000 these workers were 1.95% of a total workforce of 132,481,000; in December 2011 they were 1.8% of a total workforce of 132,965,000.
    Although technically the recession was over in 2009, when the economy began to expand, because of continued high unemployment and slow growth there is a popular perception that the recession has not yet ended.
9. T. Luo, A. Mann & R. Holden, *The Expanding Role of Temporary Help Services from 1990 to 2008*, Mthly. Lab. Rev. 3, 5 (Aug. 2010).
10. BLS, *Occupational Outlook Quarterly* 35 (Fall 2010).
11. T. Luo, A. Mann & R. Holden, *The Expanding Role of Temporary Help Services from 1990 to 2008*, Monthly Lab. Rev. 3, 7 (Aug. 2010); M. Vidal & L. Tigges, *Temporary Employment and Strategic Staffing in the Manufacturing Sector*, Indus. Rel. 55, 68 (January 2009) (finding a general pattern of use of temporaries to achieve numerical flexibility in staffing manufacturing plants).
    The cost of laying off regular workers may include voluntary severance benefits or statutory severance pay if required prior notice is not given. See description, below, of the Worker Adjustment and Retraining Act.
12. BLS, Current Employment Statistics Highlights October 2012, p. 10 (Nov. 2012).
13. T. Luo, A. Mann & R. Holden, *The Expanding Role of Temporary Help Services from 1990 to 2008*, Mthly. Lab. Rev. 3 (Aug. 2010).
    Because most employment in the US is 'at will', arguably hiring 'regular' employees should be no different than hiring 'temporary' employees. The fact that it does appear to make a difference reveals a cultural reality that most American managers are reluctant to exercise their power to dismiss workers even though workloads have diminished.

Some forms of temporary work go unmeasured. For example, surveys in the mid-1990s found that by age 12, half of American youths had engaged in some type of work such as paid baby-sitting or lawn mowing. Although there are restrictions on the hours of the day school age minors can work and the types of tasks they can perform, such employment is common during the school year and the summer recess. By the time surveyed children were in their mid-teens, most frequently they were employed in the retail trade and services industries – often as cashiers or janitors. 'Males often worked as construction labourers or in lawn care, while their female peers often perform child care or work as general office clerks or receptionists.'[14] Although the latter type of temporary or casual work done by teenagers normally is included in employment data, unless they are illegally engaged 'off-the-books',[15] baby-sitting and individually performed lawn care generally is unrecorded.

Overall, women and young workers are over-represented in the non-traditional work force, though older workers are the ones most represented in the independent contractor category of contingent workers. Some of these older workers have retired from traditional jobs. Also, non-traditional workers generally are less educated than the traditional workforce. These broad characterizations, however, can be misleading since patterns vary depending on the industry in which workers are employed and the nature of their participation in the contingent workforce. For example, college students often seek summer or part-time employment through temporary help agencies and college and graduate educated teachers who do not have annual or tenured contracts often work on-call as substitute teachers. Similarly, some independent contractors are used because of their superior education and there has been an increase in employment of higher skilled-higher wage workers who find jobs through temporary help agencies.[16]

Temporary work arrangements are not a new phenomena. It has been noted that the first format for employment most likely was temporary employment that aided in such activities as gathering crops, rocks, and wood; digging irrigation trenches; raising roof beams; or cutting timber for a boat mast. There are historical records of people gathering in public places in search of work during the Middle Ages. For example in England in the 1100s, workers seeking short-term employment went to the local market place.[17] However, temporary arrangements were not the only form of employment. In earlier centuries regular or long-term employment was common in skilled trades and on larger farms including the communal relationships of those living on feudal estates or plantations.[18]

---

14. BLS, D. Rothstein & D. Herz, *A Detailed Look at Employment of Youths Aged 12 to 15*, in *The Report on the Youth Labor Force* 20 (2000).
15. The term refers to cash payment for services so as to evade paying payroll taxes and insurance premiums.
16. C. von Hippel et al., *Operationalizing the Shadow Workforce*, in *The Shadow Workforce* (S. Gleason ed., Upjohn Inst. Press 2006) 29, 35–37; T. Luo, A. Mann & R. Holden, *The Expanding Role of Temporary Help Services from 1990 to 2008*, Mthly. Lab. Rev., 3, 5 (Aug. 2010).
17. A. Valenzuela Jr., *Day Labor Work*, 29 Annual Rev. Sociology 307, 312 (2003). In the US records of temporary hiring go back at least to 1780. A. Valenzuela, Jr. *supra* at 316.
18. A. Martinez Jr., *The Palatinate Clause of the Maryland Charter, 1632–1776: From Independent Jurisdiction to Independence*, 50 Am. J. Leg. History 305, 309–310 (2010).

Chapter 3: Regulating Temporary Work in the United States

In more recent centuries the growth of work methods such as the factory system, long distance merchandizing by seagoing vessels, the exploitation of distant cod fishing grounds and the whaling trade, required long-term commitments and temporary employment took on the character of a non-traditional or inferior work arrangement often ignored or scarcely noticed in the worker protective laws in the United States.

Because of the insecurity of irregular, short-term, and part-time work arrangements, temporary and other contingent employment often is thought of as undesirable employment. However, that assumption can be misleading. A 2005 survey found that 35.5% of all contingent workers said they preferred their non-traditional work arrangement. The extent of preference varied by the type of arrangement. For example, over four-fifths of independent contractors and a majority (56.2%) of temporary help agency referred workers reported preferring that arrangement to a traditional job.[19]

From the worker's perspective, temporary or other contingent employment sometimes is a means of obtaining new training and skill enhancement, exploring whether the work is suitable to the individual, and gaining an opportunity to demonstrate potential as a regular hire. Workers whose efforts are performed under an arrangement in which their work is leased to another employer may prefer the reduced risk of unemployment while maintaining their permanent ties and longevity benefits.[20] Another attraction for some is that temporary and other contingent employment offers variety in work activities or allows workers the independence to adjust their work schedule to other demands or desires including family commitments, volunteer activities, recreation, formal education or to pursuing low paid or unpaid creative endeavours. However, too often a temporary or other contingent work arrangement is the only work available to an individual who would prefer long-term, traditional employment.[21]

From the employer's perspective there are a variety of reasons why it is preferable to enter into a contingent employment arrangement. Some involve exploitation of the contingent worker's lack of bargaining power. Often contingent workers are drawn from those who have no savings or other employment and, therefore, are willing to be employed at reduced wages. They also are more likely to accept employment without benefits, such as paid vacation, medical insurance, and retirement fund contributions, that are contractual, traditional or statutory based expectations or requirements linked to job longevity.[22]

In other situations the employer's motivation is based on operational efficiency. Employers can gain from the flexibility resulting from their ability to use non-traditional workers to adjust workforce size and activity to the anticipated short-term

---

19. C. von Hippel et al., *Operationalizing the Shadow Workforce*, in *The Shadow Workforce* 29, 42 (S. Gleason ed., Upjohn Inst. Press 2006).
20. M. Lundy, K. Roberts & D. Becker, *Union Responses to the Challenges of Contingent Work Arrangements*, in *The Shadow Workforce* 99, 102 (S. Gleason ed., Upjohn Inst. Press 2006).
21. C. von Hippel et al., *Operationalizing the Shadow Workforce*, in *The Shadow Workforce* 29, 49–51 (S. Gleason ed., Upjohn Inst. Press 2006).
22. C. von Hippel et al., *Operationalizing the Shadow Workforce*, in *The Shadow Workforce* 29, 45–46 (S. Gleason ed., Upjohn Inst. Press 2006). D. Miller & J. Barney, *Employer Perspectives: Competing Through a Flexible Workforce*, in *The Shadow Workforce*, 65, 66–67 (S. Gleason ed., Upjohn Inst. Press 2006).

changes in the volume of demand for the employer's services or products and thereby avoid the costs of employing idle workers. (The related contention that employers use temporary workers to buffer their core workforce from job fluctuations, however, was rejected in one study of manufacturing enterprises.[23]) Flexibility is also gained for the employer when meeting temporary, occasional or non recurring needs for specialized skills or knowledge.[24]

Additionally, short-term employment arrangements can provide access to potential recruits with a minimum of commitment or can offer quick access to a trained workforce.[25] And, from the reverse perspective, short-term employment arrangements enables employers to lease their own core workers to others while retaining ties to them during slack periods.[26]

No doubt, too, some employers favour non-traditional work arrangements because the very temporariness of the arrangement makes union organizing more difficult due to both the greater difficulties in identifying and communicating with the workers and their unwillingness to invest in collective efforts that they perceive will at best bring them only transitory returns.[27] As seen below, the National Labor Relations Board's rules regarding contingent employees encourages this strategy. Related both to the desire for numerical flexibility, recruitment strategies, and, possibly, union avoidance strategies, a study of manufacturing enterprises found that enterprises with multiple plants and with human resources departments were significantly more likely to use temporary employees.[28]

Inasmuch as the availability of temporary employees can undermine job security and expansion of the regular workforce, not surprisingly, studies show that unionization in manufacturing facilities substantially reduces the use of temporary employees.[29]

§3.01 LAW

The extent to which temporary and other contingent workers are protected in the US varies with the type of protection at issue. Some laws treat these workers in the same manner as other workers, some have special provisions respecting such workers, and

---

23. M. Vidal & L. Tigges, *Temporary Employment and Strategic Staffing in the Manufacturing Sector*, Indus. Rel. 55, 69 (January 2009).
24. M. Lundy, K. Roberts & D. Becker, *Union Responses to the Challenges of Contingent Work Arrangements*, in *The Shadow Workforce* 99, 100 (S. Gleason ed., Upjohn Inst. Press 2006); M. Vidal & L. Tigges, *Temporary Employment and Strategic Staffing in the Manufacturing Sector*, Indus. Rel. 55, 68 (January 2009) (study found that manufacturers strategically and systematically used temporaries to achieve numerical flexibility in their workforce).
25. D. Miller & J. Barney, *Employer Perspectives: Competing Through a Flexible Workforce*, in *The Shadow Workforce* 65, 69 (S. Gleason ed., Upjohn Inst. Press 2006).
26. C. von Hippel et al., *Operationalizing the Shadow Workforce*, in *The Shadow Workforce* 29, 46–47 (S. Gleason ed., 2006).
27. C. von Hippel et al., *Operationalizing the Shadow Workforce*, in *The Shadow Workforce* 29, 47–48 (S. Gleason ed., Upjohn Inst. Press 2006). See discussion below concerning how this goal is facilitated by the National Labor Relations Board's bargaining unit determinations.
28. M. Vidal & L. Tigges, *Temporary Employment and Strategic Staffing in the Manufacturing Sector*, Indus. Rel. 55, 70 (January 2009).
29. M. Vidal & L. Tigges, *Temporary Employment and Strategic Staffing in the Manufacturing Sector*, Indus. Rel. 55, 68 (January 2009).

some laws withhold protection from at least some categories of temporary and other contingent workers.

[A] Collective Bargaining and Collective Representation

The National Labor Relations Act (NLRA) and Railway Labor Act (RLA) protect the rights of most non government workers to engage in concerted activities for mutual aid and protection and to bargain collectively if a majority of workers select a bargaining representative in a unit that is administratively found to be appropriate for collective bargaining.[30] Most federal government workers have similar rights (though not the right to strike) and state laws often extend similar rights to state and local government workers (often, though, with provisions for strike substitutes). Not all temporary and other contingent workers are treated alike under these laws.

Because contingent work often is performed by persons who one party or the other claims to be an independent contractor, it is important to note that independent contractors are expressly excluded from the protections of the NLRA, the statute that regulates labour organizing and employer–labour organization relations in most industries. Functional tests, rather than self-described labels, determine whether this exclusion applies. No single test is determinative. Rather, the principle factors weighed are: whether the person in question independently performs work for multiple businesses or for a single entity; whether the person in question obtained the needed training or experience independently of the entity in question; whether the person does business in the entity's name; whether the purported independent contractor receives considerable assistance and guidance from the managerial personnel of the entity for which the work is done; whether the terms and conditions under which the worker operates are promulgated and changed unilaterally by the entity for which the work is done; whether the worker governs the finances of his or her work activities; whether the worker receives the benefits of the entity's vacation plan, group insurance and pension fund; whether there is an arrangement under which the worker may continue as long as performance is satisfactory; and whether the alleged employer has the right to control both the ends to be achieved and the means used to achieve those ends.[31]

Although the RLA does not explicitly exclude independent contractors from its protections, and the issue has not received much attention from the courts, the exclusion of independent contractors from the RLA has been treated as implicit and

---

30. 29 U.S. Code §§ 151–169 and 45 U.S. Code §§ 151–185. Expressly excluded from coverage by the NLRA are a proprietor's children and spouse, household domestic servants, agricultural workers, government workers, independent contractors, management personnel, and very small business operations, as measured by the volume of business that directly or indirectly involves interstate or foreign commerce. 29 U.S. Code § 152 (3).
    Bargaining units most often are confined to a specific workplace or to an individual enterprise.
31. *NLRB v. United Insurance Co.*, 390 U.S. 254 (1968); Lakes Pilots Assn., 320 NLRB 168 (1995); Standard Oil Co., 230 NLRB 967 (1977). For illustrative case decisions in several industries, see NLRB, AN OUTLINE OF LAW AND PROCEDURE IN REPRESENTATION CASES pp. 209–12 (2008).

case law under the NLRA has provided guidance in ascertaining who fits that exclusion.[32]

The National Labor Relations Board (NLRB), which administers the NLRA, excludes temporary workers from bargaining units even though temporary workers are employees protected by the Act. (Situations in which the worker is provided by a temporary help agency are discussed below.) Their exclusion from bargaining units is because it is assumed that temporary workers do not, to a sufficient degree, share the interests of regular employees in establishing a collective bargaining relationship or adopting a collective agreement.[33]

One significance of excluding temporary hires from a bargaining unit is that they do not get to vote in elections to determine if a majority of workers wish to be collectively represented by a particular labour organization. Another affect of their exclusion is that the bargaining agent designated by a majority of the bargaining unit employees lacks a legitimate claim to bargain on behalf of temporary workers.[34] Nevertheless, it can be argued that the bargaining agent can protect bargaining unit work by insisting on a contract provision that bars the employer from hiring temporary employees at terms and conditions of work less favourable than those provided to regular employees under the collective agreement.[35]

The NLRB determines whether there is a temporary employment relationship based not on the job classification or title but on 'whether ... the employee's tenure is finite and its end is reasonably ascertainable, either by reference to a calendar date, or the completion of a specific job or event, or the satisfaction of the condition or contingency by which the temporary employment was created'.[36] Even though hired for a period of short duration, the NLRB will not exclude an employee as a temporary if the facts show a reasonable contemplation that the employment will continue beyond the stated period.[37] Thus, if the employer repeatedly re-hires employees for short durations, the NLRB will include them in a bargaining unit of regular employees.[38] Accordingly, seasonal employees are part of the bargaining unit if they have a reasonable expectation of re-employment at the same facility in the next season.[39] Similarly, a worker hired for a stated short duration but who is retained for an indefinite period beyond that term is treated by the NLRB as no longer a temporary employee.[40]

Although excluded from participating in a bargaining unit, a temporary employee has the same rights as other workers to protection against discrimination for engaging in mutual aid and protection including union organizing activities. For example, in

---

32. *Hargis v. Wabash R. Co.*, 163 F.2d 608 (7th Cir. 1947).
33. Fall River Gas Works Co., 82 N LRB 962 (1949); Weston Biscuit Co, Inc., 81 NLRB 407 (1949).
34. The statutory authority to bargain collectively is based on being the representative selected by the majority of the bargaining unit employees. 29 U.S. Code § 159 (a).
35. No case on point has been found. However, there is conceptual support for this proposition in *National Woodwork Manufacturing Ass'n v. NLRB*, 386 U.S. 612 (1967).
36. Marian Medical Center, 339 NLRB 127, 128 (2003).
37. *Ibid.*, 339 NLRB at 128n.4.
38. NLRB, *An Outline of Law and Procedure in Representation Cases* 249 (2008).
39. L & B Cooling, 267 NLRB 1, 2 (1983).
40. MJM Studios of New York, 336 NLRB 1255 (2001); Mediplex of Connecticut, Inc., 319 NLRB 281 (1995).

Crown Zellerbach Corporation, 284 N.L.R.B. 111 (1987), the Board held that it was an unfair labour practice to dismiss a temporary employee who requested the union's assistance when the employee was denied holiday pay even though he was not a member of the bargaining unit and was not entitled to grieve under the collective agreement. Also, in *Pennsylvania Electric Co.*, 289 N.L.R.B. 1200 (1988), the Board ruled that although not covered by the collective agreement, it was an unfair labour practice to refuse future work to temporary workers because they complained that they were not paid at the wage level established by the collective agreement. And, in *Sharp ex rel. NLRB v. Koronis Parts*, 927 F. Supp. 1208 (D. Minn. 1996), a court agreed with the NLRB's contention that it is an unfair labour practice if an employee sent by a temporary help agency is dismissed for supporting union organizing activities.[41]

When a temporary help agency refers contingent workers to a job, or when they are assigned by their employer to do the work of another employer, a question can arise respecting which employer is responsible for compliance with the NLRA. There is dual responsibility, as joint employers, if the temporary help agency and contracting employer, or the lessor and lessee employers, each separately or together participate to a substantial degree in determining such matters as hiring, termination, rates of pay and benefits, or if they pay such remuneration, make contributions and deductions required by law, determine qualifications for job assignments, provide job instruction and training, establish work schedules and workloads, and generally supervise work performance.[42] In summary, a lower court has explained that under the NLRA: 'Employers are joint employers when they "share or codetermine those matters governing essential terms and conditions of employment" for bargaining unit employees.'[43] However, if the sharing of control over workers is found to be insufficient to constitute joint employment, the NLRB has held that absent the express consent of all employers and the workers' labour organization, a bargaining unit must be confined to the employees of the single employer that controls their terms and conditions of employment.[44]

Nevertheless, in temporary help agency referral situations the NLRB has allowed elections in a unit in which the referral agency is treated as the employer of those being referred for employment even though it has no control over the place where work is performed and ultimately does not pay their remuneration. The Board has explained that it is not necessary that the temporary help agency be 'the' employer; it is enough that it controls some matters relating to the employment of the referred workers.[45]

---

41. See, too, Glaziers, Architectural Metal and Glassworkers Local Union No. 513 (National Glass & Glazing, Inc.), 299 NLRB 35 (1990) holding that it was an unfair labour practice for a union to insist that 'visiting' workers who were members of a different local union be laid-off prior to laying off members of the local union with which the employer had a bargaining agreement.
42. Manpower, Inc., 164 NLRB 287, 288 (1967). See also Capitol EMI Music, Inc., 311 NLRB 997, 999 (1993).
43. Peck ex rel. *NLRB v. Horizons Youth Serv.*, LLC, 186 LRRM 3112 (E.D. Calif. 2009) quoting from Oakwood Care Center, 343 NLRB 659, 662 (2004) and *NLRB v. Greyhound Corp.*, 368 F.2d 778, 780 (5th Cir. 1966).
44. Oakwood Care Center, 343 NLRB 659 (2004).
45. Recana Solutions, 349 NLRB 1163 (2007). Also, All-Work, Inc., 193 N.L.R.B. 918 (1971).

The construction industry and longshoring industry present additional special situations with respect to the rules governing temporary employment. Customarily in the US, skilled and unskilled work on a construction site is of relatively short duration because the subcontractors who oversee work by the various trades specialize in a single trade and hire workers for the specific project. When the work of that trade is finished they move on to other jobs or are unemployed. Stevedoring companies that hire longshore workers assign them to the loading or unloading site where their work is directed by the shipping company or owner of the goods being loaded or unloaded. Once the ship has been loaded or unloaded, the relationship with the owner of the ship or the cargo ends. The NLRA, implicitly acknowledging that the temporary nature of construction work does not impair the workers' right to engage in collective bargaining, expressly permits bargaining agents in that industry to negotiate the terms and conditions of their employment prior to the employees being hired.[46] Pre-hire collective agreements are prohibited in all other industries because a majority of employees have not yet selected their bargaining agent.

In the case of longshore work, the NLRB has resolved the issue of the temporary nature of the work by treating the stevedoring company as the employer despite its lack of role in overseeing work performance.[47] Thus, it has taken an approach akin to that used in dealing with those hired through a temporary help agency.

Frequently, if a labour organization represents workers in an industry in which employment typically is of short duration, the labour organization provides placement services through a registry or hiring hall. This is common, for example, in the construction industry, the performing arts, and nursing. Although such registries and hiring halls can favour workers based on longevity of experience, they cannot discriminate on the basis of union membership.[48]

Workers who do only occasional work in an on-call status with an employer are protected when they engage in activities involving mutual aid and support of other employees including holding union membership.[49] Moreover, the NLRB has ruled that an employee who does occasional work and has averaged four or more hours of work per week for the last three months prior to the eligibility date for an NLRB election, will be included in the bargaining unit on the ground that there is a sufficient continuing interest in the employer's terms and conditions of employment.[50] Part-time employees are included in the bargaining unit subject to the same conditions.[51] The above formula is adjusted if warranted by circumstances such as when the employer's operations involve irregular patterns of employment[52] or when the employer and labour organization agree that particular employees should or should not be part of the

---

46. 29 U.S. Code § 158 (f).
47. Tamphon Trading Company, Inc., 88 N.L.R.B. 597 (1950).
48. A. Goldman & R. Corrada, *United States of America*, in *International Encyclopedia Of Labour Law* ¶ 406 (Wolters Kluwer 2009).
49. *Yellow Freight Sys. v. NLRB*, 37 F.3d 128 (3d Cir. 1994).
50. Wadsworth Theater Management, 349 NLRB 122 (2007).
51. Arlington Masonry Supply, Inc., 339 NLRB 817, 819 n. 13 (2003).
52. Columbus Symphony Orchestra, Inc., 350 NLRB 523, 524 (2007).

bargaining unit (unless that agreement conflicts with fundamental principles of the NLRA).[53]

Temporary employment status takes on special significance under the NLRA when there is a work stoppage. If an employer hires permanent replacements during a work stoppage, at the end of the stoppage an employee in the pre-stoppage work force does not have a right to return to work so long as the permanent replacement remains at the job. However, if the replacement was hired on a temporary basis, under most circumstances the replaced worker is entitled to return to his job at the end of the stoppage.[54]

[B] Minimum Wage and Overtime Pay Law

Most American workers seek minimum and overtime premium pay under federal law. Two principal inter-related federal statutes, commonly referred to as the Fair Labor Standards Act (FLSA), set those standards.[55] Very small businesses, as measured by the monetary volume of business activity, are excluded from FLSA coverage but their workers may find protection under the minimum wage and overtime pay laws of the state where they work. (If a state law is more protective than federal law, it supplements federal law for those covered by the FLSA.[56]) State law can be very significant for some categories of contingent work, such as casual day labour for very small businesses, because such work often is excluded from FLSA coverage.

The FLSA has a number of total or partial exemptions for various work classifications. For example, excluded from FLSA protections are those employed in household domestic service engaged in tasks such as cooking, serving, cleaning, gardening, driving, childcare and the like, if the worker works less than eight hours in a week for all persons by whom so employed.[57] All other domestic service is covered by the FLSA.

Of some significance to temporary and other casual workers is an FLSA provision that employees under age 20 years may be employed at a reduced minimum wage for the first ninety days of employment so long as not employed to displace work performed by those employed under the full minimum wage.[58]

Because the federal wage and overtime laws protect 'employees', independent contractors are not covered by the FLSA. In order to ascertain whether an individual will be treated as an independent contractor under the FLSA, an appellate court in *Baker v. Flint Eng'g & Constr. Co.* stated that courts 'focus on whether the alleged

---

53. *Desert Hosp. v. NLRB*, 91 F.3d 187, 192 (D.C. Cir. 1996).
54. *Belknap, Inc. v. Hale*, 463 U.S. 491 (1983); *Local 825, International Union of Operating Engineers v. NLRB*, 829 F.2d 458, 462 (3d Cir. 1987); *Eads Transfer, Inc. v. NLRB*, 989 F.2d 373 (9th Cir. 1993). For a more detailed discussion see R. Gorman & M. Finkin, *Labor Law* §§ 17.6, 20.09 (2d Ed., 2004).
55. Fair Labor Standards and Portal-to-Portal Acts, 29 U.S. Code §§ 201–262. Additional legislation sets wage standards for those performing various types of government contract work.
56. State minimum wage and overtime pay standards, but not scope of coverage, can be found at: http://www.dol.gov/whd/minwage/america.htm.
57. 29 U.S. Code §§ 206((f), 207(l).
58. 29 U.S. Code § 206(g). The reduced rate currently is USD 4.25 an hour as contrasted with the normal minimum rate of USD 7.25 an hour.

employee, as a matter of economic reality, is economically dependent upon the business to which he renders his services'.[59] The factors weighed in applying the economic dependency test have been summarized as: (1) the degree of control exerted by the alleged employer over the worker; (2) the worker's opportunity for profit or loss; (3) the worker's investment in the business; (4) the permanence of the working relationship; (5) the degree of skill required to perform the work; and (6) the extent to which the work is an integral part of the alleged employer's business.[60]

Although generally looking at the same factors, judicial conclusions regarding their significance have differed. For example, in the *Baker* decision the court noted that though the list of factors weighed in an earlier decision by a different appellate court[61] were 'strikingly similar', it rejected that court's contention that important factors in establishing independent contractor status are the ability to profit from controlling supply costs and the ability to find alternative work. Rather, the court in *Baker* asserted that the relevant test of independent status is ability to make a profit or sustain a loss by bidding on projects at a flat rate and completing them by exercising independent judgment as to how to perform the work.[62]

The Secretary of Labor has statutory authority to prohibit or regulate industrial 'homework', in order to prevent circumvention of minimum wage rates through purported independent contractor arrangements.[63] That authority has been exercised to require administrative issuance of a work certificate for individual arrangements to produce goods in a broad range of clothing and other apparel categories in the worker's home.[64]

As with labour-management relations law, determining which entity is responsible for compliance with wage and overtime pay requirements can raise issues of joint employment when contingent workers obtain jobs through a temporary help agency or are in a leased worker arrangement. The Third Circuit Court of Appeals applies a four factor test for determining whether a joint employer relationship exists under the FLSA. It states that a court must consider: (1) each alleged employer's authority to hire and fire the employees; (2) the alleged employer's authority to promulgate work rules and assignments, set the workers' conditions of employment including compensation, benefits, work schedules, and the rate and method of payment; (3) each employer's involvement in day-to-day supervision, including employee discipline; and (4) which alleged employer has actual control of employee records such as payroll, insurance, or taxes. The court has emphasized that this is not an exhaustive list and cannot be 'blindly applied'.[65] The Court of Appeals for the Eleventh Circuit has adopted a test that additionally considers the degree of permanency and duration of the relationship of the

---

59. 137 F.3d 1436, 1440 (10th Cir. 1998) citing with approval *Brock v. Mr. W Fireworks*, Inc., 814 F.2d 1042, 1043, 1054 (5th Cir. 1987).
60. *Baker v. Flint Eng'g & Constr. Co.*, 137 F.3d 1436 (10th Cir. 1998).
61. 998 F.2d 330, 332 (5th Cir. 1993).
62. 137 F.3d at 1444.
63. 29 U.S. Code § 211.
64. Wage and Hour Division, 'Fact Sheet #24: Homeworkers Under the Fair Labor Standards Act (FLSA)' (July 2008).
65. *In Re: Enterprise Rent-A-Car Wage & Hour Employment Practices Litigation*, 2012 U.S. App. LEXIS 13229 (3d. Cir. 2012).

workers with the alleged employing entities, whether the activities the workers perform are an integral part of the overall business operation of each employer, which entity's premises is the location of work performance, and the extent to which the work is integrated with that commonly performed by the entity's other employees.[66]

Generally, federal pay standards law makes no distinction based on the permanency or duration of employment with a particular employer. However, special interest legislation has carved out a number of exemptions to the minimum wage or overtime pay requirements, or both, and some of these remove protections from temporary or other contingent workers. For example, fully excluded from protection are employees of enterprises operating seasonal entertainment and amusement facilities, organized camps, and non-profit or religious conference centres. Also excluded are persons employed in fishing, farming of aquatic plants and animals, and in the initial processing of those products. Similarly excluded from protection are farm labourers working for farms using not more than 500 annual man-days of such labour.[67] Another category of expressly excluded work is casual baby-sitting.[68]

Special overtime pay exemptions apply to seasonal work in such activities as the collection and processing of maple sugar and work on agricultural irrigation ditch and waterway maintenance, crop storage facilities, crop transportation to processors and timber harvesting, transportation, and processing operations with eight or fewer employees.[69]

[C] Migrant and Seasonal Farm Labourers

The Migrant and Seasonal Agricultural Worker Protection Act offers some special protection for temporary agricultural workers. It establishes for the benefit of seasonal and migrant farm workers a system of employer certification, record keeping, and inspection, as well as minimum standards for pay practices, work safety, worker transportation safety, and safe, healthy conditions of employer-provided housing. The Act applies both to farmers and to businesses that contract farm labour.[70]

Excluded from the Act's protections are family farms that contract their own labour and smaller farms that are exempted from the FLSA (see above) as well as local farm labour contractors that operate for no more than thirteen weeks a year.[71] Other exclusions relate to such situations as specialized farm servicing operations including hay harvesting; sheep shearing; and poultry harvesting, breeding, debeaking, and desexing.[72]

---

66. *Layton v. DHL Express (USA), Inc.*, 2012 U.S. App. LEXIS 13978 (11th Cir. 2012).
67. 29 U.S. Code § 213 (a)(3), (5), and (6).
68. 29 U.S. Code §213(a)(15); 29 Code Fed. Reg. Pt. 552.
69. 29 U.S. Code § 213(b)(12), (13), (15), (16), and (28).
70. 29 U.S. Code § 1801 et seq.
71. 29 U.S. Code §§1803 (a)(2), (3)(D).
72. 29 U.S. Code § 1803 (3)(E) and(F). In effect this exclusion treats these services as independent contracting operations.

[D] Employment Discrimination

Although temporary and other contingent workers can obtain relief from race discrimination by any employer,[73] most employment discrimination claims are brought under statutes that exempt very small employers.[74] As with other employee protective legislation, in some states local anti-discrimination law is not as limited by the size of the employing establishment as are the federal protections.[75] So long as the size of the employer's workforce satisfies the requirements of the protective legislation, claims can be brought regardless of the casual or temporary nature of the employment.[76]

[E] Pension, Disability and Health Care Insurance

A few categories of private sector workers, such as railroad employees, federal government workers and some state workers have special statutory disability and pension protections. However, mandatory retirement, long-term disability, and old age health care insurance (Medicare) for most workers, including self-employed persons, is provided by the Social Security Act.[77] Additionally, the Employee Retirement Income Security Act (ERISA) provides some guaranties that employer sponsored pensions and other employee benefit programmes are fair in substance and operations and abide by rules of financial integrity.[78]

The benefits provided by the Social Security Act largely are financed by a payroll tax on the employer and employee (double tax for those who are self-employed). The amount taxed is credited to the employee's account and serves as the basis for determining if that person or a spouse or dependent is eligible to receive retirement and survivor benefits and in determining the benefit amount. Medicare benefits are available to retirees and their spouses who receive retirement income under the Social Security Act, Railroad Retirement Act, or certain pension programmes for government workers.

Most individuals qualify as fully insured under the Social Security Act if the payroll tax has been paid for a minimum of forty calendar quarters. (A shorter period

---

73. 42 U.S. Code § 1981.
74. 42 U.S. Code § 2000e et seq., which prohibits discrimination based on race, sex (including pregnancy and related medical conditions), religion, or national origin applies only if the employer employs fifteen or more workers for each work day for at least twenty weeks a year. 42 U.S. Code 12101 et seq. which prohibits discrimination against disabled workers uses the same threshold respecting the size of the employer's operation. 29 U.S. Code § 621 et seq. which protects workers 45 years and older from age discrimination applies only if the employer pays 20 or more workers for each work day for at least 20 weeks a year. In contrast, the Equal Pay Act, 29 U.S. Code § 206(d), which prohibits lower pay based on gender, applies to all workers covered by the federal minimum and overtime pay laws (see above).
75. The National Conference of State Legislatures has a summarized compilation of such laws at: http://www.ncsl.org/documents/employ/DiscriminationChart-III.pdf.
76. See, for example, *Branham v. Management Analysis & Utilization*, 2012 U.S. Dist. LEXIS 47410 (D. S.C. 2012) and *Daniel v. Sargent & Lundy*, LLC, 2012 U.S. Dist. LEXIS 34013 (N.D. Ill. 2012).
77. Officially the Old-Age, Survivors, and Disability Insurance Act. 42 U.S. Code § 7 et seq. An estimated 90% of US workers, their spouses and dependents are covered by this Act.
78. 29 U.S. Code §§ 1001 et seq.

of qualification is required for long-term disability income protection.)[79] The minimum qualifying amount varies year to year based on a statutory formula and the concept of calendar quarters has been modified to consolidate all annual earnings.[80] For example, in 2012 an individual is credited with one calendar quarter of earnings for every US Dollars (USD) 1,120 of earnings subject to the payroll tax. Accordingly, workers who are and have been primarily employed in temporary or contingent positions will find it more difficult to qualify for the Social Security Act's retirement and long-term disability benefits – a problem that also affects the ability of a spouse or dependent to make claims under this statute.[81]

The ERISA fairness protections for employer sponsored retirement and other employee benefit plans establish both maximum employment periods after which the worker cannot be denied participation in a pension plan for which he or she otherwise qualified and maximum periods after which the employee's pension claim becomes vested. These provisions allow an employer to wholly exclude from benefit programmes workers under age 21 and workers who have been employed by the enterprise for less than a year. The ERISA also specifies that a year of service 'means a 12-month period during which the employee has not less than 1,000 hours of service'.[82] If the benefit is 100% vested immediately upon becoming a participant in the pension plan, the employer can defer participation for two years. The Act also allows the Secretary to establish special 'period of service' rules for seasonal businesses and for the maritime industry that substitute 125 days of service for the 1,000 work hours eligibility criteria. This, of course, means that most temporary workers and many other contingent workers can be employed without receiving the retirement benefits given other workers. Moreover, courts have held that whole categories of employees, including part-time workers, temporaries, leased employees and other contingent workers, can be excluded from a pension plan so long as the exclusion is not based on age or length of service.[83]

Even if a contingent worker satisfies the employer's minimum service requirement to participate in a pension plan, the ERISA permits employers to vest only a portion of benefits each year with the result that full vesting in such a plan can be delayed for as much as seven years.[84] Thus, if employment is terminated before that time, the retirement plan can provide for the elimination of part of the benefit.

---

79. Actually, if the employer was legally required to pay the tax, but did not do so, the employee is credited as though payment had been made.
80. 42 U.S. Code § 413.
81. This is less of a problem for those who qualified as a regular employee prior to shifting to temporary or other contingent work and to those who have collateral coverage because a spouse or supporting parent is eligible for benefits.
82. 29 U.S. Code § 1052.
83. *Abraham v. Exxon Corp.*, 85 F.3d 1126 (5th Cir. 1996) (leased employee who worked for a long period for the lessor could not claim benefits because was not in a participant category under the lessor's plan); *Clark v. E. I. Dupont De Nemours & Co.*, 1997 U.S. App. LEXIS 321 (4th Cir. 1997) (leased employee who worked for a long period for the lessor could not claim benefits because was not in a participant category under the lessor's plan); *Kolling v. Am. Power Conversion Corp.*, 347 F.3d 11 (1st Cir. 2003) (even though a contractor was a common law employee, he could be excluded from plan benefits).
84. 29 U.S. Code § 1053.

Health care in the US is the most expensive in the world and for most Americans is largely unaffordable unless they have health insurance (except for emergency room treatment which is subsidized by health insurance paid by others and by the government). Prior to the adoption of the Patient Protection and Affordable Care Act in 2010,[85] employer sponsored group health insurance was the primary source of health insurance in the US because negotiated group premiums generally are much less expensive than those charged for individual health insurance. Additionally, those with poor health histories often cannot obtain health insurance unless they are covered by a group plan.[86] Under the relatively freewheeling insurance system in place when the Act was passed, the types and scope of health insurance benefits, if any, was determined unilaterally by the employer (or through collective bargaining) and often large segments of an employer's workforce were not included in the insurance programme. Moreover, small employers often were unable to obtain insurance at favourable group rates. Accordingly, as previously observed in this paper, temporary and other contingent workers typically were among those most commonly excluded from such benefits. In addition, as a cost saving measure, in recent years a growing number of employers of all sizes were discontinuing this benefit. This situation has continued through 2012 since most provisions of the new law do not come into effect until 2013.

The new Act, which was supported by congressional Democrats and President Obama, substantially alters the rules for health care insurance by greatly expanding the availability and affordability of such insurance regardless of employment or health status. President Obama's success in the 2012 election, and a continued Democratic majority in the US Senate should insure full implementation of the new health insurance legislation which should enable most workers, including contingent workers, to obtain health insurance coverage.

[F] Family and Medical Leave Act

The Family and Medical Leave Act (FMLA)[87] requires employers to grant minimum annual periods of unpaid leave due to a serious health condition involving the employee or close family members or due to the need to care for a new-born or a newly placed foster child. However, because of the Act's threshold requirements concerning employer size and, more importantly, worker eligibility to make claims, FMLA protections are unlikely to apply to contingent workers other than leased employees and to some employees referred by temporary help agencies. This is because the FMLA right to take a leave is available only to those who have worked for the current employer at least 1250 hours in the past twelve months (an average of slightly more than twenty-four hours a week), a threshold that most temporary and other contingent workers are unlikely to satisfy. In addition, the FMLA excludes entities that employ fewer than fifty employees on each working day for twenty or more calendar

---

85. Public Law 111-148.
86. Even then, absent the protections of the Affordable Care Act, the group insurance plan could exclude coverage for health problems existing at the time coverage began and impose ceilings on the amount of coverage for particular treatments or for lifetime benefits.
87. 29 U.S. Code § 2601 et seq.

workweeks in the current or preceding calendar year. Part-time employees are counted in ascertaining whether the employer had the minimum fifty employees and part-time employees can claim FMLA protection if they have worked the requisite hours.[88] Thus, FMLA protection is unavailable for those employed by smaller enterprises that rely on on-call, temporary, or casual workers and in most situations contingent workers employed by larger enterprises lack the requisite work hours to qualify under the FMLA.

Independent contractors have no protection under the FMLA. An appellate court has held that whether a claimant is excluded as an independent contractor is determined by the extent to which the alleged employer had the authority to control the alleged contractor's activities.[89] Other courts have stated that a multi-factor test should be used which weighs: (1) the hiring party's right to control the manner and means by which the product is produced or the service is accomplished, (2) the skill required by the hired party, (3) the duration of the relationship between the parties, (4) the hiring party's right to assign additional projects, (5) the hired party's discretion over when and how to work, (6) the method of payment, (7) the hired party's role in hiring and paying assistants, (8) whether the work is part of the hiring party's regular business, (9) the hired party's enjoyment of the hiring party's employee benefits, and (10) tax treatment of the hired party's compensation.[90]

Department of Labor regulations addressed to the FMLA characterize temporary placement agency arrangements as joint employment and state that the primary employer has the responsibility of FMLA compliance. In determining which is the primary employer, factors to be weighed include 'authority/responsibility to hire and fire, assign/place the employee, make payroll, and provide employment benefits'. The regulations further state that in temporary placement agency arrangements 'the placement agency most commonly would be the primary employer'.[91]

Nevertheless, a temporary employee who seeks FMLA benefits would still have to have had the requisite minimum number of work hours assigned by the agency during the previous twelve months.[92]

[G] Occupational Safety and Health

The federal Occupational Safety and Health Act (OSHA) protects employees from recognized hazards likely to cause serious physical harm (including death) or working

---

88. 29 Code of Fed. Reg. § 825.105(c).
89. *Demers v. Adams Homes of Northwest Fla., Inc.*, 321 Fed. Appx. 847 (11th Cir. 2009).
90. *Holliday v. Vacationland Fed. Credit Union*, 2004 U.S. Dist. LEXIS 5655 (N.D. Ohio 2004), citing *Simpson v. Ernst & Young*, 100 F.3d 436, 443 (6th Cir. 1996).
91. 29 Code Fed. Reg. § 825.106(c).
92. In *Miller v. Defiance Metal Prods., Inc.*, 989 F. Supp. 945 (N.D. Ohio 1997), the court held that when a worker referred by a temporary placement agency later becomes permanently employed by the client employer, because of the joint status during the temporary placement, the period of employment in that capacity counts toward satisfying the threshold number of work hours employed. Accord, *Mackey v. Unity Health Sys.*, 2004 U.S. Dist. LEXIS 8830 (W.D. NY 2004). Also, *Frees v. UA Local 32 Plumbers & Steamfitters*, 589 F. Supp. 2d 1221 (W.D. Wash. 2008) (work for various contractors combined where the claimant had been placed in jobs as part of an industry sponsored apprentice programme).

conditions that do not comply with federally established health and safety standards including providing mandatory safety equipment, training, and labelling information. The OSHA legislation created a system of inspection, corrective orders to remove violations, and fines.[93] The Act's protection extends to all employees regardless of the duration or type of service so long as they are employed by an entity engaged in a business that affects commerce. That leaves some very small enterprises beyond the Act's requirements. Nevertheless, about half of the states have adopted coordinate OSHA laws and in many cases the state laws are broader in coverage than the federal Act. Thus, generally, temporary and other contingent employees have the same OSHA health and safety protections as other workers.

Particularly noteworthy is that in establishing standards under the Act, the safeguards for agricultural workers, an area of considerable temporary employment, are not as comprehensive as in other industries. The few safety and health safeguards for seasonal and migrant farm labourers do not extend to small farming, fishing or marine harvesting operations. In addition, a series of annual appropriations laws have long barred the Occupational Safety and Health Administration from applying the Act to farms that employ ten or fewer employees during the last twelve months and that have not had an active temporary labour camp during the preceding twelve months.[94] In this age of farm mechanization, very large farms can operate with ten or fewer employees with the result that the data shows that in fact almost all farms qualify as exempt from OSHA enforcement.[95]

[H] Workers Compensation

Federal law provides for medical and disability benefits for work related injuries or illness of those employed in the maritime and rail industries and in the work of building repairing, loading, and unloading maritime vessels. Seafarers can claim the benefit of the maritime law doctrines of unseaworthiness and the duty of maintenance and cure.[96] In addition, pursuant to the Jones Act[97] they are entitled to the protections found in the Federal Employers' Liability Act (FELA)[98] and also are covered by the Death on the High Seas Act.[99] Rail industry workers who suffer work related injuries can recover under the FELA and those injured on the job who build, repair, load and

---

93. Criminal prosecution is possible under limited circumstances involving death due to false statements, giving advance notice of inspections, or wilful violations causing death. 29 U.S. Code § 666 (e), (f), (g).
94. Department of Labor Directive CPL 02-00-051 Memorandum 'Enforcement Exemptions and Limitations under the Appropriations Act', 23 Dec. 2011.
95. In 2007, of all farms that employed farm labour, barely 9% had 10 or more workers and only 3% had 10 or more workers who worked 150 days or more in the year. U.S. Department of Agriculture, Census of Agriculture 2007, Table 7, 336. Since a worker working five days a week for 30 weeks works 150 days (less than 12 months during the year) and since the criteria for a farm's exemption from OSHA is '10 or less,' not 'less than 10', some of the farms counted toward the 3% figure would have been exempt from OSHA enforcement.
96. *Mahnich v. Southern S.S. Co.*, 321 U.S. 96 (1944); *Vella v. Ford Motor Co.*, 421 U.S. 1 (1975).
97. 46 U.S. Code § 30104 made FELA available to seafarers.
98. 45 U.S. Code § 51 et seq. This Act primarily protects railroad workers.
99. 46 U.S. Code § 30104.

unload vessels are protected by the Longshore and Harbor Workers Compensation Act (LSHWCA).[100] The latter statute excludes, among others, office clerical, on-shore security personnel, and those employed in servicing smaller recreational vessels and very small commercial vessels – categories of work that may often include contingent workers such as clericals obtained through a temporary hiring agency or casual or on-call workers.

The grounds for recovery and measures of recovery differ among these various federal laws. Recovery for injury under the FELA generally provides more generous remedies than state workers' compensation law or the LSHWCA. However, unlike worker compensation claims, recovery under the FELA is available only upon proof of the employer's or a fellow worker's fault; that is, it must be shown that a duty of care was not performed or was negligently performed. In those FELA suits that are based on maritime law, proof of wrong must establish the unseaworthiness of the vessel or crew—proof of negligent performance in the specific instance is insufficient to establish liability. Although none of these federal protective measures expressly requires any particular duration of employment before an employee can claim its benefits, the Supreme Court has held that in order to claim the benefits available to a seafarer, an employee must 'have a connection to a vessel in navigation (or to an identifiable group of such vessels) that is substantial in terms of both its duration and its nature'.[101] Accordingly, temporary or casual workers employed aboard a vessel may have more limited prospects for recovery than regularly employed fellow workers. However, the worker may still be entitled to recover for work related illness or injury under the federal or a state workers' compensation law.[102]

State law governs liability for work related injuries in all other industries. In most work related injury or illness situations it often is difficult to establish the employer's tort liability. Each state has adopted a workers' compensation system that grants mandatory insurance type medical and disability benefits for all job related illness or injury claims without proof of fault. If a workers' compensation remedy is available to an employee it bars a tort action against the employer.[103] However, the remedy of a workers' compensation benefit is almost always considerably less generous than would be a tort remedy if it was possible to prove tort liability.[104] Therefore, where a tort cause of injury or illness cannot be proved, alleged employers or their insurer sometimes attempt to avoid responsibility for the workers' compensation insurance

---

100. 33 U.S. Code § 901 et seq.
101. *Harbor Tug & Barge Co. v. Papai*, 520 U.S. 548 (1997) and *Chandris, Inc. v. Latsis*, 515 U.S. 347 (1995). *Zertuche v. Great Lakes Dredge & Dock Co.*, LLC, 306 Fed. Appx. 93 (5th Cir. 2009) held that the job assignment at the time of injury or illness must involve at least 30% of the worker's time spent aboard a vessel.
102. The applicable federal law is the LHWCA which requires showing that the worker was engaged in loading or unloading vessels or in ship building, repair, or disassembly. For further discussion see, A. Goldman & R. Corrada, *Labour Law in the USA* §§ 233–45 (3d Rev. ed., 2011).
103. There are exceptions in the event of a wilful injury to the worker.
104. Tort remedies include payment for pain and suffering and full reimbursement for lost wages. Workers' compensation insurance rejects recovery for pain and suffering and only partially reimburses the lost wages (usually two-thirds with a cap based on average earnings in the jurisdiction).

claim by asserting that the claimant was not an employee. Where a tort cause of injury or illness can be proved, alleged employers often try to reduce the degree of remedy by attempting to prove that the claimant was an employee and, therefore, entitled only to the insurance benefit.[105] Thus, contingent workers can benefit from being treated as something other than an employee of the responsible entity if it can be proved that the injury was the fault of that entity or its agents. However, if the injury of illness was the worker's own fault or fault cannot be proven, the worker is without any protection unless treated as an employee.

Workers' compensation statutes often exclude various types of temporary and casual employees and generally do not provide benefits for an independent contractor. For example, the state of Idaho's workers' compensation statute expressly exempts from mandatory coverage, among others, household servants, casual employees, aircraft operators who apply fertilizers or pesticides to agricultural crops, volunteer ski patrollers, and officials of athletic contests involving secondary schools.[106] The definition of a covered 'employee' in the Arkansas workers' compensation statute excludes those engaged on a casual basis except when employed in the course of the employer's trade, business, profession, or occupation.[107]

In contrast, the high court in Maine, a state in which fishing is an important industry, has held that the workers' compensation system protects casual workers who unload, sort, cull, and weigh fish from fishing vessels and are paid by the pound for the amount of fish handled.[108] Similarly, Louisiana's law expressly rejects treating one who does manual labour as an independent contractor, as do some other states.[109] Thus, the party for whom the work is performed must provide workers' compensation insurance coverage.[110] However, the Louisiana high court has held that this provision is limited to situations in which the work performed is part of the trade, business or occupation of the party for whom the work is done.[111] Similarly, although the state of Colorado expressly requires the party that obtains contracted work on real property or its improvements to provide workers' compensation coverage to those performing the work, it excludes home owners and renters from this requirement.[112] Accordingly, if a home owner hires someone to do casual manual labour, the worker's injury will not be covered by workers' compensation insurance and the home owner would be liable in tort if the owner's fault can be proven.

Some courts carefully examine the nature of the 'independent' engagement in order to determine whether the exemption of independent contractors from workers' compensation coverage is applicable. For example, a Minnesota court ruled that a

---

105. Although the claim is covered by insurance, the employer's interest is potentially affected because workers' compensation insurance premiums are partly based on the history of the amount of claims that have been paid on behalf of the insured employer.
106. Idaho Code § 72-212.
107. Ark. Code Ann. § 11-9-102(9)(A).
108. *Stone v. Thorbjornson*, 656 A.2d 1211 (Me. 1995).
109. Larson, *Workers' Compensation Law* § 71.02 (2012).
110. La. Rev. Stat. 23:1021.
111. *Lushute v. Diesi*, 354 So.2d 179 (La. 1977).
112. Colo. Rev. Stat. 8-41-402.

casual worker was not an independent contractor and, therefore, workers' compensation benefits were owed, where the worker was compensated with a meal and the work was done for someone who retained control over the means and manner of performance even though the worker used his own tools and fixed his own hours.[113]

A common issue under workers' compensation statutes is determining which entity has insurance responsibility for temporary work performed as a result of being assigned to that work by another entity. In Michigan this issue is resolved by weighing, among other factors, which entity has the right to control the work, which pays the worker's wages, and which maintains worker discipline. In the case of temporary help agency assignments, the Michigan high court has ruled that the parties' activities are so integrally related to common objectives that for purposes of the workers' compensation statute, the referred employee is to be treated as employed by both the referral agency and the entity to which the worker is referred.[114] In contrast, the Virginia rule is that a worker, although directly employed by one entity, 'may be transferred to the service of another so that he becomes the employee of the second entity "with all the legal consequences of the new relation"'.[115] It should be noted that in applying that rule a trial court has held that under Virginia law one is a borrowed servant when injured only if performing work for the benefit of the alleged borrower and under the borrower's control when injured.[116]

[I] Unemployment Insurance

Federal law imposes an unemployment tax on all payrolls. In order to encourage states to adopt a programme of unemployment insurance benefits, employers are excused from paying up to 90% of the federal tax to the extent that they contribute to a federally qualified state unemployment insurance programme. The credit has induced every state to establish such a programme to which most employers in the state must participate.[117] (All but three states impose on the employer all of the payroll tax for unemployment insurance; employees pay a portion of the tax in the other three states.)

---

113. *Dawson v. Eayrs*, 210 N.W.2d 311 (Minn. 1973).
114. *Farrell v. Dearborn Mfg. Co.*, 330 N.W.2d 397 (Mich. 1982).
115. *Metro Machine Corp. v. Mizenko*, 419 S.E.2d 632, 634 (Va. 1992) quoting *Standard Oil v. Anderson*, 212 U.S. 215, 220 (1909). Standard Oil was a tort action in which a worker was injured while loading a ship due to another worker's negligence. The LHWCA had not yet been adopted so the court was addressing general borrowed servant rules respecting employer liability for a tort. In its explanation, the court stated that if a worker is furnished to work in the manner directed by the borrower, the latter is 'responsible for their negligence in the conduct of the work, because the work is his work and they are for the time his workmen'. However, an employer who 'agrees to furnish the completed work through servants over whom he retains control is responsible for their negligence in the conduct of it, because, though it is done for the ultimate benefit of the other, it is still in its doing his own work'. 212 U.S. at 221.
116. *Slater v. Skyhawk Transp., Inc.*, 187 F.R.D. 185 (D.N.J. 1999).
117. Because the full federal levy is imposed if the state does not have a qualified unemployment insurance programme, states adopt such programmes so that the major part of the revenue will be transferred to unemployed state residents. The 10% of the tax retained by the federal government is used for grants to states to defray the costs of administering their unemployment insurance programmes.

Some aspects of temporary and other contingent employment are affected by the rules that state unemployment insurance programmes must satisfy so that employers in that state will qualify for the federal tax credit. For example, the federal law prohibits undocumented aliens, who generally work in temporary or other contingent jobs, from receiving unemployment insurance benefits.[118]

Additionally, the federal Act does not imposed the payroll tax on some 'small' farmers, thereby encouraging state programmes to exempt them from having to provide employees with unemployment compensation insurance. Under the criteria used, over 90% of farms are exempt from this payroll tax,[119] with the result that few temporary or seasonal farm workers qualify for unemployment insurance benefits. Farmers also do not have to pay the tax for temporary foreign farm labourers working under a programme that is federally approved for such labour.[120]

Exempt from the unemployment payroll tax, too, are employers of persons who perform domestic service in private homes, college clubs, fraternities and sororities unless the employer paid at least USD 1,000 in a calendar quarter in the current or preceding calendar year.[121] Work by a student or spouse of a student for a school, college or university is exempt if employment is part of a programme to provide financial assistance to the student.[122] Other exemptions from the payment of the federal unemployment payroll tax that are relevant to temporary or contingent employment include newspaper and newsletter delivery by those under age 18, newspaper and magazine delivery by those who pay a fixed price for the items delivered and retain the excess of the amount collected,[123] crews of most types of small fishing and marine cultivation or harvesting vessels,[124] and full time students employed for not more than thirteen weeks a year by an organized camp that operates no more than seven months a year.[125] Also, as with most other employee protective statutes, the federal unemployment insurance scheme does not protect independent contractors.[126]

---

118. 26 U.S. Code § 3304 (a)(14). The tax, nevertheless, has to be paid on the wages they receive.
119. 26 U.S. Code § 3306 (c)(1)(A) – exempts farmers that paid farm labourers less than USD 20,000 and did not have more than nine labourers who worked each of twenty days during the year. Approximately 91% of farms reported having nine or fewer farm workers in 2007. U.S. Department of Agriculture, Census of Agriculture 2007, Table 7, p. 336. Some farms with ten or more workers undoubtedly have annual payrolls of less than USD 20,000. (At USD 7.25 an hour minimum wage, USD 20,000 would pay for 2,758 hours or over 275 hours of work each for 10 labourers.) Accordingly, well under 10% of farms are exempted from the unemployment payroll tax.
120. 26 U.S. Code § 3306 (c)(1)(B).
121. 26 U.S. Code § 3306 (c)(2).
122. 26 U.S. Code § 3306 (c)(10)(B).
123. 26 U.S. Code § 3306 (c)(15).
124. 26 U.S. Code § 3306 (c)(17).
125. 26 U.S. Code § 3306 (c)(20).
126. For example., compare In re Barnaba Photographs Corp., 43 N.E.2d 720 (N.Y. 1942) (finding photographer's model not protected because she was an independent contractor) with In re Claim of Chopik, 535 N.Y.S.2d 268 (N.Y. App. Div. 3d Dep't 1988) (finding agency that referred models had sufficient degree of regular contact and control over work opportunities to make it an employer subject to the unemployment insurance tax).

Some states include in the state unemployment insurance programme various categories, such as self-employed persons, that federal law allows to be excluded.[127]

Most states do not pay unemployment benefits unless in the first four out of the last five completed calendar quarters prior to the time a claim is filed (the base period) the claimant had at least a specified amount of employment or earnings (or both) on which the unemployment insurance tax was paid – requirements that temporary and contingent employees often cannot satisfy.[128] In addition, the claimant must be ready, willing and able to accept appropriate employment in order to remain eligible for benefits for the week in which a claim is made.[129] Refusal to accept work or failure to seek work in the geographical market that the state finds appropriate disqualifies the worker from receiving unemployment benefits.[130]

The amount of unemployment insurance benefit paid is a portion (most commonly 50%) of an eligible claimant's earnings during the base period subject to a maximum weekly amount that usually is equal to or based on the state-wide average earnings of employees covered by the insurance programme.

Temporary and other contingent workers are greatly disadvantaged by the exemptions from unemployment benefits and the eligibility requirements based on prior work or earnings. One study of the amounts paid to different claimants found that although 6.1% of those who had been employed full time in regular jobs were ineligible for unemployment insurance benefits in 2001 due to inadequate prior earnings, 30% of those who had been voluntarily employed part-time were ineligible for the same reason and 63.1% of independent contractors were ineligible.[131] Inasmuch as the study looked at data for claimants, the figures almost certainly would be more dramatic if it included those who were unemployed but did not file claims because they knew from past experience that they did not qualify for the benefits or had been so advised.

Every state allows claimants some earnings from brief episodes of employment without eliminating benefits or only partially reduce the benefits based on such earnings.[132] Thus, temporary and contingent work can be a means of supplementing income from unemployment insurance.

---

127. For a collection of case decisions respecting unemployment compensation coverage or non-coverage in various occupations and situations, see 95 American Law Reports 3d 891 (2008).
128. Office of Unemployment Insurance, U.S. Department of Labor Employment and Training Administration, 'Significant Provisions of State Unemployment Insurance Laws' (July 2011). For example, at the time of writing, in Massachusetts the minimum required earnings for benefit eligibility during the base year was USD 3,500.
129. 20 Code Fed. Reg. 604.3–604.5.
130. 20 Code Fed. Reg. 604.3 (b).
131. J. Wenger, *Public Policy and Contingent Workers*, in *The Shadow Workforce* 169, 180–181 (S. Gleason ed., Upjohn Inst. Press 2006).
132. Office of Unemployment Insurance, U.S. Department of Labor Employment and Training Administration, 'Significant Provisions Of State Unemployment Insurance Laws' (July 2011).

[J] Worker Adjustment and Retraining Act

The Worker Adjustment and Retraining Act (WARN)[133] attempts to reduce the impact on employees and communities from larger scale long-term layoffs (at least six months' duration) or dismissals, or substantial work reductions (at least 50% during each month in a six month period) when they are due to financial or operational changes. Small businesses (generally those with less than 100 employees) are exempted from the Act. The WARN Act's benefit for employees is that the employer is required to give sixty days' prior notice of impending job loss unless the employer qualifies for any one of several defences that waive or partially waive that requirement.[134] If the required notice is not given, the affected employees receive mandatory severance pay for the period for which notice should have been given.

Protected are those employees who 'may reasonably be expected to experience an employment loss as a consequence' of the business closing, layoff or reduction in work.[135] Accordingly, temporary and other contingent workers may not be able to establish their eligibility for the mandatory severance pay even if the employer is large enough to come under the Act.[136]

[K] Regulation of Temporary Hiring Agents and Agencies

Workers in the US often find contingent employment through informal means including print and electronic media advertising, referrals by acquaintances who work for the employer, contacting a potential employer's personnel office, and gathering at locations near an unemployment office or street corner where those seeking casual work are known to congregate. Contingent work placement also is provided by government placement services, including those operated by schools, by apprenticeship programmes, and by businesses that offer general job placement services or that specialize in placing workers in temporary jobs.

The regulation of businesses that place workers in employment positions is largely left to the states. One exception is a federal regulation that prohibits all government operated employment agencies from referring workers to jobs where there is a work stoppage.[137] A few states similarly have laws that prohibit private as well as government employment agencies from referring workers to such work sites[138] and at

---

133. 29 U.S. Code § 2101 et seq. This statute is popularly known as the Plant Closing Act.
134. The defences are unforeseeability of the need to reduce the workforce, the publicity of giving the notice would hamper efforts to raise capital or obtain new business that would avert the work reduction, hiring was for a specific duration, or the reduction was due to a work stoppage arising out of a labour dispute. 29 U.S. Code §§ 2102 (b), 2103.
135. 29 U.S. Code § 2101(a)(5).
136. Temporary workers if hired for a specific duration are expressly excluded under 29 U.S. Code §2103 (1).
137. 20 Code Fed. Reg. § 652.9.
138. For example, Ha. Rev. Stat. § 379-2, 820 Ill. Comp. Stat. 30/2, and Or. Rev. Stat. § 658.205(5). A few court decisions, however, have ruled that such state laws are invalid to the extent that they affect workplaces covered by the National Labor Relations Act. 520 S. Mich. Ave. Assocs. Ltd. v. Devine, 433 F.3d 961 (7th Cir. 2006) and Kapiolani Med. Ctr. V. Hawaii, 103 F. Supp. 2d 1233 (Ha. 2000).

least one state requires the employment agent to inform job applicants if they are being referred to employment covered by a collectively bargained agreement and a union security provision.[139] Additionally, some states have laws that require that workers be notified of a labour dispute at a facility for which they are offered employment.[140]

As previously noted, federal law also regulates the recruitment and job placement activities of those who contract for migrant and seasonal farm labour.[141] Because there are some exclusions in the federal legislation relating to job placement involving smaller operations, a few states have their own laws safeguarding farm labourers from various exploitive job placement practices.[142]

Federal law additionally provides financial incentives and oversight for the development of apprenticeship programmes and regulates their operations to safeguard the welfare of apprentices and promote apprenticeship opportunities. Included are regulations governing such matters as the minimum number of classroom and on the job training hours, execution of a required apprenticeship agreement, safety and health standards, progressive wage increases, and minimum instructor qualifications.[143]

State laws generally require licensing of employment agencies, including those specializing in temporary help placement. These laws vary considerably but some impose specific regulations on temporary help referral services and have special provisions for occupations that often involve contingent employment such as nursing, domestic service, farm labour, and artistic performances. The special regulations affect such things as maximum referral fees, employer responsibility for payment of such fees, and reduction of fees in the event of pre-mature termination. Exclusion from regulation of employment placement activities sometimes is given for placement services of schools, labour organizations, charitable organizations, and professional associations.[144]

[L] Other Laws

The foregoing is not an exhaustive list of all legal standards that may affect temporary and other contingent workers. There are miscellaneous other, less often used, federal and state laws that provide employees with various protections such as limitations as employer investigatory tools of polygraph and other deception detection mechanisms, common law restrictions on unfair dismissal, restrictions on the use of pre-employment health examinations, mandatory accrual of vacation benefits, employee drug testing

---

139. Or. Rev. Stat. § 658.205(6). The statute uses the undefined term 'labour contract' but in the context of the provision is likely to be construed as applying only to collectively bargained agreements.
140. For example, Cal Civ Code § 1812.509; Ann. Laws Mass. ch. 140, § 46K (9).
141. See *supra* nn. 70–72, and accompanying text.
142. See, for example, Or. Rev. Stat. § 658.405 et seq.
143. 29 U.S. Code §§ 29.4, 29.7. In recent years over 400,000 apprentices have been enrolled annually in federally registered programmes. 73 Fed. Regis. 64424 (2008).
144. See, for example, N.Y. Gen. Bus. L. Art. 11 §§ 185-86; Or. Rev. Stat. §§ 411.892(10)(e) and (13), 658.005(4)(b), 658.015, and 658.185.

regulations, and whistleblower protection laws.[145] The scope of these and other state law protections varies considerably from jurisdiction to jurisdiction. The foregoing, however, is sufficiently representative to demonstrate the lack of a comprehensive set of consistent principles guiding the scope of legal protections for temporary and other contingent workers in the US.

§3.02 CONCLUSIONS

The political process in the US is marked by a lack of clear ideological divisions and the inability of party hierarchies to command adherence to whatever policy positions are adopted by party leaders. As a result, special interest lobbies that try to persuade officials to their point of view, including providing election and re-election campaign financial support, wield considerable impact on legislative outcomes in the US. Thus, federal and state legislation in the US characteristically fails to reflect unifying social, jurisprudential, philosophical or economic principles other than the preservation of constitutionally mandated due process and the protections of fundamental liberties.

From time to time, federal and state legislative or executive bodies sponsor comprehensive studies aimed at reforming various aspects of law in a coherent manner that balances or adjusts competing interests so as to best serve the public welfare. Most of these efforts fail once the recommendations are subjected to the realities of the political process. Accordingly, inconsistent treatment of seemingly like or similar situations or interests is not unusual.

The affects of the above described worker protection laws exemplify the almost haphazard character of the US legislative process. Workforce flexibility generally is well served by the treatment of temporary and other contingent workers but worker welfare and security are far less well served for these groups.

Reduced legal burdens on employment of temporary and other contingent workers in the US no doubt expands such work opportunities, a situation that does not always ill serve workers. Both life style and life stage considerations often make such jobs welcome even if they lack the welfare and security protections of regular employment.

One practical problem that offers some justification for some situations in which temporary and other contingent workers are less protected than their regular counterparts is where the employer is too small to be able to efficiently absorb on behalf of short-term employees the administrative costs and actuarial projections for financing benefits such as employer-provided pensions, mandatory sick leave, or workers' compensation insurance. A related practical problem is the greater cost of administrative oversight and enforcement when having to inspect numerous workplaces, each with only a few workers. This is especially true in the case of engagements by

---

145. Many of these laws are discussed in M. Rothstein, C. Craver, E. Schroeder & E. Shoben, *Employment Law* (4th ed., 2009); M. Finkin, *Privacy in Employment Law* (2009); R. Covington, *Employment Law* (3d ed., 2009); J. Hood, B. Hardy & H. Lewis, *Workers Compensation and Employee Protection Laws* (5th ed., 2011).

households that do not regularly employ anyone. These justifications for not burdening, or attempting to burden, small or only occasional employers does not justify completely ignoring the needs of temporary or other contingent workers respecting particular types of personal needs. Exemptions under the guise of shielding small entities often in reality reach businesses that are well established and of significant size, especially when measured by financial resources or closely affiliated entities. Additionally, government insurance programmes to which employees directly pay premiums can provide needed alternative protections for temporary and other contingent workers.

Exemptions from standards such as minimum wage and overtime pay requirements often follow no logic or practical justification but instead are the product of effective interest group political lobbying. An irony is that some of the exemptions, such as for those engaged in fishing on small craft or labourers on what are characterized as small farms, lead to non protection of those who perform some of the nation's most onerous work under especially dangerous or very undesirable conditions.[146]

Lobbying power rather than reasoned distinctions would appear, also, to account for most of the exemptions from perceived burdens of the payroll tax financed benefits such as workers' compensation and unemployment insurance. In reality, in the long run employees are the ones who bear the full weight of such payroll taxes inasmuch as it is a remuneration expense that reduces the employer's ability and willingness to provide higher wages. Thus, when hired, or over a period of time for those already employed, the financial burden of these benefits is taken into account by the employer and reflected in the overall remuneration package. The cost, therefore, is carried by the benefited workers, not by their employers. Accordingly, if temporary and other contingent workers are to gain protection under these programmes, their advocates will have to find more effective ways to persuade employer groups and legislators of that economic reality.

In the case of occupational safety and health, more rigorous compliance with OSHA standards is induced in some states by increasing the workers' compensation disability benefit if the injury is caused by a violation of occupational safety or health standards.[147] Linking the level of the workers' compensation benefit for all workers to compliance or non compliance with OSHA standards might be one way to improve safety and health conditions for all employees covered by workers' compensation, including those temporary and contingent workers whose employment is covered by

---

146. 'Farm workers are at high risk for fatal and nonfatal injuries, work related lung diseases, noise-induced hearing loss, skin diseases, and certain cancers associated with chemical use and prolonged sun exposure.' For example, in 2010 the injury rate for farm workers was 20% higher than for all other workers and the fatality rate was seven times greater than for all other workers. http://www.osha.gov/SLTC/agriculturaloperations/index.html. The highest fatality rate for all industries in 2010 was for workers engaged in fishing. http://www.bls.gov/iif/oshwc/cfoi/worker_memorial.htm.
147. Larson, *Workers' Compensation Law*, § 105.01. See, for example, Conn. Gen. Stat. § 31-307 (b).

such insurance regardless of whether their employer is exempt from direct enforcement of OSHA.[148]

As we have seen, current NLRB doctrine respecting the right of temporary workers to vote in NLRB elections gives those referred by temporary help agencies greater protection of the right to participate in selecting a bargaining agent than is given to temporary employees hired directly by the employer whose work is to be performed. In the former case they can obtain a bargaining representative by choosing one to represent them with the temporary help agency; in the latter case they are totally excluded from such representation. The rationale for this result, that they do not to a sufficient degree share the interests of regular employees, is not necessarily true when temporary employees have hopes or expectations of becoming part of the regular work force or when they anticipate future opportunities to again work for the employer in a temporary capacity.

Moreover, treating temporary hires as not sharing sufficient interests with regular employees is inconsistent with the approach to voter eligibility respecting other situations in which an employee's ties to the work place either are tenuous or will be nonexistent once collective bargaining begins. For example, where an employee notifies the employer that he is quitting after the NLRB election, the NLRB has ruled that the employee, nevertheless, is entitled to vote.[149] Similarly, a beginner on his or her first day who has not learned where the rest rooms are when the election is ordered, and a probationary employee or a trainee who ultimately may not qualify to remain in the workforce, are eligible to vote in an NLRB ordered representation election.[150]

Allowing temporary employees to vote in a representation election does not necessarily mean they will vote. A temporary employee who feels no ties to the workplace can simply not cast a ballot. Treating temporary employees as eligible to vote, however, would allow the individual to reflect his or her own perception of workplace ties, rather than the NLRB's perceptions, either by casting a ballot or declining to vote.

In sum, there are ways to expand most employment protections so that temporary and other contingent workers are on a par with the regular workforce. Whether there is the political will to accomplish this in the US is another matter.

---

148. Insurers seeking to attract more customers by lowering their premiums often conduct their own inspections and counselling of customers to help reduce the frequency and severity of claims.
149. *NLRB v. General Tube Co.*, 331 F.2d 751 (6th Cir. 1964); *NLRB v. Hillview Health Care Center*, 705 F.2d 1461 (7th Cir. 1983); *St. Elizabeth Hospital v. NLRB*, 708 F.2d 1436 (9th Cir. 1983); Grange Debris Box and Wrecking Co., 177 LRRM 1318 (NLRB 2005).
150. Johnson Auto Spring Service, 221 NLRB 809 (1975). Normally the employee has to have been employed during the payroll period immediately preceding the date of the direction of election and be in employee status on the date of the election. NLRB, *An Outline of Law and Procedure in Representation Cases* § 20-100 (2008). Employees hired but engaged in preliminary orientation are not eligible to vote but those in a comprehensive training programme are eligible. CWM, Inc., 306 NLRB 495 (1992).

CHAPTER 4
Public-Private Partnerships on Temporary Work: The Case of Flanders

Fons Leroy

The role of private employment services in the Flemish labour market has changed considerably over the decades. The collaboration between the public employment service, the VDAB, and the private employment services has changed from 'not on speaking terms' to 'valuable partners in work'.[1]

For a long time temporary work was only tolerated on the fringes of social policy in Belgium. This type of work was strictly regulated at the national level and seen as a strict exception to regular employment. Hardly surprising when you consider that labour law and social law were based on the principles of lifetime employment, the male costwinner model and a classical Fordist/Taylorist system of employment relations. Nevertheless, temp work has gradually carved out a place for itself. Suzanne from Interlabor and Bianca from T-Interim have given temporary work a face for the man in the street.

§4.01 REGIONALIZATION IN 1980

When placement was regionalized in 1980, the regions became responsible for licensing temp agencies. The Federal Government retained, however, the power to regulate temporary work through both labour legislation and social legislation. This framework has not changed since 1987. In the state reform which is taking place, part

---

1. F. Leroy, *Uitzending door derden: Suzanne, Bianca, Saïda en de anderen. De rol van uitzendarbeid in het regionaal arbeidsmarktbeleid* in *Plus est en vous. Een halve eeuw uitzendarbeid in België* (J. Denys ed., Lannoo: Tielt 2005), 149–163. F. Leroy & H. Muyldermans, *Working in Partnership in Flanders* (Brussels: PARES – Conference 29 Sep. 2011). W. van der Beken, A. Peeters & A. van Pelt, *Meer werk door samen sterk* (Brussel: Idea Consult 2006).

of the policy on temporary work has been regionalized: within a few years the regions will be able to decide for themselves whether their government agencies and local administrations will use temporary workers and integrate temporary work in their labour market policy.

The transfer of authority in the state reform of 1980 did not immediately create a strong dynamism. It was not until 1991 that Flanders first exerted its authority over this area. The decree of 6 March 1991 and its implementing order set out the conditions that temp agencies must fulfil in order to operate within the Flemish Region. By passing this decree the government's aim was to do no more than simply separate the good from the bad within this sector. Temporary work was still not seen as a tool of regional labour market policy. Even the public temp agency T-Interim, which was set up in 1980 and served as a thorn in the flesh of the private sector, was not explicitly given any active role in delivering the political aims of government.

§4.02 *WEER WERK* (BACK TO WORK)

The sector, however, addressed the licensing regulations itself, as it sought to define its position in the Flemish labour market, as well as its position vis-à-vis the government. In 1992 the *Weer Werk* (Back to Work) campaign for long-term job seekers created the impulse for the first exploratory collaboration between the temp agency sector and the Flemish Government. UPEDI, the professional association of temp agencies and forerunner of Federgon, and Leona Detiège, Flemish Minister for Employment and Social Affairs, entered into a collaboration agreement. The VDAB (Flemish Public Employment Service) would refer long-term unemployed job seekers to the temp agency sector and UPEDI would find 250 work experience places for those job seekers. This collaboration, however, yielded little in the way of results. The differences between the public and private actors in the labour market turned out to be too profound.

§4.03 FORERUNNERS OF THE ILO CONVENTION

Around that time, a vigorous political debate was in progress on allowing private actors in the labour market to play a greater role in labour market policy, following the International Labour Organization (ILO) convention on employment mediation. This vision ran counter to the VDAB's objective of enlarging its own market share. That is because the VDAB feared that its market share would shrink if private actors were given greater opportunities in the market. The political authorities, however, were pursuing a two-track approach: both strengthening the public service and broadening the activities of the private sector. The decree of 19 April 1995 explored the limits of what was legally permissible by stating that private labour market actors would be able to play a complementary role in the labour market. This was because the new ILO convention was not yet in place.

A study conducted by the HIVA (Research Institute for a Work and Society) in 1997 and the Imago (Image) survey in 1996 showed that temporary work can serve as a springboard into permanent employment for young people and long-term unemployed. The VIB (Flemish Agency Bridging Project) then once again picked up the thread of engaging the temp agency sector in Flemish labour market policy. With this project, Flemish Minister for Employment, Theo Kelchtermans, was aiming to promote the reintegration of target groups in the labour market through temporary work. NGOs, which are referred to as third parties, offered training and guidance to target groups; the temp agency sector used its commercial network to prospect for jobs and work experience placements. Notably, this project developed entirely outside the VDAB public mediation service. The project was relatively successful: 5,300 job seekers were guided into the labour market.

§4.04   NEW IMPULSE

The decree of 13 April 1999 on private employment services in the Flemish Region gave a new impulse to policy. By means of this decree – based on ILO convention 181 and ILO recommendation 188 – the Flemish Parliament created a framework encompassing all the private actors in the labour market. The decree of 13 April 1999 integrates the existing separate sectoral licensing regulations, eliminates the regulations that create barriers between the different private actors and introduces self-regulation mechanisms and quality standards to create greater responsibility among those actors.

The ILO convention no. 181 was used by the political authorities in Flanders to encourage collaboration between the public employment agency and the private temp agencies. With support from Minister Kelchtermans, the UPEDI and the VDAB entered into their first collaboration agreement in 1999. The aim was to allow the labour market to operate more smoothly and transparently, while optimizing the allocation of labour. In this way the Flemish Government required the VDAB and UPEDI to cooperate. The arrangements that allowed the private sector to access the VDAB's KISS (candidate information and selection) and WIS (work information) systems were particularly important. This was however, not a voluntary collaboration and consequently problems with its implementation arose on a regular basis. Nevertheless it was still a breakthrough in the search for a balanced approach to all the service providers in the labour market.

§4.05   INDEPENDENCE FOR T-INTERIM

The Flemish Government agreement of July 1999 brought about a major change for the private actors in the market. This agreement gave them an unmistakeable role in regional labour market policy. The government agreement also obliged the private partners and the VDAB to work together, signposting the fact that the conductor role of the VDAB was becoming more important. Last but not least, this agreement reversed the view of complementarity: the public service was to work in a way that complemented the work of private service providers in the market. The role of the private sector as an actor in the labour market became more and more important.

Soon afterwards the Flemish Parliament decided to create independent structures to accommodate the commercial activities of the VDAB, including T-Interim. These activities were incorporated in a separate company which was intended to operate entirely under market conditions. However, the government wanted to reconcile market-based functioning with its social objectives, so it set up the *Werkholding* (Work Holding) company, a public company with a social purpose, and a public company with a commercial purpose called T-Groep to incorporate all the commercial activities in the areas of temporary work, outplacement and HR consultancy. The *Werkholding* company used the dividends generated by its commercial activities to finance or participate in projects aimed at difficult target groups. In this way the profits are not privatized but instead they are collectivized for the purpose of getting underprivileged groups in Flanders back to work.

This independence operation eliminated a situation that had hampered interaction between the VDAB and the private actors in the market for years. As a public service provider, T-Interim was exempt from value-added tax (VAT) and corporation tax. UPEDI considered that this did not represent a level playing-field.

§4.06 INSTANT A

During the 1999–2004 legislature a number of initiatives were brought forward to give the temp agency sector a more prominent role in operational labour market policy. The NGO Jeugd en Stad (Youth and City) worked with two temp agencies to set up the social temp agency Instant A. The aim was to create opportunities for young people on the fringes of society who were picked up through street-level activities and guided into suitable temporary work. The first office was established in Antwerp, and was soon followed by offices in Mechelen, Ghent, Vilvoorde and Genk. This successful formula was also copied in the Brussels Capital Region.

Other interesting collaboration projects involving the temp agency sector included the Daikin 50+ project, in which temp agencies and the VDAB worked together to create a pool of older employees. Paradox was a project initiated by a temp agency, the VDAB, an NGO and a research organization to improve awareness among small- and medium-sized enterprises (SMEs) of the management of diversity. During this period more than eighty collaboration projects were set up; all involving private temp agencies and the Flemish public employment agency VDAB.

A second area of action involving the temp agency sector was anti-discrimination policy. Following a number of complaints against temp agencies in relation to discriminatory elements in their vacancies, UPEDI and Flemish Minister for Employment, Landuyt, entered into an agreement. The result of this agreement was a manual setting out of 'how to deal with discriminatory vacancies', an awareness campaign and human resource (HR) tools on managing diversity. Through this collaboration agreement the temp agency sector came forward as a partner for the government in its efforts to combat discrimination and promote equal participation.

§4.07 BUILDING BRIDGES

Consultation Platform Flemish Labour Market Intermediaries (OVA) was set up to create a forum for consultation between public and private actors in the labour market. Through this forum Flanders found an original response to the 1997 ILO recommendation to build bridges between the private and the public sector. Specifically, training sessions in non-discrimination were organized for VDAB consultants and those working for private actors. The OVA forum also led to recommendations and streamlining of the 2002 decree on equal participation in the labour market.

The Jobs Exchange Plan (*Wisselbanenplan*) was less successful. The aim was to 'lend' long-term unemployed job seekers to companies via a temp agency on temporary employment contracts for a maximum period of two years. Unfortunately, this temporary placement formula was structured in an excessively bureaucratic way. The principle, however, was important: research has shown that employers use temporary work as a trial period. Using the 'temporary placements' scheme, the Flemish Government acknowledged this practice and recognized temporary work as a tool on the labour market, aiming at putting target groups to work.

§4.08 TEMPORARY AGENCIES AS A COMMERCIAL SECTOR IN THEIR OWN RIGHT

The sectoral agreement between the Flemish Government and the social partners in the temp agencies sector in 2002 was even more significant. This agreement contained specific commitments on employment for underprivileged groups, lifelong learning, diversity, etc. The sector took a commitment to place 750 people from target groups referred by the VDAB and its Job Centres. Due to the positive results, a new sectoral agreement was concluded in 2004–2005. The target number of jobs for people in target groups was increased to 1,125. Through this agreement the Flemish Government recognized the temp agencies sector as a commercial sector in its own right. Moreover, the sector was able to claim the same public support as other sectors, including subsidies for sectoral consultants.

It was also at this time that the idea first emerged of freeing temporary work from its straitjacket under labour and social legislation. The possibility of allowing temporary work within public service organizations was mentioned on a number of occasions. Minister Landuyt also called for permanent contracts to be permitted in temporary work. In practice changes only occurred in the construction sector: the ban on temporary work in the sector was lifted on 1 January 2002. This resulted in a modified licensing procedure for temp agencies in the construction sector, and market players immediately responded to this.

§4.09 SERVICE VOUCHERS

When the Federal Government introduced service vouchers in 2001, Flanders immediately allowed temp agencies to be recognized as service providers. Thanks to the temp agency sector, service vouchers saw a veritable boom in Flanders, creating significantly more new jobs than in the other regions. In 2003, the Flemish model was also implemented in the other regions, under the influence of Federal Employment Minister Frank Vandenbroucke.

In his 2004–2009 Policy Memorandum, the Flemish Minister for Employment, Education and Training gave a clear role to private actors in the labour market. In the context of providing a coherent approach for unemployed people, a pilot scheme was set up comprising tendering for guidance pathways. The guidance and training pathways for a proportion of long-term unemployed were contracted out. Some 6,000 pathways were entrusted to commercial and non-commercial actors in the labour market. This was followed by a whole series of outsourcing measures: the activation tender for extremely vulnerable target groups, the European Social Fund tender, the youth work plan tender, the centre cities tender and others. In 2011, the VDAB contracted out approximately 19,500 reintegration pathways for job seekers to its partners. Commercial partners were involved in 17,000 of these.

§4.10   TEMP AGENCIES GOING STRONG

The story of the temp agencies sector and the other private agencies in the labour market has not ended yet. In 2010, following an initiative by Flemish Employment Minister Philippe Muyters, a new decree on private employment mediation was passed by the Flemish Parliament. This decree satisfies the requirements of the European Services Directive on the free movement of services within the European Union (EU). Only temp agencies still have to request an explicit license from the Flemish Government in order to carry on their business. Other private mediation agencies such as recruitment, search and selection, outplacement etc. are able to operate as long as they meet the conditions set out in the above-mentioned decree.

In the Careers Agreement (*Loopbaanakkoord*), which was concluded in early 2012 within VESOC (the Flemish Economic and Social Consultation Committee), the temp agency sector is given a greater role in guiding over-50s into long-term employment. Negotiations on this are still underway, but it is clear that temp agencies will make a commitment to find long-term employment for job seekers aged over 50 who have been unemployed for more than one year.

§4.11   COLLABORATION BETWEEN VDAB AND TEMP AGENCIES: A NEW LEASE OF LIFE

Flemish Employment Minister, Frank Vandenbroucke, was convinced at the time that the various partners – VDAB, NGOs and temp agencies – ought to work together to get more people into work. This policy perspective was expressed in the policy governing the VDAB: public–private collaboration was also given a further boost within the VDAB and enjoyed the full support of the new senior management. To establish this collaboration on a firm structural footing the VDAB and Federgon (the successor of UPEDI) decided to set up a joint non-profit association. In September 2005, the non-profit association Federgon-VDAB was officially born. The most important role of this structure is to provide advice and means on possible collaboration projects.

In 2007, the VDAB and Federgon signed their second collaboration agreement. An important part of the agreement is the VDAB guarantee of equal treatment between permanent jobs and temp jobs. The VDAB has also introduced a strategic account management system to guide and monitor the collaboration. As well as online collaboration, with vacancy and CV matching, this collaboration agreement has created scope for collaboration on the field, including placement and training for job seekers, participation in job fairs, jobdatings and training and exchanges for temp agency consultants.

§4.12   ZOOMING IN ON A DIVERSE COLLABORATION

A study carried out by Idea Consult, commissioned by Federgon and in collaboration with the VDAB, showed that collaboration is taking place in many different ways. There are top-down initiatives and bottom-up initiatives; in some cases the initiative has come from the temp agency while in others it has come from the VDAB, etc. Idea Consult listed some eighty specific cases of collaboration, most of which were started up in 2006–2008. Some of these involved very new areas such as creating a flexible pool of security guards, recruitment campaigns for the temp agency offices themselves, organizing short, labour market focused training courses for forklift drivers, cleaners, packers, etc., organizing job fairs and speed dating events, etc. The study indicated that this broad-based collaboration was generating considerable added value for those involved, particularly in terms of operational efficiency, improved access to information, reputation management and knowledge enhancement. Society at large and the economic actors involved also noticed the added value resulting from better and faster matching processes, a higher proportion of bottleneck vacancies filled and improvements in placing people from target groups in the labour market. The recommendation was therefore simple: establish this type of collaboration as a common strategy and ensure that the resulting lessons are learned to best effect.

In addition to these operational collaboration initiatives, vacancy exchanges using the HR-XML standard between temp agencies and the VDAB are also particularly significant. This project was started up in 2007 and it is still running today. The HR-XML standard is a universal language for structuring HR data and documents on the web and therefore communicating these using a single language.

The VDAB has consequently made its website – which generates heavy traffic with an average of 80,000 visitors per day – available to temp agencies, allowing them to fill vacancies quickly and easily. A total of twenty-six Federgon members are making use of this collaboration opportunity. In 2011, the temp agencies sector posted 298,150 vacancies on the VDAB website.

§4.13   CERTO

Agreements were concluded in Flanders in 2008 and 2011 between the Flemish Government and the social partners on the reintegration of older job seekers (50+) into work. This agreement refers to the collaboration agreements between the VDAB and outplacement agencies.

Outplacement agencies in Flanders play an important role in finding work for job seekers aged over 45 (in cases of individual redundancy) and over 50 (in cases of collective redundancy). People over 45 who have been working for their employer for more than one year are entitled to an outplacement guidance pathway, paid for by the employer, when they are made redundant. Those aged over 50 are also entitled and in some cases even obliged to take outplacement in case of collective redundancy. In cases of bankruptcy, those over 50 (and other employees) can also get outplacement.

In 2009, to guarantee the quality of outplacement provided for those aged over 50, Federgon and the VDAB jointly set up the certification body CERTO for outplacement organizations. Using the certificate issued by this body, outplacement agencies can guarantee the quality of the services that they provide to the companies that are their clients and the employees involved. In this way the sector will regulate itself. The certificate is awarded on the basis of a number of quality criteria: subscribing to a code of conduct, communicating details of the guidance process to the VDAB, a satisfaction survey among both employers and employees who have been made redundant, the professional experience of the outplacement consultants and a competency test for them, and subscribing to a complaints procedure. Certificates have so far been awarded to thirty-nine outplacement agencies.

§4.14 YOUTH WORK PLAN

In 2006, the VDAB started a pilot project for young job seekers in thirteen cities and municipalities. This approach turned out to be successful, and in 2008 the approach was extended to all young job seekers throughout Flanders. In the context of this Youth Work Plan, temp agencies and the VDAB are working closely together to help young people mostly with low levels of education and/or in situations of long-term unemployment to find a (temporary) job. The temp vacancies are sent to the young people on a daily basis by e-mail and SMS.

Under the same Youth Work Plan, also tenders are submitted for guidance pathways for young people. During the period from September 2010 to August 2011, three commercial players each offered one year guidance pathways to 1,350 young people. One of the commercial actors was engaged in collaboration with non-commercial partners.

§4.15 SEA PORTS

The sea ports of Flanders are always looking for workers. A study concluded that the ports will be needing 13,000 extra workers by 2015. As a result, the Flemish Government immediately put an action plan in place. The VDAB is contributing to this action plan through its niche website at www.vdab.be/haven, where port companies can post their vacancies and port-related training courses can be promoted. Use of the site by port companies and other port-related businesses is free of charge. Temp agencies can also post temp vacancies directly on the port website, hosted by VDAB.

§4.16 TRAINING FOR TEMP WORKERS

The VDAB and the temp agency sector are also working together in the area of training. Temporary workers who are not currently working can take a targeted training course from the VDAB with a view to a subsequent agency assignment. They are considered as job seekers and the courses are free of charge for them. As part of its collaboration framework with *Vooruitzenden* (Agency Advance), a private training fund for temporary workers, the VDAB provided training to 297 candidate temporary workers in 2011. Six months after the course, 84% of them were working. In addition, the VDAB also has a large number of agreements with individual temp agencies.

For temp workers who are working and wish to undertake additional training, the employee training courses provided by the VDAB are available at reduced rates. The VDAB also offers a range of open web-based training courses for temporary workers, such as training courses for IT-skills, languages or forklift drivers.

§4.17 IN-HOUSE TEMP AGENCY AT THE VDAB COMPETENCY CENTRE

At the VDAB competency centre in Wondelgem, six different temp agencies are present during the week to help job seekers who have (almost) finished their vocational training to find work. This collaboration dates back to the new collaboration agreement between the VDAB and Federgon in 2007. The initiative is better known as the *Sollicitatiehuis* (House of Job Applications) in Ghent. This collaboration is still bearing fruit, since the proportion of attendees finding work after VDAB training courses in East Flanders is one of the highest among all the Flemish provinces: 68.5%.

§4.18 INTERREGIONAL MOBILITY

The VDAB works with its regional colleagues from Le Forem and Actiris, the public employment services in Wallonia and Brussels, respectively to find jobs in Flemish companies for job seekers living in Wallonia and Brussels. Unemployment in the Walloon and Brussels Regions is significantly higher than in Flanders, while Flanders has a growing number of bottleneck vacancies, even in difficult economic times. The organizations have therefore come together and set up joint teams to fill vacancies in Flanders.

The temp agency sector also participates in this collaboration. Temp agencies can call on the interregional teams from VDAB-Le Forem and the VDAB-Actiris collaboration to help to fill their vacancies. In concrete terms, temp agencies can participate actively in job dating events, where job seekers from Wallonia and Brussels are prepared (language skills, etc.) and preselected to meet the criteria for the jobs that are on offer at job dating events.

§4.19 HIGH-PROFILE JOBSEEKERS

Despite a number of measures introduced in Flanders and at the federal level to improve job opportunities, 'available high-profile individuals' do not always benefit from the economic recovery. This is certainly true in the case of older job seekers, job seekers of ethnic origin and job seekers who do not have a higher education degree but do have experience of working in senior roles.

The VDAB and Federgon have decided to set up an experiment in which the CVs of available high-profile individuals are sent to the Federgon members participating in the experiment who are active in headhunting, recruitment and selection. This makes it possible to engage a wider network of organizations and/or partners to help these job seekers to find work. The project was started up in March 2011. Around 300 highly trained individuals were screened by the VDAB and referred to the recruitment and selection sector.

§4.20 MEET & GREET, HANDS ON, LEARNING EXCHANGE

The VDAB and temp agencies organize Meet & Greet events at the local level to get to know each other better. At these Meet & Greet events the VDAB explains the services that it provides. In 2010, there were eleven Meet & Greet events involving a total of 200 participants.

In the 'Hands On' initiatives, temp agency consultants find out about the training courses available at VDAB competency centres so that they can subsequently make better referrals. The temp agency consultants not only acquire information but they also roll up their sleeves and become immersed in the job. This is why it is called Hands On. A total of twelve sessions were organized in 2011, involving sixty-seven temp agency consultants.

In some regions, consultants from the VDAB change places with temp agency consultants. This allows them to become more familiar with each other's work. The VDAB trains temp agency consultants so that they register vacancies more effectively.

§4.21 TEMP AGENCIES AND THE VDAB: EVERY DAY LIFE

Collaboration between temp agencies, outplacement, recruitment and selection takes place every day in Job Centres, temp agencies, outplacement agencies, etc. This is where the 'win-win' structure takes shape: work for job seekers, workers for employers, satisfied customers for temp agencies and good employment results for the VDAB.

The most concrete initiatives are in the areas of multiple placements and training: major recruitment campaigns for a company involving an (in-house) temp agency, training courses aimed at specific multiple placements, job fairs or job dating events (where a limited number of jobs are offered by one or more companies with a similar activity). Here are a few examples from the wide range of collaboration initiatives:

Temp agencies and the VDAB: 'soused herrings'
In May 2012 VDAB Sint-Niklaas worked with an temp agency to find two hundred fish filleters for a large customer for the soused herring season (which begins on 6 June). It was all hands on deck at VDAB Sint-Niklaas, which organized information sessions for job seekers in Sint-Niklaas, Lokeren, Dendermonde and ultimately also Antwerp. They showed a film of how the soused herrings come here from the far north and how they are processed. Brief aptitude tests were also administered during these information sessions. Those who were selected were given a short two-day course in fish filleting.

The unique aspect of this recruitment project is that the company did not require a diploma or any language skills. Job seekers with low or very low levels of education and no knowledge of the Dutch language were able to attend. The project therefore attracted a very diverse range of people: Flemings, Nepalese, Afghans, Turkish women with no knowledge of Dutch at all ... even the hidden labour market reserve was opened up. The Turkish women, for example, brought along their mothers, sisters or other family members, who were not registered as job seekers. The only requirement made by the company was: hard work and a willingness to get up early. People from this recruitment campaign are still working for the company today.

Temp agencies and the VDAB: 1+1=10
Early this year an temp agency in Limburg was given an assignment to find electrical engineers for three different companies. VDAB Limburg, the temp agency and the companies then set up a recruitment and training campaign.

The VDAB vacancies consultant from the regional job centre contacted the company to gather information about the vacancy and the competencies that were required. The VDAB competency centres developed a short training module, tailored to suit the needs of the three companies.

Together with the temp agency, the VDAB organized a speed dating event with a brief meeting between job seekers and the temp agency/companies. The companies then selected those candidates that they were willing to take further. These people took the tailored training course and subsequently began training placements at the company. Afterwards the temp agency employed them in the company on agency contracts.

The campaign involved ten individuals in all. It began in March 2012 and the ten participants are still working, although not all of them for the same company. The temp agency had committed to actually employ all the people who were trained and it made a special effort to achieve this.

§4.22 CONCLUSION

To conclude, you can see that we made a strong shift during the past decade: from no cooperation at all towards a broad partnership not only with the sector of temporary work agencies but more global with the sector of private employment services. Our only goal as VDAB, as a public employment service and as labour market conductor, for this approach is to offer more and better job opportunities for our clients-jobseekers and to fulfil the vacancies of our clients-companies.

CHAPTER 5
Regulating Temporary Work in Belgium

Frank Hendrickx & Piet Van den Bergh

§5.01 GENERAL INTRODUCTION

In essence, temporary jobs have been used since long in Belgium. Since the existence of modern labour law, employers can hire employees for the performance of a temporary job or for a fixed period of time. However, more recent in concept is the use of 'temporary work'. This concept refers to the business of temporary work agencies, whereby the agency puts employees at the disposal of users. In this construction, the employer's authority is 'delegated' to the user, but the temporary work agency remains the legal employer of the worker. This concept has been gaining legal meaning with the growing of a sector which was initially regulated by some collective agreements and a *provisional* law of 28 June 1976. The latter law covered only a period of four years, maximum five years. When the 1976 Law expired, the legal gaps were filled up by collective agreements. These were concluded in the National Labour Council, meaning that they became legally binding for all employers and employees of the private sector in Belgium. These agreements carried the number 36. The drive for more flexibility extended the use of temporary work and, eventually, in 1987 a new law – this time a permanent law – was passed. This is the Law on Temporary Work of 24 July 1987, which established the core of the prerequisites for the use of temporary work by the user as well as the basic working conditions for temporary workers.[1]

After the law of 1987 was passed, the prerequisites for the use of temporary work were further specified in the National Labour Council by a new set of collective agreements, this time carrying number 58. These collective agreements nail down the procedures that have to be followed by the user company (e.g., agreement of the workers representation) and the duration of temporary work. For the use of temporary

---

1. Belgian State Gazette, 20 Aug. 1987.

work in exceptional circumstances, part of the old collective agreement number 36 remained applicable. The National Labour Council also took care of the working conditions and remuneration of the temporary workers until 1993, when the Joint Committee number 322 was established for this purpose. (see section §5.06)

During the 1980s there have been important constitutional reforms in Belgium. Belgium became a federal state, with three Regions (Brussels, Flanders, Wallonia) and three Communities (Flemish, French, German) each having competences on their own conferred upon them by the federal constitution. Although labour law and social security have remained – and are still – national matters, employment policies have been transferred to the regions, including employment intermediation. This latter notion has been interpreted as also covering the competence to regulate the recognition of temporary work agencies. This competence led to a number of regional decrees – laws in the Regions are called 'decrees' – mostly in the 1980s and 1990s. As these decrees regulated other forms of employment intermediation such as recruitment and outplacement as well, they had to be revised in the shadow of the Services Directive 2006/123/EG of 12 December 2006 before 28 December 2009. Temporary agency work being excluded from the scope of the Services Directive, the provisions regarding temporary agency work were mostly taken over unchanged in new decrees. These regional laws will be discussed below.

Temporary work can be used in a *direct relationship between employer and employee* or can be used in a *triangular relationship*, i.e., whereby an employer calls on a temporary work agency who provides a temporary worker. This contribution will mainly concentrate on temporary work in the framework of a triangular relationship, meaning that the concept will be used in terms of *temporary agency work*. We will however, for some elements, refer to the situation of temporary work outside such triangular relationship.

In legal terms, *temporary work*, governed by the Law of 24 July 1987 on Temporary Work, is the activity performed under *an employment contract* so as to carry out one of the following tasks:

(1) replace a permanent employee;
(2) respond to a temporary increase of the workload;
(3) perform an exceptional work.[2]

In practice however, *temporary agency work* is also being used as a way to *recruit* permanent staff. Rather than directly hiring new staff with a trial period, companies often fill in vacancies with temporary agency workers. Only after having worked a certain period as temporary agency worker, a fixed contract may be concluded. In certain cases, this way of recruiting staff can be qualified as the replacement of a permanent employee, while this is not the case when e.g., a new position is put vacant.

Acknowledging this practice, a the social partners in the National Labour Council agreed in July 2012 to introduce recruitment as a fourth reason to make use of

---

2. Article 1, §1 Law on Temporary Work.

temporary agency work.[3] Equally part of the agreement in the National Labour Council is an open norm provision to limit the use of daily contracts. The legislative changes as a result of the agreement are expected to enter into force on 1 July 2013. At the same time, a new collective agreement will coordinate the provisions of the collective agreements 36 and 58.

Some facts on temporary work within the Belgian labour market for the year 2011 can be mentioned.[4] In that year, there were 176 million working hours in the temporary work sector. With regard to the activity of temporary work, Flanders represented 67%, Wallonia 24% and Brussels 9% of the complete volume. As far as the structure of the temporary work sector is concerned, there were about 1,356 of temporary work agencies[5] in 2011, 547,259 temporary workers, on average 89,941 temporary workers per day and there was an employment share of temporary work of about 2.36%.

§5.02 TEMPORARY WORK

[A] Notion

As explained above, the concept of temporary work is defined in the Law of 24 July 1987 on Temporary Work. Temporary work is the activity performed under an employment contract so as to carry out one of the following tasks:

- replace a permanent employee;
- respond to a temporary increase of the workload;
- perform an exceptional work.

Unlike these three reasons for temporary work that allow for temporary work both in a direct and in a triangular relationship, recruitment will be introduced in the Law of 24 July 1987 on Temporary Work as a reason for temporary agency work only.

[B] Cases in Which Temporary Work Is Allowed

[1] Replacement of a Permanent Employee

The replacement of a permanent employee is possible in the following instances:[6]

(1) The temporary replacement of a permanent employee whose employment contract has been suspended. Such replacement is not possible if the employment contract of the permanent employee has been suspended for reasons of lack of work for economic reasons or bad weather.[7] An

---

3. Advice n° 1.807 of 17 Jul. 2012 on Temporary Agency Work (www.nar-cnt.be).
4. Federgon, *De arbeidsmarkt van morgen vormen. Jaarverslag 2011* 24 (Brussels 2012); available from Federgon, federation of temporary work agencies: www.federgon.be.
5. All local branches included.
6. Article 1, § 2 Law on Temporary Work.
7. See also the collective agreement concluded in the joint committee on temporary work on 14 May 1997.

employment contract for temporary work is legally permitted, however, in case of sickness, pregnancy leave, etc.
(2) The temporary replacement of an employee whose employment contract was ended.
(3) The temporary replacement of a civil servant whose employment has been partly or fully suspended.
(4) The replacement of an employee who has temporarily diminished his working time in accordance with the legal provisions regarding reduction of the professional career.

Except for the replacement of an employee whose employment contract was ended, the length of the replacement is *not limited in time*. *No permission* beforehand is required either.

In the case of an *employee whose employment contract was ended*, the procedures and periods of temporary work are further determined by collective agreement, concluded in the National Labour Council.[8] A distinction can be made between temporary work without interference of temporary work agencies and temporary work through a temporary work agency.

[a]   *Temporary Work Without Interference of a Temporary Work Agency*

   [i]   Procedure

   (1) The temporary replacement of an employee whose employment contract has been terminated with a *term of notice* or because of dismissal for *serious cause*, can only take place when specific conditions and procedures are followed.[9]

   The temporary replacement of an employee whose employment contract has been terminated otherwise, is not subject to the specific conditions or modalities, but the prolongation thereof is subject to the specific conditions and procedures.

   (2) The replacement can only take place with the *prior permission of the trade union delegation* of the enterprise where the employee is replaced. Within a period of three working days after the permission has been received, the employer must inform the local labour inspectorate.

   In case there is no trade union, the employer needs to obtain the permission of the *trade union organizations* that are represented on the level of the Joint Committee which is applicable to the enterprise. If there is no

---

8. Collective agreement n° 58, concluded in the National Labour Council on 7 Jul. 1994, extended by Royal Decree of 23 Sep. 1994, Belgian State Gazette, 18 Oct. 1994; amended by collective agreement n° 58*bis*, concluded in the National Labour Council on 25 Jun. 1997, extended by Royal Decree of 14 Sep. 1997, Belgian State Gazette, 15 Nov. 1997 (www.nar-cnt.be).
9. Article 3 collective agreement, n° 58.

such Joint Committee, or if there is no active Joint Committee, then such permission should be obtained from the unions represented in the *National Labour Council*.
(3) In case there is no trade union delegation, and in case the employment contract is terminated because of death of the employee, agreement of the parties, or dismissal for serious cause, the employer may provisionally replace the employee by a temporary worker during a period of maximum fifteen days, to start on the moment on which the request has been directed to the trade union organizations.

[ii]   Duration

The duration of the replacement of the permanent employee is limited.[10]
In case of replacement of a permanent employee whose employment contract has been terminated, the duration of the replacement is limited:

- To a period of *three months*, starting from the moment of termination, in case of termination with a term of notice.
- To a period of *six months*, starting from the moment of termination, in case of termination for serious cause.
- To a period of *three months*, starting from the moment of termination, in case of other forms of termination. In this case, there is a possibility of prolongation for a *total* duration of three months.

[b]   *Temporary Work Through a Temporary Work Agency*

[i]   Procedure

(1) The temporary replacement, via a temporary work agency, of an employee whose employment contract has been terminated with a *term of notice*, or for *serious cause*, can only take place following specific modalities and procedures mentioned below. The same counts for *prolongation* of a replacement.
   The temporary replacement in case of other forms of termination of the employment contract, there are no such specific modalities and procedures, except for the *prolongation* of such replacement.
(2) In case there is a *trade union delegation* in the enterprise, the same procedure must be followed as explained above (hypothesis that temporary work is not performed via a temporary work agency).
   If there is *no trade union delegation*, the temporary work agency must inform the *Social Fund for Temporary Workers* of the name and address of the

---

10. Article 6 collective agreement, n° 58.

user as well as the number of the applicable Joint Committee. This communication should take place at the latest on the twentieth of the month following the temporary employment of the temporary worker with the user.

The user must communicate the same information if this is provided in the written agreement with the temporary work agency. The user must also provide the name of the temporary work agency.

[ii] Duration

Also in these cases, the duration of the replacement of the permanent employee is limited.[11]

The replacement of a permanent employee whose employment contract has been terminated, is limited:

- To a period of *six months* – with the possibility of extension for another six months – starting from the moment of termination, in case of termination with a term of notice.
- To a period of *six months* – with the possibility of extension for another six months – starting from the moment of termination, in case of termination for serious cause.
- To a period of *six months* – with the possibility of extension to a total maximum duration of six months – starting from the moment of termination, in case of other forms of termination.

[2]   Temporary Increase of the Workload

Temporary work is possible in the case of a *temporary increase of the workload*. In the original version of Law of 24 July 1987, temporary work was made possible in order to cope with *an extraordinary increase* in the workload. This notion of 'extraordinary' increase in workload is also used in the 1971 Labour Act. According to this 1971 Act, overtime is possible in order to respond to an extraordinary increase in the workload.[12] The Law of 26 July 1996 modified the Law of 1987. It replaced the notion of 'extraordinary increase' by the much broader notion of 'temporary increase'.[13] It gave, in other words, broader possibilities to make use of temporary work.

Procedures and periods of temporary work are determined by collective agreement n° 58, concluded in the National Labour Council on 7 July 1994.[14]

---

11. Article 5 collective agreement n° 58.
12. Labour Act of 16 Mar. 1971, Art. 25.
13. Law of 26 Jul. 1996, Art. 47.
14. Belgian State Gazette, 18 Oct. 1994.

[a] Temporary Work Without Interference of a Temporary Work Agency

In the event of a temporary increase of work, temporary work is permitted, provided the *trade union delegation* or, in the absence of a union delegation, the *trade union organizations* agree in advance. Within three working days of the receipt of such agreement, the employer shall inform the labour inspector thereof.

In his request, the employer shall state the number of employees involved and the duration of the temporary work. The request can only be made for a *maximum period of one calendar month*, except in the case of employment abroad, but it is *renewable*.

If the trade unions do not reply within seven days following the request, the employer may proceed to employ temporary labour, provided he so informs the labour inspector.

In the absence of a union delegation, the employer may *provisionally* have recourse to *temporary work for a maximum period of fifteen days*, following the request for temporary work. During one calendar year however, this provision shall apply only to the *first request* made for the same technical production unit and the same occupational category of workers (e.g., blue-collar or white-collar). If the employer is not authorized to have recourse to temporary work, he shall immediately end this provisional engagement. The employee, however, will receive any remuneration that remains due to him up to the end of his employment contract.

[b] Temporary Work Through a Temporary Work Agency

The procedure is alike but the equally *renewable period of temporary work can be longer than one month*. In his request the employer shall state the number of the employees involved and the duration of the temporary work. The *trade union delegation* has to agree both with the number of employees involved as with the duration of the employment.

If there is no trade union delegation, temporary work is possible for a maximum period of six months, renewable with a second period of maximum six months. The procedure is the same as for the temporary replacement of an employee whose employment contract was ended. If the employer wants temporary work for a period longer than six or twelve months or longer than the shortened period in accordance with the above mentioned procedure, he has to follow the same procedure as for temporary work for a temporary increase of work without a temporary work agency.

[3] Exceptional Work

Temporary work is also allowed in order to perform exceptional work. By exceptional work is understood, the activities determined in a collective agreement concluded in the National Labour Council. The concept is defined in *collective argreement n°36*, concluded in the National Labour Council on 27 November 1981.[15] These provisions

---

15. Extended by Royal Decree of 9 Dec. 1981, Belgian State Gazette, 6 Jan. 1982.

are expected to be taken over in a new collective labour agreement from 1 July 2013 onwards.

Insofar as it does *not relate to the usual activities* of the user undertaking, the following activities are considered to constitute exceptional work:

- work regarding the preparation, running and winding up of trade fairs, congresses, workshops, seminars, public events, parades, exhibitions, receptions, market research, inquiries, elections, special promotions, interpretations, removals;
- the unloading of lorries, provided the union delegation of the user agrees in advance;
- the secretarial work for businessmen staying temporarily in Belgium;
- work for embassies, consulates and international bodies, provided the Belgian representative trade unions have agreed in advance;
- the performance of short and specialized tasks which require special professional qualifications. In this case the user shall inform the labour inspector twenty-four hours beforehand and must have the agreement of the union delegation or, in the absence of a union delegation, of the trade unions. If the unions disagree, agreement can be obtained by the competent joint committee;
- the performance of new functions, when the employer has not yet been able to engage permanent employees, after having made an appeal to the director of the Regional Employment Service. This activity will no longer be considered as exceptional work from 1 July 2013 onwards, with the introduction of recruitment as a reason to make use of temporary agency work;
- work in urgent cases (e.g., accident or imminent accident, repair machines or material, circumstances beyond control);
- to take stock, to draw up the balance sheet. The duration of such work shall not exceed seven days per calendar year.

[4]   Recruitment

The recruitment of permanent staff will be introduced from 1 July 2013 onwards as a reason to make use of temporary agency work. Though the parliamentary debate[16] was not yet finished at the time of writing, the main conditions had already been set out by the National Labour Council on 17 July 2012.[17]

This legislative change will allow for temporary agency work which aims to directly hire an employee, who filled in the same vacancy for a certain period of time as an agency worker, with a permanent contract by the employer, i.e., the former user.

There are neither specific procedures nor permissions required for the use of temporary agency work as a means of recruitment. A set of strict rules ought to prevent

---

16. Legislative proposal N° 53-2740/001 of 8 april 2013 to amend the Law of 24 Jul. 1987 regarding temporary work (www.dekamer.be).
17. Advice N° 1.807 of 17 Jul. 2012 on Temporary Agency Work (www.nar-cnt.be).

abuses such as the use of 'recruitment' to circumvent the procedures previously discussed, or the use of temporary agency work where it is not allowed at all. These rules are:

- Only three attempts, i.e., three different temporary workers, are allowed per vacancy. The temporary work contract has to mention the number of attempts. (e.g., two for the second temporary worker, when the first temporary worker for the same vacancy was not given a permanent contract).
- If the employer, the former user, decides to give the employee a direct contract, he has to offer a contract for an indefinite period of time. Contracts for a definite period of time are only allowed in sectors where the custom exists, confirmed by collective agreement, to give one or more fixed term contracts after one or more temporary work contracts.
- An agency worker can only be given temporary contracts for six months. After this period, the employer has to take a decision: end the collaboration, or give a permanent contract.
- However, the agency worker has to be guaranteed a certain period of employment. This is the responsibility of the temporary work agency, which can place a temporary worker at different users, always with weekly contracts as a minimum. If the temporary work agency fails to complete the guaranteed period of employment, it has to pay the remuneration of the remaining period to the temporary worker. The guaranteed period of employment will equal the minimum period of employment for regular workers in a trial period. As a result of a judgment of the Belgian Constitutional Court of 7 July 2011,[18] the duration of this has to be laid down before 9 of July 2013. The duration is expected to not exceed one month, the current guaranteed period of employment for white collar workers.
- In the event a permanent contract is concluded subsequently between the worker and the employer, a trial clause in the permanent contract is only possible for the remainder of the trial period which was *ab initio* possible. A worker who can be given a trial period for six months according to the Law of 3 July 1978 on Labour Contracts[19] and worked already three months as an agency worker, can only be given a trial period for three months in his permanent contract.
- Per vacancy, temporary work is only allowed for nine months. If the employer e.g., decided not to hire the first temporary agency worker after six months of temporary work, only three months remain for the two attempts left.

Beyond these limits, temporary work is not allowed. After three failed attempts, an employer seeking to fill in a vacancy, has no other choice than to directly hire an employee. If he wishes to do so, this can of course be done via a recruitment company.

---

18. Constitutional Court, 7 Jul. 2011, case n° 2011/125 (www.const-court.be).
19. The duration of trial periods are currently under discussion as well, as a result of the above mentioned judgment of the constitutional court.

[C] Cases in Which Temporary Work Is Prohibited

Even when the conditions to allow temporary work as explained above would be met, the employment of temporary workers through a temporary work agency may still be prohibited in some cases.

The most important exception is the prohibition to use temporary workers in case of *strike*. Temporary work cannot be undertaken in case of strike in the enterprise of the user. The collective agreement n° 58 of 7 July 1994 concerning the procedure and the period of temporary work, concluded in the National Labour Council, implements this provision.[20] Directive 2008/104 of 19 November 2008 on temporary agency work is without prejudice to such a prohibition.[21]

In order to avoid abuses, temporary work has been traditionally prohibited in some particular *sectors of industry* and for some categories of workers, like in the construction industry and removal companies (blue-collar workers).[22] As far as the construction industry is concerned, collective agreement n° 36 quaterdecies of 19 December 2001 made temporary work possible in this sector.

Furthermore, these prohibitions had to be reviewed in the light of Article 4 of Directive 2008/104 by December 2011. The social partners in the joint committee number 140 for the transport sector – to which the removal companies belong – expressed the view on this occasion that the prohibition of temporary work in the removal companies is justified on the grounds of health and safety at work and the functioning of the labour market.[23] Nevertheless, although the business association representing the temporary work agencies claimed a review of restrictions or prohibitions, this has not been fully carried out, as the majority of the existing restrictions or prohibitions have been maintained.[24]

§5.03 THE TEMPORARY WORKER

[A] Legal Qualification Relationship Worker-Agency

There is a legal presumption that the temporary worker is an employee of the temporary work agency. This is a presumption *juris et de jure*, which means that it cannot be refuted.

Article 7, 3° of the Law of 1987 provides that 'the temporary employee is an employee who enters into a contract of employment with a temporary work agency to

---

20. Extended by Royal Decree of 23 Sep. 1994, Belgian State Gazette, 18 Oct. 1994. See Art. 8 of the collective agreement.
21. Recital 20 of the Directive.
22. Law of 24 Jul. 1987, Art. 23 and collective agreement n°36, concluded in the National Labour Council on 27 Nov. 1981, extended by Royal Decree of 9 Dec. 1981, Belgian State Gazette, 6 Jan. 1982, Art. 18. See also the collective agreement concluded in the joint committee for temporary work on 14 May 1997, Reg. No.: 44282/cob/322, Belgian State Gazette, 11 Jul. 1997.
23. Letter of 23 Dec. 2010 of the representatives of the removal companies to the National Labour Council regarding the prohibition of temporary agency work in their sector.
24. Federgon, *De arbeidsmarkt van morgen vormen. Jaarverslag 2011* 9 (Brussels 2012).

[1] Object and Nature of the Employment Contract

The object of the contract is the performance of *legally permitted forms of temporary work* (see above). The contract can be concluded, as far as its nature is concerned, for a fixed duration of time, for a specific work, or for the replacement of a permanent worker. Therefore, the contract is in principle not a contract for an indefinite period. However, according to some authors, the conclusion of a contract for indefinite period is not excluded either.[25] It is also possible for the temporary worker and the temporary work agency to conclude successive fixed term contracts. In practice, the vast majority of contracts cover one (working-)week. Until 30 june 2013, no legal provisions existed with regards to the minimum duration of the contracts. The earlier discussed legislative will change this:

- As a general rule, successive contracts for the duration of one day are prohibited, unless the user can prove the need for the flexibility for the use of such successive contracts.
- Using agency work for the recruitment of permanent staff, contracts cannot cover a period shorter than a week.

[2] Form of the Employment Contract

The Law of 1987 stipulates that parties must conclude *two separate contracts*. The first of these contracts will indicate *that the parties intend to conclude* an employment contract for temporary work. This contract must be in writing, and must be concluded before the commencement of the first employment for the temporary work agency. However, it does not have to be renewed every time the temporary employee accepts a new job with the same employer.

The second contract, also in writing, is the actual *employment contract for temporary work*. This contract shall be confirmed in writing at the latest within two working days from the commencement of the work.

If there are no such written contracts, the only rules applicable to employment contracts for an indefinite period shall be applicable. However, in such case, the employee may still terminate the contract without notice or payment in lieu of notice, within seven days of the ending of the period of two days after the commencement of employment.

[3] Trial Clause

Unless otherwise stated, the *first three working days* constitute a trial period, during which each party may terminate the contract without notice or compensation.

---

25. R. Blanpain, *Arbeidsmarktrecht* 133-135 (Brugge, die Keure 2008).

When a temporary employee works with consecutive employment contracts for a definite period for the same user in the same function, consecutive trial periods are not allowed.[26]

[4] Contents of the Employment Contract

The employment contract for temporary work must contain *various items*:[27]

- the name of the user;
- the reason for the contract and, where applicable, the duration of the contract;
- the reason for the replacement;
- the occupational qualifications of the temporary employee;
- the place of employment;
- the working time;
- the agreed upon remuneration and the benefits to which the employee is entitled.

The absence of one of the required items renders the temporary work contract null and void and the employee is considered to be the employee of the temporary work firm, engaged on the basis of an employment contract for an indefinite period of time. According to the law of 24 July 1987, the temporary employee should also receive information relating to the contract between the temporary work firm and the user. In order to avoid the exchange of a supplementary document between the agency and the worker, a collective labour agreement concluded in the Joint Committee n° 322 envisages this information to be included in the labour contract.[28]

[B] Remuneration, Seniority and Social Advantages

The principle of equal treatment of Article 5 of Directive 2008/104 of 19 November 2008 on temporary agency work has always been found in the Law of 27 July 1987. Article 10 states that the *remuneration* of the temporary employee may not be lower than that to which he would be entitled if he had been hired directly by the user as a permanent worker under the same conditions. Departure from this stipulation is permissible however, if equivalent benefits are granted by a collective agreement concluded in the joint committee for temporary work and extended by Royal Decree. Application of this provision has been made by collective agreement of 3 October 2011 concluded in the joint committee n° 322, granting a thirteenth month pay under a set

---

26. Collective agreement concluded in the joint committee on temporary work on 30 Jun. 1995, extended by Royal Decree of 6 Jun. 1997, Belgian State Gazette, 28 Nov. 1997.
27. Article 9 Law on Temporary Work.
28. Article 17 § 2 Law on Temporary Work and Collective agreement n° 72.231/co/322 of 10 May 2004 establishing a standard labour contract for agency work, Belgian State Gazette, 4 Nov. 2005.

of uniform rules for all temporary agency workers.[29] Such collective labour agreements, while respecting the overall protection of temporary agency workers, are in line with Article 5 paragraph 3 of the Directive.

Seniority is usually only acquired on the basis of employment with the same employer, without interruptions. So normally, a temporary employee will be losing his seniority once he will be working for another temporary work firm, or when he has a period of inactivity between two assignments for the same temporary work firm. The Law of 1987 has tried to remedy this situation partly, and sets out specific rules for the calculation of the seniority of the temporary employee.[30] In order to determine the seniority of the temporary worker, the following periods will also be taken into account:

- periods of suspension of the execution of the employment contract during which the temporary employee was covered by the social security system and insofar as he has not been employed by another employer;
- a period of inactivity for one week or less (e.g., between two assignments with the same temporary work firm).

As a general rule, periods of temporary work with a user do not count as seniority with the user in case the temporary worker would become employed by the user.[31] In case the temporary worker would subsequently be fired however, the former user should under certain conditions take the periods of temporary work into account for the calculation of the notice period, up to maximum one year.[32]

[C] Termination of the Contract

In principle, the general rules which apply to the termination of an individual labour contract also apply in case of temporary work. In principle, a contract for a *fixed term* ends at the expiration of the period which was provided for; the contract for a *specific work* ends when the work is finished; the *contract for replacement* ends when the replaced (permanent) employee returns to his job.

> (1) When a contract is for a *fixed term or* for a *specific work*, the party that terminates the contract before the expiry of its term, and without serious cause, is required to pay to the other party compensation equal to the amount of the remuneration due up to the expiry date, provided that this amount shall not exceed twice the amount of the remuneration corresponding to the

---

29. With the exception for agency workers in the construction sector, for whom the thirteen-month pay of the construction sector remains applicable; Collective agreement n° 106.667/co/322 of 3 Oct. 2011 establishing a thirteen-month pay for agency workers.
30. Article 13 Law on Temporary Work.
31. Labour Tribunal Brussels 4 Mar. 1982, J.T.T. 1982, 233.
32. Articles 65/4 and 86/2 § 4 Law 3 Jul. 1978 on Labour Contracts. Specific provisions will be included in the Law on Temporary Work with regards to the use of agency work for the recruitment of permanent staff.

period of notice that would have governed the contract had it been one of indefinite duration.[33]

This compensation is not due in case the underlying service agreement is terminated by the user, if the temporary work agency, for the remaining period, provides another job to the temporary worker which entitles him/her to the same remuneration and working conditions of an equal value.

(2) If the employment contract was concluded as a *contract for replacement* of a permanent employee for a non-specified period, the premature termination (i.e., before the end of the period of replacement) will give rise to a compensation of three months' pay. This compensation is not due if the user is responsible for the premature termination and the employee receives comparable work from the temporary work agency for a period of three months.[34]

If the employment contract was concluded as a contract for replacement of a permanent employee for a non-specified period, the temporary worker can terminate the contract with a *term of notice of seven days* in case he/she has found another employment.[35]

[D] Employment with the User

Temporary workers are always free to alter their relationship and to conclude an employment contract with the user. According to the Law of 1987, *clauses* in the employment contract prohibiting the hiring of a temporary worker by the user, are considered to be null and void.[36]

However, clauses in the contract between a temporary work agency and a user obliging the user to pay a compensation to the agency when a direct employment contract is signed before a certain period of temporary agency work has been completed, are no longer prohibited.[37]

§5.04 THE TEMPORARY WORK AGENCY

Temporary work agencies can only supply temporary workers as defined in the Law of 24 July 1987. If these businesses would operate outside the scope of the law, they may lose their license and incur penal sanctions. Indeed, in order to operate as a temporary work agency, a governmental license is required. Such license is provided by the Flemish, the Walloon, or the Brussels' regional government upon the fulfilment of certain conditions.

---

33. Article 14 Law on Temporary Work.
34. Article 15 Law on Temporary Work.
35. Article 15 Law on Temporary Work.
36. Article 16 Law on Temporary Work.
37. Article 18 of the Law on Temporary Work which prohibited such clauses, has been abolished by Law of 5 Sep. 2001.

[A] Licensing

In order to have the maximum guarantee that the firm will respect its obligations to its temporary employees, as well as to the users, the law provides that temporary work firms can only operate in Belgium after a license has been granted. This competence, given the federalization of Belgium, lies with the three regions. As a consequence, a temporary work agency wishing to operate on the entire Belgian territory, theoretically needs three licenses, one in each region. The subtleties of the Belgian state structure falling outside the scope of this contribution, we will not dive into the delegation of this competence by the Walloon region to the (small) German speaking community.[38]

Contrary to the Flemish region, the Walloon and the Brussels region accept a license in another region as an equivalent to fulfil this requirement.[39] Hence, a temporary work agency can ask for a license in the Flemish region only, and, once this has been granted, for a declaration of equivalence in the other two regions. At first sight, the slightly stricter requirements for temporary work agencies in the Walloon and the Brussels region (cf. *infra*) easily could be circumvented this way. A distinction can be made however between the vesting conditions, of which de facto the fulfilment in the Flemish region suffices, and the other conditions which need to be fulfilled in every region in which the work agency operates.[40]

As requirements with regard to licensing are explicitly excluded from the scope of Article 4 of the Directive 2008/104, the licensing requirements have not been reviewed in the light of the Directive.

[1] Flemish Region

In Flanders, the rules regarding licensing are laid down in a Decree of 10 December 2010 concerning private employment mediation.[41] This decree does not only cover temporary work, but various forms of private employment intermediation services or employment finding services, i.e., private employment agencies understood in the broad sense. The decree also covers recruitment and selection businesses, headhunters, outplacement businesses, sports agents, etc. The Flemish government found its inspiration in International Labour Organization (ILO) Convention 181. When it comes to private employment mediation other than temporary work, reference is equally made to the Services Directive. The Flemish regulation is only applicable in the Flemish

---

38. Leading to the Decree of 11 May 2009 of the German speaking community regarding the licensing of temporary work agencies and the inspection of private employment agencies, Belgian State Gazette 13 Jul. 2009.
39. Articles 5 and 6 of the Walloon Decree of 3 Apr. 2009 and Art. 9 of the Brussels Decree of 14 Jul. 2011; In the Brussels region only insofar the temporary work agency does not have a (branch) office in the Brussels region.
40. For the Walloon region: the vesting conditions are listed in Art. 4 (*conditions d'octroi de l'agrément préalable*), e.g., the maximum concentration of 40% (cf. *infra*), the other conditions in Art. 11 (*obligations à charge de l'agence de travail intérimaire agree*), e.g., the annual report (cf. *infra*).
41. Belgian State Gazette, 29 Dec. 2010.

Region, which excludes the Walloon and Brussels Region. The Decree of 10 December 2010 has been further implemented in a Decision of 10 December 2010.[42]

The exploitation of a temporary work agency as understood by the 2010 Decree is subject to *prior recognition* by the (Flemish) government. This formal license must be obtained before any exploitation or publicity regarding the business or its services. The governmental license is issued by the Flemish Minister of Employment upon the advice of the so-called Advisory Commission. This is a governmental body, established by law in the framework of the Social Economic Council of Flanders, in which the most representative trade unions and employers' organizations are represented. Every application for recognition as a private employment agency will be treated by this Advisory Commission, which holds hearings at which files can be presented and defended. In principle, a license is given for an indefinite period and stays valid until governmental withdrawal.

Furthermore, there are *various conditions* to be met, such as:

(a) not to be either in a state of bankruptcy, nor the subject of bankruptcy proceedings, nor having requested or received a judicial agreement;
(b) the managers, business managers or persons having the authority to commit or to represent the company:
 - may not have been held liable for the obligations or debts of a bankrupt company, during the period of five years preceding the request for recognition or renewal of recognition;
 - may not have been repeatedly or seriously in breach of the law respecting tax duties, social duties or the performance of the activity of a private employment agency;
 - may not have lost their civil or political rights.
(c) fulfil all duties with regard to taxes and social security;
(d) no employment contrary to public order or contrary to social or tax legislation;
(e) consider all employees in an objective, respectful and non-discriminatory manner; not draft or publish job vacancies that may give rise to discriminatory treatment;
(f) respect the privacy of employees;
(g) no fee from the employee for services;

Temporary work agencies operating in the construction or the artistic sector need a specific license to operate.[43] Remarkably, the requirement for temporary work agencies in the construction sector to operate within a distinct legal entity was abolished by the Flemish Minister, reasoning that such a requirement was incompatible with the free

---

42. Belgian State Gazette, 29 Dec. 2010.
43. Article 6 Decision of 10 Dec. 2010.

movement to provide services as guaranteed by Article 56 of the Treaty on the Functioning of the European Union.[44]

The licenses are granted for an indefinite period. In some cases, the Government can withdraw the license, e.g., in case of violation of the provisions of the 2010 Decree, after advice of the Advisory Commission.

[2] Walloon Region

For the Walloon Region, the rules are laid down in the Decree of 3 April 2009[45] and the Decision of the Walloon Executive of 30 April 2009[46] and of 10 December 2009.[47] The requirements are similar to those in the Flemish Region. Moreover, the following vesting conditions are imposed:

- to be properly formed as a commercial company, with temporary work as an activity according to the bylaws; (rather theoretically, a physical person could also obtain a license);
- not to concentrate 40% or more of its activities on one client.[48]
  The recognition can be withdrawn when the firm:[49]
- no longer complies with the conditions laid down in the Decree of 3 April 2009; it is unclear whether this includes the actual vesting conditions of the Walloon region, in case the temporary work agency operates in the Walloon region with a Flemish or Brussels license;
- is in breach of the social legislation and the legislation respecting temporary work;
- asks for or receives a compensation from the temporary agency worker;
- fails to send yearly a detailed report of activities to the Walloon government;
- fails to deliver, at the request of the jobseeker, a document stating the date and time of the visit of the jobseeker at the temporary work agency.

The temporary work agency shall be heard or at least be offered a hearing.

[3] Brussels Region

For the Brussels Region, the rules are laid down in the Brussels Decree of 14 July 2011[50] and the Ministerial Decision of 12 July 2012.[51] The conditions are similar to those in the Walloon Region.

Equally the withdrawal of the license is similarly regulated.

---

44. Parliamentary question n° 675 of 6 Jun. 2012 of F. Watteeuw to Flemish Minister P. Muyters (www.vlaamsparlement.be).
45. Belgian State Gazette, 5 May 2009.
46. Belgian State Gazette, 25 May 2009.
    30 October 1991.
47. Belgian State Gazette, 21 Dec. 2009.
48. Article 4 of the Walloon Decree of 3 Apr. 2009.
49. Article 13 Walloon Decree of 3 Apr. 2009.
50. Belgian State Gazette, 10 Aug. 2011. Brussels (bilingual) decrees are actually called 'Ordannance' in French and 'Ordonnantie' in Dutch.
51. Belgian State Gazette, 1 Oct. 2012.

[B] The Agency as an Employer

The temporary work agency is employer of the temporary worker. This implies the duty to comply with all obligations arising from normal labour and employment laws as well as social security laws. As indicated above, according to the Law of 1987, there is a legal assumption that the contract between the agency and the worker is a contract of employment.

§5.05 THE USER

[A] The Relationship User: Temporary Work Agency

The relationship between the user and the temporary work agency is based on a contract. It concerns a service contract whereby the temporary work agency agrees to put a temporary worker at the disposal of the user for the performance of temporary work and whereby the employer's authority is delegated to the user. In case law, this service agreement is often labelled as a contract sui generis.[52] The relationship is strictly regulated by the Law on Temporary Work of 24 July 1987.

The contract entered into between the temporary work firm and the user must be established *in writing* at the latest within seven working days after the date of the commencement of the employment of the temporary worker.[53]

The contract must include at least the following items:

(1) the temporary work agency's recognition number;
(2) the registration number under which the temporary work agency is registered with the National Social Security Service;
(3) the designation of the joint committee or the joint sub-committee applicable to the user;
(4) the reasons for employing the temporary employee;
(5) the place and the duration of the employment;
(6) the working time regulation in the user's undertaking;
(7) the professional qualifications of the temporary employee;
(8) the remuneration of the permanent employee with the same qualifications in the user's undertaking;
(9) the manner in which the remuneration is paid;
(10) the specific characteristics of the assigned workplace.[54]

Within at least two working days after the date of the commencement of his/her employment, the *temporary worker* must receive a written communication containing the items which have to be included in the contract between temporary work agency and user.[55] As discussed earlier, a collective labour agreement concluded in the Joint

---

52. Cf. Court of Appeal Ghent 23 Dec. 1998, T.G.R. 1999, 74.
53. Article 17 Law on Temporary Work.
54. Article 17, §1 Law on Temporary Work.
55. Article 17, §2 Law on Temporary Work.

Committee n° 322 envisages this information to be included in the labour contract in order to avoid the exchange of a supplementary document.

[B] The Relationship User: Temporary Worker

The user is not the employer of the temporary worker, but is delegated by the temporary work agency to exercise the employer's authority.

[1] Labour Protection and Collective Facilities

For the period during which the temporary employee is at the disposal of the user, the latter is responsible for the observance of those provisions of labour regulation and protection that apply to the workplace.

These cover:

- working time;
- public holidays;
- Sunday rest;
- employment of women;
- employment of young people;
- night work;
- work rules;
- health and safety of employees;
- the salubrity of the work and the work place;
- legal provisions regarding non-discrimination, including equal treatment of men and women;
- the protection of pregnant women and nursing mothers.

The latter two provisions were introduced in order to comply with Article 5 of Directive 2008/104.[56] At the same time, Article 6, paragraph 1 regarding the information of vacant posts and paragraph 4 regarding collective facilities were copied into the Law of 24 July 1987.

A Royal Decree of 15 December 2010 indicates the respective duties of the user and the temporary work agency with regard to health and safety.[57] The user, the temporary work agency and the temporary worker have to exchange information on the risks of the job and the precautions that have to be taken. According to the Royal Decree, the user shall supply working clothes and personal protective equipment. The user's medical service as well as the medical service of the temporary work agency have to take care of the medical surveillance of the temporary worker. A centralized medical dossier is to be kept.

---

56. Law of 9 Jul. 2012 implementing Directive 2008/104, Belgian State Gazette, 26 Jul. 2012.
57. Belgian State Gazette, 28 Dec. 2010.

[2] Temporary Nature of the Relationship

The relationship between user and temporary worker may change. The temporary worker and the user are always free to alter their relationship and to conclude an employment contract. As indicated above, according to the Law of 1987, contractual clauses prohibiting the hiring of a temporary worker by the user, are considered to be null and void.[58]

It may also be that the user will be held to be (or to have become) the employer of the temporary worker. This is provided by the Law of 1987 as a form of sanction.[59] The user and the temporary employee shall be considered to be bound by a contract of employment for an indefinite period if:

(1) the user continues to employ a temporary employee even though the temporary work firm has informed the user of its decision to withdraw the employee;
(2) the user employs temporary employees in breach of the 1987 Law.

[3] Representation of Temporary Agency Workers

Article 7 of Directive 2008/104 gives Member States the option to count temporary agency workers for the threshold above which bodies representing workers are to be formed in the *user undertaking*, rather than in the temporary work agency. For the calculation of the threshold above which works councils (100 employees) and committees for prevention and protection at the workplace (50 employees) are to be established in Belgium, the temporary employees are indeed considered to be employed by the user. A similar rule exists with regard to union delegation thresholds.[60]

A rather broad exception is made however, when temporary employees replace permanent employees whose contract is suspended: such temporary agency workers are not counted for the threshold. As this exception is much wider for temporary agency workers than for permanent workers, trade unions question the conformity of this exception with Article 7 paragraph 2 of the Directive.[61]

The Belgian highest court, the Cour de Cassation, decided that temporary agency workers have to be counted equally as permanent staff for determining the *number* of workers representatives in the user undertaking.[62]

---

58. Article 13 Law on Temporary Work.
59. Article 20 Law on Temporary Work.
60. Collective agreement n°58, concluded in the National Labour Council on 7 Jul. 1994 concerning the procedure and the duration of temporary work, extended by Royal Decree of 23 Sep. 1994, Belgian State Gazette, 18 Oct. 1994, Art. 10. This collective agreement was amended by the collective agreement n°58*bis*, concluded in the National Labour Council on 25 Jun. 1997, extended by Royal Decree of 14 Sep. 1997, Belgian State Gazette, 15 Nov. 1997.
61. ACV-studiedienst, *Sociale Verkiezingen 2012. Juridische aspecten*, Brussel, 2011, p. 22.
62. Cass. 30 maart 2009, *Soc. Kron.* 2010/3, p.132.

§5.06 COLLECTIVE LABOUR RELATIONS ASPECTS

The Law of 24 July 1987 provides that a specific Joint Committee will be established for the sector of temporary work.[63] It concerns Joint Committee n°322, established by Royal Decree of 8 April 1988. The Joint Committee is competent for temporary work agencies and temporary workers.

This joint committee, like other joint committees established at sectoral level, is competent to establish wages and working conditions for temporary workers by way of collective bargaining agreements concluded between the representative employers' associations and the unions which are represented in the committee. If such an agreement is extended by Royal Decree, all temporary work firms are legally bound by it, and can be enforced through criminal sanctions.

Many collective bargaining agreements have been concluded within Joint Committee n° 322.

In addition to this general competence, the 1987 Law specifically provides that the joint committee has the task to set up a Livelihood Guarantee Fund for temporary workers. This Fund was set up by collective agreement n° 36*bis*, concluded in the National Labour Council on 27 November 1981.[64] In the event that a temporary work firm fails to meet its financial obligations vis-à-vis temporary workers, the Fund, financed by contributions from the temporary work agencies, guarantees payment to the temporary workers involved of:

(1) the remuneration payable under individual contracts of employment or collective bargaining agreements;
(2) the allowances and benefits payable by law or under collective bargaining agreements.

§5.07 THE ROLE OF THE GOVERNMENT

As indicated above, the operation of temporary work agency requires a prior *governmental recognition*, which implies a role of the regional governments (Flanders, Wallonia, Brussels) in Belgium. If the temporary work agency does not live up to its duties under the social legislation, the recognition may be withdrawn.

Besides the competences of the *social inspection*, the Social Penal Code of 6 June 2010[65] provides for *civil and criminal sanctions* in case of violations of certain provisions of the Law of 24 July 1987 on Temporary Work.

On the basis of a collective agreement of 8 July 1993, a *Commission of Good Services* has been established. This Commission is competent to deal with any problem

---

63. Article 27 of the Law on Temporary Work.
64. Extended by Royal Decree of 9 Dec. 1981, Belgian State Gazette, 6 Jan. 1982. Here, the National Labour Council acted as a joint committee. At that time the joint committee for temporary work was not yet established. According to Article 7 of the Act of 5 Dec. 1968 respecting collective agreements and joint committees, an agreement may be concluded in the National Labour Council for a branch of activity where no joint committee functions.
65. Article 176 of the Social Penal Code, Belgian State Gazette 1 Jul. 2010.

with regard to the application of legal and regulatory provisions by which temporary work agencies are bound. The Commission is composed of an equal number of representatives of the employers' and workers' organizations that have a seat in the sectoral Fund mentioned above.

§5.08 DIRECTIVE 2008/104 AND CONCLUSION

The impact of Directive 2008/104 of 19 November 2008 on temporary agency work on the Belgian legislation has been fairly modest. The equal pay principle as found in Article 5, is part and parcel of the Belgian legislation on temporary agency work. Legislative changes occurred with regards to the equal treatment of some non-pay related matters, such as non-discrimination and the protection of pregnant women. Access to employment and collective facilities to be guaranteed by Article 7 of the Directive, was copied into the Law of 24 July 1987 on temporary work at the same occasion.

Is this the end of the discussion? Trade unions claim the Belgian implementation of the representation of temporary agency workers is not fully satisfactory, as temporary agency workers are not counted (exactly) the same way as permanent workers for the threshold of bodies representing workers. The business association representing the temporary work agencies claim the review of restrictions or prohibitions has not been fully carried out, as the majority of the existing restrictions or prohibitions have been maintained.

However, almost a decade of (interrupted) negotiations between social partners led to a new agreement, introducing the recruitment of permanent staff as a fourth reason to make use of temporary agency work. Arguably mirroring the spirit (or ghost?) of the Directive, labour contracts of an indefinite duration remain the general form of employment in Belgium, while temporary agency work can play its role in job creation and integration into the labour market.

CHAPTER 6
Regulating Temporary Work in Germany

Manfred Weiss

§6.01 INTRODUCTION

The European Council (EC) Directive on temporary agency work has been transposed into German law by an amendment of 2011 of the Act on Temporary Agency Work (ATAW) which first legalized and regulated in detail temporary agency work in 1972. The amendment is in force since 1 December 2011. This amendment has not only transposed the Directive but was also motivated by two other aspects. First, Germany was not prepared for the freedom of movement for the employees of the countries who joined the European Union (EU) in 2004. Since Germany still does not have a comprehensive statutory minimum wage, it was necessary to develop a safeguard against social dumping by transnational temporary agency work. Second, a special pattern of abuse which happened and created big controversies had to be prevented. There were groups of companies creating temporary agencies within the group. They terminated employment relationships. These employees were hired by the agency as temporary workers and assigned to the original company who dismissed them before. This strategy to simply save costs was considered to be a scandal.

Already, before 2011 the original legal framework of 1972 was modified by quite a few amendments. The most significant change happened by an amendment of December 2002, in force since 1 January 2003. The driving force behind this amendment was the idea to develop a tool to decrease the amount of unemployment.

In order to understand the impact of the amendment transposing the Directive on temporary agency work it is necessary to sketch briefly the legal situation as it developed until the end of 2011. Only by doing this it will be possible to show the relevance of the Directive for the legal situation in Germany.

§6.02 THE SITUATION BEFORE THE TRANSPOSITION OF THE DIRECTIVE

[A] The Situation between 1972 until the End of 2002

In Germany, temporary agency work refers to employees who have a normal contractual relationship with an enterprise whose role it is to hire-out (hirer-out) the employees temporarily to a third party (user) where the employees are at work. The ATAW only applied to agencies hiring-out in a profit oriented manner, acting on a gainful commercial basis.

In spite of several amendments the ATAW of 1972 has kept its basic structure up to the amendment of 2002. The Act intended to provide a minimum of protection for employees engaging in temporary work. In a very important branch of the economy, the construction industry, this temporary work has been banned since 1982 for blue-collar workers. This ban for the construction industry was a reaction by the legislator to the ever increasing abuses of this system in this industry. The administrative control of the abuses in that area turned out to be ineffective. However, in 1994 the ban for the building industry has been significantly weakened. It has been made possible for companies of the building industry being covered by the same collective agreement to temporarily hire-out blue-collar workers among each other.

A tendency to facilitate temporary work in order to increase flexibility became effective. The first step in this direction was the Act on Improvement of Employment Opportunities (AIEO) of 1985. In 1994, in 1997 and in particular in 2001 the ATAW was amended again in order to facilitate even more this type of work, always without changing the basic structure. The change of paradigm only happened by the amendment of 2002.

[1] *Licensing*

The hiring-out enterprise according to law needs a license. Applicants can be persons, legal entities under public law (i.e. churches or a municipality) and legal entities under private law (i.e. joint-stock companies) and groups of persons. The license is bound to the person or legal entity to whom or to which it is issued.

In principle, the applicant is entitled to get a license if none of the statutory reasons for refusal is given. The reasons for refusal were and still are exclusively laid down in a specific section of the Act so that the issuing authority is not entitled to refuse a license for other reasons. The statute contains several reasons why a license must not be issued in any case. If these reasons are given, the issuing authority is obliged to refuse the license.

According to the law as it was before the 2002 amendment, a license could not be issued or extended if there was reason to believe that the applicant (a) does not have the required reliability for performance of activities of temporary work business, in particular because he fails to obey provisions of social insurance legislation, provisions concerning deduction and transfer of wage tax, provisions concerning placement, recruitment abroad or work permits or provisions of industrial safety legislation or fails to fulfil his obligations under labour law; (b) is according to the organization of his establishment incapable of properly fulfilling the usual employers' obligations; (c) concludes with temporary workers' employment contracts of limited duration unless there is a justification for the limitation and the limitation refers to an employment contract which follows immediately to previous one with the same employee; (d) concludes with temporary work employees unlimited employment contracts, dismisses and re-engages them, however, within three months after the termination of the employment relationship; (e) limits repeatedly the duration of the employment relationship to the period of the first assignment to a user unless the temporary work employee engages in an employment relationship with the user enterprise immediately after its stay there if the Federal Employment Agency (FEA) has recognized this person to belong to a group with specific difficulties at the labour market; (f) hires a temporary worker out to a user for a period longer than twenty-four consecutive months, including any time immediately preceding this period during which the hired-out employee has been assigned to the same user by a different temporary employment business.

Furthermore, the issuing authority had to refuse to issue or to extend a license if the establishments, parts of establishments or subsidiary establishments provided for the performance of the temporary work activities are not situated in a Member State of the EU. Applicants from EC Member States can obtain licenses under the same conditions as Germans.

The burden of proof for the existence of facts justifying the assumption that reasons for refusal exist is on the issuing authority. The decisive point of time to answer the question if a statutory reason for refusal exists, is the moment when the authority's decision is made. Licenses may be issued subject to conditions and requirements in order to preclude circumstances which would justify the refusal of licenses.

Licenses shall be issued for a period not exceeding one year. An application for extension of a license has to be made not later than three months before the end of the year. A license is extended for a further year unless the issuing authority refuses to extend it before the end of the year. If the issuing authority refuses to extend a license, it is regarded as continuing its validity for not more than six months in order to permit the termination of contracts lawfully concluded. Only if a temporary work organization has been operating lawfully for three consecutive years licenses may be issued for an indefinite period.

The hirer-out has a legal duty to inform the administrative authority on all the relevant facts referring to the preconditions of the license. In addition, every half year the hirer-out has to deliver to the administrative authority a report containing the number of temporary employees, their citizenship, their occupation before becoming temporary worker, the occupation performed as temporary worker, the number of cases where temporary workers were sent to users, the number of users, the number and length of employment relationships etc.

According to the Act a license which does not comply with law may be withdrawn with effect from the date of its repeal. Since most licenses are of limited duration the most important reason for expiry of licenses is simply expiry of time.

[2] The Employment Relationship

The hiring-out enterprise is the temporary worker's employer. In principle, the employment relationship between the hiring-out enterprise and the temporary work employee is to be an indefinite one. The legislator's idea was to establish a stable relationship. It especially should be prevented that the period of the employment relationship could be limited to the period the temporary employee works for a specific user (prohibition of synchronization). According to the amendments before 2002 it was possible to once conclude a contract for a definite period without any problem. Only the repetitive conclusion of such a contract in principle was forbidden. It, however, was exceptionally permitted if a specific justification could be given. The exact meaning of such a justification of course was subject to interpretation. The principle of prohibiting synchronization became extremely controversial.

There is only a contractual relationship between hiring-out enterprise and the user enterprise. This contract has to be in written and fulfil specific conditions. A contractual relationship between the temporary employee and the user does not exist. If, however, the hiring-out enterprise has no license or loses its license, the law treats the user as if there would be a contractual employment relationship between the user enterprise and the temporary work employee in order to protect the latter one.

The period for which a temporary employee can be hired-out to a user has been extended constantly: the original maximum amounted to three months and climbed up to twenty-four months.

[3] The Relationship to the User

Even if there is no contractual employment relationship between temporary employee and user enterprise it has to be stressed that the user nevertheless has certain rights and duties towards the temporary employee. The contract between user and hirer-out leads to a splitting of the employer's function between hirer-out and user. The user has especially all the rights in reference to the performance of work: to specify the contractual obligations by giving orders and instructions to the temporary employee. This of course implies duties: the duty to give assistance and to respect all the protective regulations concerning the temporary employee's integration in the user's enterprise. The user especially has to make sure that the health and safety rules are observed. But, of course, the usual employer's rights and risks remain with the hiring-out enterprise.

The hiring-out enterprise is the temporary work employee's exclusive contractual partner. All the temporary work employee's contractual claims (wage, benefits, annual vacation etc.) only can be directed against the hiring-out enterprise. And of course the hiring-out enterprise has to pay the employer's share of social security contributions.

Already before the transposition of the Directive 91/533/EEC on an employer's obligation to inform employees of the conditions applicable to the contract of employment relationship into German law, the ATAW stipulated that specific working conditions are to be contained in a written document given to the temporary worker. The content of this document in the meantime has been extended in line with the

Directive's requirements. It, however, has to be stressed that this document is to be given to the temporary employee already before he or she begins to perform the work as contractually agreed. In case the hiring-out enterprise is not fulfilling this duty the contract is not becoming void. The sanction is a different one: the Act provides for a fine.

The works council of the user's enterprise has a right to be informed and consulted before every assignment of a temporary work employee. In this context the user has to present a written declaration by the hiring-out enterprise confirming that it has a license. Under certain conditions enumerated in the Act on Works Constitution (AWC) the works council is entitled to refuse its consent to bring in temporary workers. It, however, has to be admitted that this mainly is possible if the user violates legal provisions referring to the employment of temporary workers. Therefore, the works council's role in this context may be described as mainly consisting in the monitoring of legality. But it has to be stressed that the works council's possibility to prevent the occupation of temporary workers might go further. One of the reasons allowing the refusal to consent consists in the fact that due to the temporary work employee's employment 'there is a probability that employees of the respective establishment are to be dismissed or to suffer other disadvantages'. If such a link can be demonstrated the works council can refuse its consent in order to protect the already existing employees of the respective establishment. It, however, has to be mentioned that in actual practice the proof of such a link is very difficult.

A temporary work employee is not obliged to work for a user which is directly affected by a strike or lock-out. In such a case, the hiring-out enterprise has to inform the temporary work employee about his or her right to refuse work performance.

[B] The Situation since 2003 Up to the Transposition of the Directive

[1] *Deregulation*

The amendment of 2002, in force since 1 January 2003, abolished the prohibition of synchronization, the special rules on fixed term contracts for temporary work employees and the maximum amount of time to be spent in the user's enterprise. Thereby the hiring-out enterprises' chances to obtain a license and to act in a more flexible way have increased significantly. The amendment has not totally abolished the prohibition of temporary work in the construction industries but significantly facilitated it. In addition, the use of temporary work employees between enterprises of the construction industries has been further facilitated, in particular in view of enterprises of the construction industries seated in other Member States of the EU and hiring-out temporary work employees to German enterprises in the construction industries. In addition the hiring-out enterprises as well as the user-enterprises have been liberated of some administrative duties.

[2] Equal Treatment

The trade-off for this far-reaching deregulation was the equal treatment of temporary work employees as comprehensively and as early as possible. According to the respective section of the statute the temporary work employee is entitled 'for the time of his or her stay in the user enterprise to the same essential working conditions, including remuneration, of comparable employees in the user's enterprise'. Remuneration is to be understood in its broadest sense, including fringe benefits etc.

The principle of equal treatment does not apply for the first six weeks 'if the temporary work employee before was unemployed and is paid by the hiring-out enterprise as net remuneration at least the amount he or she got from the unemployment insurance'. This, however, does not apply if any time in the past there has been an employment relationship between this temporary work employee and the same hiring-out enterprise. Much more important is the second exception: the equal treatment principle does not apply if a collective agreement allows for a different treatment. This shifts the responsibility for the final pattern which will be relevant in actual practice to the social partners, to the trade unions and the employers' associations and/or the individual employers. There is no restriction for the scope of deviation from the principle of equal treatment by collective agreement. It has to be kept in mind that normative clauses contained in collective agreements in Germany only apply to those employees who are unionized and are employed by an employer who either is member of the concluding employers' association or party of the collective agreement. All others are not bound. However, according to the amendment employers and temporary work employees who are not bound by such a collective agreement are entitled to extend its content by so called reference clauses in the individual employment contract.

If the hiring-out enterprise is not fulfilling its duties in reference to the essential working conditions the temporary work employee is entitled to claim these conditions from the user. In addition to the written information already to be given the hiring-out enterprise has to provide written documentation also on 'the kind and amount of remuneration and other working conditions for periods in which the temporary work employee is not working in a user enterprise'. The user is obliged to include in the written contract with the hiring-out enterprise information on the essential working conditions, including remuneration, of comparable employees in the user's enterprise. Finally, the temporary work employee is entitled to claim this very same information from the user.

[3] Collective Bargaining

Due to the legislative amendment of 2002 the focus was on collective bargaining. After the amendment collective agreements with trade unions belonging to the German Confederation of Trade Unions (DGB) were concluded fixing the amount of remuneration at around 80% of the equal treatment level. The trade unions did not negotiate as a separate group but jointly as a bargaining team. However, these collective agreements were undercut by collective agreements concluded with a marginal trade union movement, the Christian Trade Union (CTU), fixing the level below 60%. Since the unionization rate in this sector is rather low, the reference clauses in individual employment contracts became important. And there in most cases reference was made to the collective agreements concluded with the CTU. However, in Germany trade unions do have to meet specific requirements to be allowed to conclude a collective agreement. Most important in this context is the requirement of sufficient power to exert pressure on the employers' side. The necessity of sufficient power is based on the assumption that proper functioning of the autonomous system of collective bargaining would be undermined if powerless trade unions were allowed to participate in collective bargaining. Today a trade union is considered to possess the necessary power if it is taken seriously by the employers' side. When this requirement is met, is difficult to decide. According to the Federal Labour Court (FLC) all circumstances of the respective case have to be taken into account.[1] The number of members is an important indicator. However, as the FLC emphasizes, a small number of members may be sufficient if the ability to exert sufficient pressure on the employers' side results from the fact that the trade union's members are specialists who work in key positions and, in case of industrial action, cannot or can only hardly be replaced on short notice. The uncertainty of this criterion shows the wide range of the FLC's leeway in allowing or preventing a trade union to participate in collective bargaining.

By a judgment of the FLC of 15 December 2010[2] it was denied that the Christian trade unions have sufficient power to be an actor in collective bargaining. This led to the effect that all these collective agreements are null and void which implies that the temporary agencies have to repay the workers also for the past the difference between the wages fixed therein and equal pay. And they also have to repay social security contributions for this difference to the social security authority.

§6.03 INNOVATIONS INTRODUCED BY THE TRANSPOSITION OF THE DIRECTIVE

The sketchy overview of the situation as it was up to 2011 should be sufficient to show that already before the transposition the concept of the German law on temporary agency work was very much in line with the Directive. Nevertheless, a few innovations have been introduced by the transposing amendment which are rather important.

[A] Scope of Application

The scope of application of the Act and, thereby, the need for the respective agencies and user companies to get a license and to abide to all the protective standards of the ATAW has been extended. Now the law no longer only applies to profit oriented agencies and user undertakings but in line with the Directive to all those engaged in economic activities whether or not they are operating for gain.

---

1. FLC of 14 Dec. 2004, Arbeitsrechtliche Praxis, No. 1 § 2 TVG Tariffaehigkeit.
2. FLC of 14 Dec. 2010, Arbeit und Recht 2011, 41.

Already before the amendment some types of hiring-out between employers were exempted from the core requirements of the ATAW. This has not been changed but extended to a new type: if the hiring-out between employers only happens occasionally and if the employee is not employed for being hired-out. This is considered to be problematic because 'occasionally' is much too vague. A much more precise description would have been necessary.[3] It remains to be seen how case law will be able to specify this vague notion.

The already mentioned prohibition of temporary agency work in the construction industry has remained. It is very doubtful whether this restriction can be justified under Article 4 paragraph 1 of the Directive.

[B] Period of Assignment to a User Company

One of the big problems in Germany consisted in the fact that to an ever bigger extent temporary agency workers got an assignment for an indefinite time, thereby substituting employees in the user company. This was strongly opposed by the trade unions. Now in line with the Directive German law now specifies that the temporary agency worker only can be assigned to a user company 'temporarily'. Thereby, it has become clear that a timely unlimited substitution for employees of the user company is no longer possible. Nevertheless this notion has become the by far most discussed topic.[4] The interpretation of 'temporarily' has become difficult since the legislator has not put a maximum limit into the law. There is only consensus that the assignment has to be for a limited time. The big majority also agrees that 'temporarily' implies that the relationship between temporary agency worker and temporary work agency has to last longer than the assignment to a user company. This would mean a revival of the prohibition of synchronizing the employment relationship with the agency and the assignment to a user. It, however, is not only unclear which maximum time would be possible for the assignment to a user (two years as before 2003 or more or less?) and under which conditions repetitive assignments to the same user are allowed. In short: the interpretation of 'temporarily' has become the main battlefield. It remains to be seen how the courts will handle the term.

The result of this debate is important because an assignment which is not 'temporarily' is against the law and gives the works council of the user company the power to prevent the assignment.

[C] Equal Treatment

The pattern already existing before in German law has been kept. But the exception for the first six weeks if the temporary work employee before was unemployed has been abolished. In line with the Directive the derogation by collective agreement is as possible as before. In the meantime the DGB trade unions have started to improve their

---

3. See W. Hamann, *Die Reform des AUEG im Jahr 2011*, Recht der Arbeit 321–341 (333) (2011).
4. See for example W. Hamann, *supra*, 324–326 and more recently R. Zimmer, '*Voruebergehender' Einsatz von Leiharbeitnehmerinnen*, Arbeit und Recht 422–426 (2012).

collective agreements by adding supplements to come close to the equal pay level. In some big companies collective agreements were concluded to simply confirm the equal treatment principle to its full extent.

The possibility to derogate from the principle of equal treatment by collective agreement, however, is excluded for the case mentioned in the beginning of this sketchy article. If an employee's employment relationship in a company is terminated and the same employee is hired-out to this same company by a temporary work agency within less than six months, there is no possibility to derogate the principle of equal treatment by collective agreement. The same applies if the employee's employment relationship is terminated and the same employee is hired-out to a company which is part of a group with the original company where the employee was employed. In such a case equal treatment applies for the whole time of the assignment, even if there is a derogating collective agreement. Thereby a strategy whereby companies simply exchange the status of employees to save costs is prevented.

As mentioned above unionization of temporary agency workers always has been and still is marginal. Therefore, the still existing possibility of extending the derogation to non-unionized temporary workers by reference clauses in individual employment contracts is the decisive instrument. It, however, is doubtful whether this possibility of extension by an instrument of individual labour law is in line with the spirit of the Directive.[5] If the European Court of Justice (ECJ) would consider it to be a violation of the Directive, the possibility of derogation from the principle of equal treatment would have almost no practical effect in Germany.

[D] Minimum Wage

A new provision provides for a minimum wage which has to be the same for times of assignment and non-assignment in between of assignments. In a very complicated procedure trade unions and employers' associations who have concluded collective agreements on minimum hourly wage are entitled to jointly propose the Federal Ministry for Labour and Social Affairs to make them general binding by way of a legal order. In case there are several proposals, the representativeness of the trade unions and employers' associations have to play a decisive role in the evaluation of what to take. This minimum wage applies to all temporary agency workers, be they unionized or not. It becomes particularly relevant for temporary work agencies residing outside of Germany in other countries of the EU. Presently this minimum remuneration fixed by the Federal Ministry amounts to Euros (EUR) 8.19 for West Germany and EUR 7.50 for East Germany per hour. It goes without saying that derogation of the principle of equal treatment by collective agreement cannot go below this level.

This minimum wage only fixes the minimum for the lowest wage category. The DGB trade unions would have liked a minimum wage also for higher wage categories

---

5. For a discussion of this problem see B. Waas, *A Quid pro Quo in Temporary Agency Work: Abolishing Restrictions and Establishing Equal Treatment – Lessons to be learned from European and German Labour Law?*, Comparative Lab. L. & Policy J. 47–61 (59–60) (2012).

to make sure that there cannot be social dumping by bringing in skilled workers. However, they did not succeed.

[E] Additional Information and Access to Collective Facilities

In addition to the already far-reaching information rights of temporary agency workers and in line with the Directive two new provisions have been introduced, one providing for information of any vacant posts in the user undertaking and one providing access to the amenities or collective facilities in the user company. As far as the latter are concerned, the law lists up some examples as are child care institutions, canteens and transport systems.

§6.04 CONCLUSION

The transposition of the Directive into German law mainly has strengthened the principle of equal treatment, has reduced the former excessive degree of deregulation and has eliminated possibilities for abuse. There are, however, still serious doubts whether after the amendment everything is in line with the Directive. The amendment definitely has not succeeded to stop the debate on the question, how far temporary agency work should be allowed. While employers still welcome it as a tool of flexibility according to the needs of the market and plead for utmost flexibility, trade unions consider it to be mainly a mechanism for precarious work and, therefore, try to restrict it further. Trade unions also point to the difficulties of integrating temporary agency workers into systems of collective representation, in particular the works council system which somehow is the backbone of German labour law.

The trade unions have already started to further restrict the possibility of assignments to user companies by concluding collective agreements.[6] Therefore, in particular in the metal and chemical industries collective agreements were concluded which try to make sure that the assignments in user companies are limited. They contain in particular clauses for maximum periods of time in the user company, ranging from three up to six months). Other collective agreements contain a duty to offer an indefinite employment relationship by the user company after a certain time. Other collective agreements go further and try to restrict temporary agency work as such. According to some collective agreements assignments are only allowed if there are: (a) extraordinary circumstances (unforeseen events) and (b) no alternatives (as are overtime work, use of working time accounts, fixed term contracts etc.). Another type of collective agreement fixes a maximum quota (15% to 25% of the total workforce) for temporary agency workers. And again another type increases the power of the works council in monitoring the assignment up to co-determination. All these restrictions are considered to be in line with the Directive since 'public interest' as reason for justification of restrictions in Article 4 paragraph 1 refers to 'the protection

---

6. For these different types of collective agreements see R. Krause, *Tarifvertraege zur Begrenzung der Leiharbeit und zur Durchsetzung von Equal Pay*, HSI Schriftenreihe Bd. 2, Saarbruecken (2012), 35–42.

of temporary agency workers' and 'the need to ensure that the labour market functions properly and abuses are prevented'. Whether this view will be shared by the ECJ will be seen.

In Germany the indefinite employment relationship for an indefinite period is still considered to be the goal to be achieved. Therefore, temporary agency work and other forms of external flexibility still are considered to be the exception which is supposed to be restricted as much as possible. Nevertheless, the number of temporary agency workers is steadily increasing, presently ranging around 1 million.

CHAPTER 7
Regulating Temporary Work in the Netherlands

Mijke Houwerzijl

§7.01 APPROACH AND STRUCTURE

This paper presents an overview and analysis of the evolving regulatory and legal framework of temporary agency work (TAW) in the Netherlands in light of two dominant trends: TAW as a means of achieving flexicurity and TAW in the context of cross-border service provision within the European Union (EU).

The article is structured as follows: after an introduction into these two key drivers of regulatory change in TAW in the last fifteen years (§7.02 and §7.03), the paper proceeds with a more detailed and technical account of the legal and self-regulatory developments they provoked in the Netherlands (§§7.04–7.09), including the implementation of the Temporary Agency Work Directive (2008/104/EC). However, the transposition only concerns minor changes, due to the fact that the Dutch law is perceived as being already largely in conformity with the Directive (see below §7.05). The paper ends with some concluding remarks, including an observation on the question to what extent the two identified key drivers of regulatory activity on TAW interact with each other or may even be envisaged as mutually reinforcing (§7.10).

§7.02 TAW AS A MEANS OF ACHIEVING FLEXICURITY

The main features of the current regulatory regime of TAW in the Netherlands can only be explained against the backdrop of the social policy debate on 'Flexicurity'.[1] The

---

1. Flexicurity refers to both the employer's demand for flexibility and the employee's demand for security. Thus, the term refers to a win-win flexibility–security trade-off. Ton Wilthagen & Frank Tros, *The Concept of 'Flexicurity': A New Approach to Regulating Employment and Labour Markets*, 2 Transfer 166–186 (2004).

pursuit of a (new) balance between flexibility and security has, over the years, become more prominent in the framework of the European Employment Strategy (EES). The 2001 European Employment Guideline 13, under the Adaptability pillar, already explicitly addressed both flexibilization and security goals. In 2005 it became a goal in itself and from 2006 on the term 'flexicurity' is being used. Furthermore, the December 2007 European Council endorsed the agreed common principles of flexicurity. In this year, EU Member States have agreed on the following main elements of an EU flexicurity strategy: flexible contractual arrangements, reliable and responsive lifelong learning, effective labour market policies and modern social security systems.[2]

In the Netherlands the relaxation of the regulation on TAW at the end of the 1990s was part of a broader 'flexicurity trade-off' which attracted much attention of European policymakers.[3] The (win-win) trade-off involves more external labour market flexibility for companies and at the same time more employability and thus employment security, for starters and employees 'with a distance' to the labour market. Accordingly, temporary agency workers are kept out of unemployment while simultaneously increasing their employability. One of the most common phrases used to describe the aim of such a 'flexicurity deal' is of 'TAW as a stepping stone towards regular (long-term) employment'.[4] The *stepping stone* function of TAW is often contrasted with TAW as a source of '*dead end* and precarious jobs'.[5]

Recently, the European sectoral social partners EuroCiett,[6] and Uni Europa,[7] emphasized the positive role of TAW in increasing the chances of agency workers for long-term employment in the labour market as a result of job placement and the possibility of vocational a training provided by temporary employment agencies

---

2. Sonja Bekker *Flexicurity: The Emergence of a European Concept*, Social Europe Series, volume 30 (Intersentia 2012); Pacelli et al., *Employment Security and Employability: A Contribution to the Flexicurity Debate* (European Foundation for the Improvement of Living and Working Conditions 2008). See for an analysis of actual examples implemented in the Member States, Irene Mandl & Funda Celikel-Esser, *The Second Phase of Flexicurity: An Analysis of Practices and Policies in the Member States* (European Foundation for the Improvement of Living and Working Conditions 2012).
3. The flexicurity debate in the EU drew partly on this Dutch Flexibility and Security law and policy construct. See Green paper on labour law, *Modernising Labour Law to Meet the Challenges of the 21st Century* (2006); *European Expert Group on Flexicurity* (2007); European Foundation, *Varieties of Flexicurity: Reflections on Key Elements of Flexibility and Security* (2007).
4. However, academic research into the validity of this claim shows no consistent results. See recently e.g., Kristina Håkansson, Tommy Isidorsson & Hannes Kantelius, *Temporary Agency Work as a Means of Achieving Flexicurity?*, 2 Nordic J. Working Life Stud. 153–169 (2012); Marloes de Graaf-Zijl, Gerard J. van den Berg & Arjan Heyma, *Stepping Stones for the Unemployed: The Effect of Temporary Jobs on the Duration Until (Regular) Work*, 24 J. Population Econ. 107–139 (2011).
5. Giovanni S.F. Bruno, Floro E. Caroleo & Orietta Dessy, *Stepping Stones versus Dead End Jobs: Exits from Temporary Contracts in Italy after the 2003 Reform*, IZA Discussion Paper No. 6746 (2012).
6. Eurociett gathers thirty-one national federations from EU and European Free Trade Association (EFTA) countries, and seven of the largest international staffing companies as corporate members. See http://www.eurociett.eu/.
7. Representing 7 million workers in 330 European trade unions. See http://www.uniglobalunion.org/.

(TEAs).[8] In this respect, they refer to the preamble of the EU Directive on Temporary Agency Work, where it is stated that this form of employment '[...] meets not only undertakings' needs for flexibility but also the need of employees to reconcile their working and private lives. It thus contributes to job creation and to participation and integration in the labour market'.[9]

§7.03 TAW IN THE CONTEXT OF CROSS-BORDER SERVICE PROVISION WITHIN THE EU

Notwithstanding the importance of TAW as facilitator of transitions on the national labour market, recent changes in the Dutch regulatory regime on TAW were triggered by negative effects of 'TAW transitions' across borders of national labour and services markets. When, for example, a TEA recruits Polish workers for jobs in the Netherlands, the actual circumstances may not change according to whether the TEA is established in Poland or the Netherlands, but the legal situation does. This creates a clear incentive to look for the easiest and cheapest way (for the employer, the worker or both). Labour law is but one of the points to be taken into consideration; social security, pension and tax law being at least as important. Notably, only a hard core of labour standards may apply mandatorily during the temporary posting in the host country.[10] Next to this, the posted worker stays insured under the social security schemes in the sending state.[11] When posted from 'low wage' to 'high wage' countries, this[12] makes posted workers (far) less costly than locally hired (agency) workers.

Until 2004, cross-border labour mobility within the EU used to consist of a comparatively small group of migrant workers, mainly frontier workers, who made use of their right to free movement of workers.[13] Facing the inflows of workers in

---

8. See their joint recommendations, Press release 19 Dec. 2012 Temporary Agency Work Facilitates Labour Market Transitions.
9. Directive 2008/104/EC of the European Parliament and of the Council of 19 November 2008 on temporary agency work, preamble para. 11.
10. Pursuant to Art. 3 of the Posting of Workers Directive 96/71/EC.
11. Pursuant to Art. 12 of Regulation 883/2004 on the coordination of national social security systems, which deals with the issue of affiliation to a social security system in case of movement to another Member State. In principle, during the first twenty-four months of posting, the worker remains affiliated to the social security system of the Member State where he normally works.
12. Taxation of workers lies within the competence of Member States. Bilateral agreements exist between most of the Member States in order to avoid double taxation. These agreements set out the rules according to which taxes must be paid either in the country of residence of the worker or in the country of posting. Normally, for posting up to 183 (calendar)days income taxes are paid in the country of residence of the worker. In case of posting beyond 183 days income tax has to be paid in the country where the worker is posted. However, for posted agency workers the tax regime of the host state may apply from day 1.
13. Due to a decline in economic motivations, such as differences in wage-levels, living standards and employment opportunities across EU Member States, the geographical mobility of EU citizens in the 1970s, 1980s and 1990s was lower than that existing in the 1950s and 1960s. In 2002, only 600,000 people, or 0.4% of the total employed population, worked in a country different from their country of residence. However, cross-border commuting was continuing to grow. See Report 'The Social Situation in the European Union 2002', 23. The last data for

recent years from new into old Member States, this image had to be revised. Despite the existence of transitional arrangements in most of the old Member States, demand factors, such as the demand for low-skilled and flexible labour, led to a steady increase of intra-EU labour mobility from new to old Member States. Also supply factors, such as the chance for improvement of living standards, were strong drivers behind (the size of) this trend.

The transitional restrictions undeniably influenced the places where most workers went.[14] In exploring their opportunities to move to EU-15 countries with transitional restrictions, EU8/EU2 workers often seem to have opted for 'diversification strategies'.[15] Part of the available low-skilled labour has moved to the desired country of destination through illegal channels or even by 'grey' use of legal routes meant for non-economically active migrants such as the family migration or student route.[16] Others went abroad through alternative legal routes, namely as posted worker or (bogus) self-employed.[17] High demand for 'cheap labour' on the demand side combined with scarce information about possibilities to move on the supply side, seems to have encouraged the reliance on migration facilitators, ranging from bona fide temporary agencies and subcontractors to middlemen and gang masters operating in the

---

mobility within the EU-15 showed that about 1.5% of employed people (including legally residing third country nationals) within the EU-15 moved in one year from another region *within* their Member State *or* from another Member State. See EC Press Release IP/04/267.

14. According to a recent study commissioned by the European Commission, there is clear evidence that the pattern of transitional restrictions in place at the beginning of the 2004 enlargement diverted mobile workers away from traditional destinations – namely Germany – and towards the more easily accessed labour markets in the UK and Ireland. The research findings also suggest that, due to network effects, transitional arrangements can have permanent effects on the pattern of migration. See Dawn Holland et al., *Labour Mobility within the EU. The Impact of Enlargement and the Functioning of the Transitional Arrangement* (National Institute of Economic and Social Research London 2011) http://ec.europa.eu/social/main.jsp?langId=en&catId=89&newsId=1108&furtherNews=yes.

15. Support for this stance is delivered by socio-legal studies such as the dissertation of Samantha Currie, *Migration, Work and Citizenship in the Enlarged European Union* (Ashgate 2008) and the dissertation of Cathelijne Pool, *Migratie van Polen naar Nederland in een tijd van versoepeling van migratieregels* (Bju 2011). Based on qualitative interviews with various key-actors in the field, both studies highlight tangible experiences of Polish migrant workers in respectively the UK and the Netherlands and show how the legal framework and the formal status they are granted shapes their attitudes and experiences. The term 'diversification strategies' is from Hein de Haas, *The Determinants of International Migration*, IMI Working Papers Series 32 (University of Oxford 2011) http://www.imi.ox.ac.uk/pdfs/imi-working-papers/wp-11-32-the-determinants-of-international-migration.

16. Martin Ruhs & Bridget Anderson, *Semi-compliance and Illegality in Migrant Labour Markets: An Analysis of Migrants, Employers and the State in the UK*, 16 Population, Space and Place 195–211 (2010).

17. See the study commissioned by the European Commission of Aukje van Hoek & Mijke Houwerzijl, *Comparative Study on the Legal Aspects of the Posting of Workers in the Framework of the Provision of Services in the European Union* (Radboud University Nijmegen 2011), especially Annex I. ec.europa.eu/social/BlobServlet?docId=6677&langId=en. The choice for illegality was observed by the Bureau of European Policy Advisers and the Directorate-General for Economic and Financial Affairs, *Enlargement, Two Years After: An Economic Evaluation*, European Economy Occasional Paper 24 (European Commission 2006). http://ec.europa.eu/economy_finance/publications/publication7548_en.pdf.

shadow economy.[18] Many research studies have shown, that this new mobile EU-labour force is vulnerable as regards exploitation, especially in the lower segments of the labour markets. Their employers have often strong incentives for 'non-compliance' with labour law,[19] whereas the workers involved often face many barriers to insist on their rights.

It is estimated that about 200,000 'labour migrants' from Central and Eastern European countries (CEE countries) are at work in the Netherlands by now. This number may increase after 1 January 2014, when work permits are no longer required for workers from Bulgaria and Romania. Half of the labour migrants from the CEE countries work in the Netherlands via intermediaries such as TEAs. Part of these TEAs are guilty of mala fide and fraudulent practices.[20] There is a great variety of mala fide practices in the TAW sector, varying from incorrect administration to serious exploitation of workers, through (international) 'creative' constructions (e.g., via establishments of Dutch TEAs in the new Member States or foreign TEAs).[21] The (perceived threat of) social dumping and diminishing opportunities for Dutch jobseekers[22] that comes along with it, provides a source for political tensions, especially in times of economic downturn. The scapegoating of Polish workers by the PVV-hotline in the Netherlands is a radical example of it.[23]

§7.04 THE EVOLUTION OF TEMPORARY AGENCY WORK IN THE NETHERLANDS

Paradoxically, it was also the growth of illegal labour brokers in the 1960s that encouraged the Dutch government to introduce legislation to regulate the TAW business, by means of a permit system that was established in the Act on the Provision of Temporary Labour in 1965. With that regulatory initiative, the Netherlands was the first Member State of the EU which acknowledged and allowed bona fide TAW. At the time, the TAW sector criticized the strict license conditions that were introduced, arguing against the assumption that the sector was only a poor arrangement for

---

18. Jan Cremers, Jon Erik Dølvik & Gerhard Bosch, *Posting of Workers in the Single Market: Attempts to Prevent Social Dumping and Regime Competition in the EU*, 38 Indus. Rel. J 524–541 (2007).
19. The term 'labour law' refers in this paper to both collective labour laws and individual employment standards.
20. Kamerstukken II 2010/11, 29 407, nr. 118, p. 2.
21. Report Setting the Limits. Extent of and measures against mala fide practices in the temp agency sector ('*Grenzen stellen. Omvang van en maatregelen tegen malafide praktijken in de uitzendbranche*'), Research voor Beleid, 2010. Hereinafter referred to as 'Report Mala fide practices in the temp agency sector 2010', 22.
22. See for example newspaper articles on replacement of Dutch workers in 'sheltered' professions: Poolse buschauffeurs in dienst bij GVB, Parool 2009; Polen schoffelen bij WSW-bedrijf TBV, Vlaardingen, De Echo, 20 juli 2010, http://www.echo.nl/ro-vl/zorg-enwelzijn/ ingezonden/ 1052759/polen.schoffelen.bij.wsw.bedrijf.tbv/?utm_campaign=rss&utm_source=rss&utm _medium=rss.
23. This provoked a statement of Commissioner Viviane Reding on (and against the content of) the PVV's website http://ec.europa.eu/commission_2010-2014/reding/multimedia/news/2012/ 02/20120211_en.htm accessed 13 Aug. 2012 and a European Parliament resolution of 15 Mar. 2012 on discriminatory internet sites and government reactions (2012/2554(RSP)).

workers. The companies in the sector worked hard to change their image by showing that the sector also brings about positive effects like additional income and independence for the agency worker.[24] The continued growth of TAW in later years led to collective labour agreements (CLAs). Consequently, the Dutch regulatory model that was developed over the years, was based on a combination of general regulation in statutory law and detailed and specific arrangements in collective agreements concerning the employment conditions at the agency. In addition to the growing demand for TAW as a consequence of the high degree of employment and in particular strict dismissal protection of regular employees, the pragmatic stance of the trade union movement has been a crucial factor to the early acceptance of TEAs in the Netherlands.[25]

In 2009, the proportion of temporary agency workers was estimated at approximately 1.5% of the total labour force in the EU, ranging from less than 1% in some countries up to around 3% in others, such as in the Netherlands. These figures may seem low, but the proportion of workplaces using temporary agency workers is considerable, ranging from approximately 20%–40% of all private and public workplaces in a country.[26]

Currently, the total Dutch TAW market amounts to more than 734,000 agency workers, 1.4 million placements and a turnover of more than 10 billion annually. Hence, the temporary agency work sector plays a prominent role in the Dutch economy, society and labour market.[27] The largest volume of temp work through agencies includes rather low-skilled jobs for manufacturing, transport, cleaning and administrative work, although most large temp work agencies also have specialized departments for outsourcing nurses, secretaries, managers, and other professional medical or technical staff; activities deployed by specialized agencies too.[28] Given the competitive pressures among temporary employment agencies (TEAs), the trend is to look for new, more differentiated market niches. Another strong trend, signalled some five years ago, is the further internationalization of the sector, especially since the accession to the EU of CEE countries.[29]

---

24. See C. Passchier, *Loon naar werkgever of naar werkvloer*, SMA 7-41 (2002).
25. See E. Sol, *Targeting Transitions: Employment Services in the Netherlands*, 23 Comparative Lab. L. & Policy J., 81–128 (2001).
26. See Kristina Håkansson et al., *Report: The Representation of Agency Workers in Europe at National and Local Level in France, Netherlands, Sweden, Poland and the UK* (Goeteborg 2009).
27. The temporary agency work sector in the Netherlands, ABU February 2012.
28. According to the Eurociett 2012 report, in countries where the manufacturing sector covers an important segment of the economy, it also represents a higher share in agency work: 70% of agency workers in Poland are assigned to manufacturing, 61% in Hungary, 52% in the Czech Republic, 46% in Germany. In other countries, such as Spain, the Netherlands, and in the UK, over 50% of the temporary agency workers are in the services sector. The share of temporary agency workers in agriculture is generally low across Europe.
29. ABU 2000/2008 Marktmonitor.

§7.05 CURRENT STATUTORY FRAMEWORK OF TAW IN THE NETHERLANDS[30]

We now turn to the more detailed and technical analysis of the Dutch legal and self-regulatory framework for TAW.

The regulatory framework for temporary agency work (TAW) in the Netherlands comprises a structure of legal and contractual measures that have been adopted in legislation, covenants, and collective labour agreements (CLAs) by the end of the 1990s. Since 1999, TEAs are seen as regular employers and, following a certain term of service, agency workers are treated as regular employees.

The legislation is to be found in the Civil Code (introduced by the so-called Flexibility and Security Act), the Placement of Persons by Intermediairies Act (hereinafter WAADI) and the Works Councils Act. The WAADI regulates the TAW market as allocator on the labour market and has abolished the license system. The Flexibility and Security Act (hereinafter F&S Act) has created clarity in the labour relations concerning TAW. The intended result of all these measures was to inject additional flexibility into the labour market by relaxing dismissal laws and the rules to start a temporary work agency on the one hand, while generating a higher level of security for employees in flexible jobs on the other.[31] Two collective agreements are applicable, one of which as a rule is declared generally binding.

Since 1 January 1999, the legal position of agency employees is enhanced by classifying the relationship between an agency employee and the agency as an employment contract, as stipulated in the Dutch Civil Code (Article 7:690). Nevertheless, there are some exceptions to the general rules pertaining to ordinary employment contracts. The first exception is that parties may agree in writing that the contract of employment will end without notice at the moment that the user firm states that there is no more work. However, this exception is limited in time. The second is the exception to the provision in the Civil Code (Article 7:668a) which for ordinary workers states that after three fixed-term contracts he automatically is entitled to a permanent contract. This entitlement is postponed for an agency worker. Next to this, it is possible to make further deviations in CLAs. Finally, the Flexibility and Security Act introduced, combined with a revision of the Works Councils Act (WOR), agency workers codetermination rights in the agency and in the user firm (Article 1(3)(a) Works Councils Act) similar to those of the 'regular' Dutch workforce.[32]

---

30. The sections 5–7 draw partly on earlier publications. See Houwerzijl & Sol, the Dutch national part of the report (written together with Dr E. Sol, HSI, University of Amsterdam) on the Representation of Agency Workers in Europe at national and local level in France, Netherlands, Sweden, Poland and the UK, authors: Kristina Håkansson et al. (Goeteborg 2009); E. Sol en M. Houwerzijl, *The Articulation of the Interests of Temporary Agency Workers in the Netherlands: Current Trends. The Role of Social Dialogue and Collective Bargaining Structures and Labour Organisations* 30 pp. (HSI Discussion Paper 2008); Wilthagen et al., *Flexicurity in the Dutch Temporary Work Sector: A Positive Sum Game?* (2008) – Paper available through SSRN elibrary.
31. See R. Knegt et al., *Tweede evaluatie Wet flexibiliteit en zekerheid* (HSI UvA ism TNO, maart 2007).
32. More precisely, persons who have worked in a user company for at least twenty-four months, on the basis of a temporary employment contract concluded with another company (for instance a TEA) as meant in Art. 7:690 CC, are granted the same information and consultation

The WAADI which came into force on 1 July 1998, changed the regulation of the position of intermediaries, including TEAs. The distinction between secondment (posting) and agency work was abolished. Moreover, the WAADI abolished the permit system and the maximum tenure of the agency worker with the user firm. Also abolished were the authorization procedure and most sector restrictions for agency work, but some special regulations remained in force, such as the equal wages clause (Article 8), the prohibition to demand something in return (such as a fee) from agency workers for the placement at the user firm and the prohibition to post agency employees in user firms where a strike is going on (Article 10).

Recently, the WAADI and the WOR were amended in order to implement the Temporary Agency Work Directive (2008/104/EC).[33] This concerns only minor changes, due to the fact that the Dutch legislation is perceived as being already largely in conformity with the Directive. Actually, Article 5(1) of the Directive, which deals with the equal treatment of temporary agency workers with regard to certain employment conditions is transposed by Article 8(1)(b) WAADI. Next to this, Article 5(5) of the Directive is transposed by Article 8(3)(a) WAADI, allowing social partners to deviate from the rules on equal treatment by collective agreement, for as long as the collective agreement foresees in measures preventing misuse of, in particular, successive assignments designed to circumvent the provisions on equal treatment. Article 6 of the Directive is transposed by Article 8b of the WAADI. This new inserted article stipulates that agency workers should be clearly and timely informed about vacancies in the user undertaking in order to give them the same opportunity to find permanent employment as other workers in that undertaking. Article 6(2) of the Directive, which provides that every direct clause that prohibits or has the effect of preventing the conclusion of a contract between the user undertaking and the temporary agency worker after the assignment is null and void, is transposed by Article 9a WAADI.[34] The new inserted Article 8a WAADI transposes Article 6(4) of the Directive, giving agency workers equal access to amenities or collective facilities of the user undertaking. Article 31b of the WOR is amended with the obligation for the user company to provide

---

rights in the user company. These rights are granted on the condition that the work performed by these temporary workers falls within the sphere of the normal business activities of the user company. Furthermore, these persons are also considered to be workers of the supplier company (for instance a TWA or secondment company). As a result of these extensions of the definition of 'worker', persons who are posted/seconded by a TWA or other suppliers of staff to the same user company for a longer period of time, can claim information and consultation rights in the companies of both the supplier and the recipient.

33. The summary below is taken from the website of the European Labour Law Network (http://www.labourlawnetwork.eu/). For further information in Dutch see Handelingen I 2011-12, nr. 26 item 3; K.H. Hermans & M.S. Houwerzijl, *Verbeterde positie uitzendkracht en uitzendarbeid*, TRA 60 (2009); M. Hennevelt, M. Louisse & W. Bijveld, *Nederland en gelijke bezoldiging: in lijn met de Uitzendrichtlijn?*, TRA 58 (2011); Kamerstukken II, 2010/11, 32 895. On 17 Apr. 2012, the First Chamber of Parliament accepted the proposal unanimously without taking a formal vote.
34. This is actually a re-codification of Dutch law that existed until 1 Jul. 1998 (Art. 93 Arbeidsvoorzieningswet 1990) and a codification of the jurisprudence of Dutch Supreme Court that based on Art. 6:248 Civil Code declared such clauses as unreasonably onerous meaning that it is therefore null and void (HR 4 April 2003, LJN: AF2844, NJ 2007/351 with note Heerma van Voss).

information on the use of temporary agency workers, such as on how many temporary agency workers are employed or are expected to be employed in the future. In this way Article 8 of the Directive is implemented. As required by Article 4 of the Directive, a review has taken place with respect to restrictions or prohibitions on the use of temporary agency workers, in both laws and collective agreements. However, since there were hardly detected any of such restrictions, this has so far not resulted in actual changes.[35]

§7.06 COLLECTIVE LABOUR AGREEMENTS IN THE TAW SECTOR

As was already noted, by means of CLAs it is possible to deviate from a number of these provisions, namely when they are laid down in the Civil Code (as most of the measures are) under the condition that they are not of a fully mandatory character. The Dutch Civil code permits social partners to deviate from mandatory law by collective agreements also *in peius*. It concerns the so-called three quarter mandatory stipulations.[36]

Regarding the social partners involved in TAW, on the employers' side TEAs have structured themselves into a separate sector. On the employees' side there are no separate unions for agency workers. Employees are mainly organized in three sectoral unions: FNV Allies, affiliated to the FNV Confederation, De Unie (affiliated to the MHP confederation) and CNV services union, affiliated to the CNV confederation). Jointly they organize about 7% of the agency workers. Employers are organized in the association of agency workers (ABU) and the Dutch Association of intermediary and agency companies (NBBU). ABU represents more than 65% of the market in turnover. ABU is by far the largest employers' organization within the private employment agencies industry.[37]

Besides the two statutory changes described above, in 1999 two new CLAs were agreed upon, which were evaluated and renewed in 2004, 2009 and very recently, in 2012. The main CLA is a result of bargaining between the ABU, representing the employers, and the sectoral trade unions, representing the employees. This so-called ABU-CLA is as a rule declared generally binding and covers (without extension) more than 60% of the branch of TAW.[38] The second collective agreement, concluded between employers' organization NBBU and the sectoral trade unions covers about 25% of the TAW branch. This CLA is not extended. Both CLA's may be seen as a sectoral follow-up of the national flexicurity package deal: At the same time that the social partners agreed upon the flexibility and security legislation, the employers and

---

35. See: Analyse van de STAR ten behoeve van de heroverweging met betrekking tot beperkingen en verbodsbepalingen op de inzet van uitzendarbeid in cao's, February 2012. See also Kamerstukken II 2011-2012, 32895, nr. 6, p. 1 en 2 with appendix: 'Rapportage heroverweging overheid', 1-3.
36. See for instance G.J.J. Heerma van Vos, *Driekwart dwingend recht*, in *CAO-recht in beweging*, 121-133 (R. Duk ed., Den Haag: SDU 2005).
37. See Sol, Houwerzijl, *supra* n. 31, 2009.
38. See http://www.abu.nl/abu/organisatie and https://www.nbbu.nl/pagina/over-nbbu.

trade unions in the temporary agency sector made a gentlemen's agreement (covenant) on how to deal with the new legislation.[39] Below, we only refer to the ABU-CLA.

What are the most important deviations? First of all, a deviation from the law stipulating that flexible workers are entitled to a permanent contract after three years or after three consecutive fixed-term contracts (Article 7: 668a Civil Code). This stipulation was transformed in the ABU-CLA by introducing a so-called phases-system that agency workers have to pass through before becoming for an indefinite period of time employed by the temp agency. Another important deviation is the extension of the period that an agency worker is lent out under mere agency work conditions. The law states that this period should be twenty-six weeks, but it is possible to deviate from this provision in a collective agreement.

In the ABU-CLA, the system is currently divided into three phases.[40] The agency employee stays in phase A until he has worked seventy-eight weeks for the agency. In this phase the agency employee may have an unlimited number of contracts. When an interruption of twenty-six weeks between two contracts occurs, the counting of the seventy-eight weeks starts again. The employee in phase A works under a so-called *agency or employment clause*. This has several consequences. One is that the contract with the agency in principle ends when the contract between agency and user firm ends. After three months of work, the user firm has to give notice before terminating the contract with the agency. This notice period increases with the duration of the work. The employment clause also gives the employee the right to stop working with one day notice. Phase B starts after the period of seventy-eight weeks and lasts two years (or eight consecutive contacts, whichever comes first). In this period the employee may have a maximum of eight fixed-term contracts. If the agency employment contracts in phase B are interrupted by a period of less than three months, the period of the interruption counts as part of the total duration of phase B. During phase B, the temporary employment contract ends on the agreed expiry date. The employment clause may no longer be included in the employment contract. This means that if the user firm ends the contract with the agency, the temporary employment contract of the employee with the agency does not automatically end and the agency has to find a suitable job for the agency worker and pay for the period in between jobs whilst the contract is not yet ended. The period of notice is also longer for the agency worker. From phase B on the agency worker starts building up pension rights. After two years or eight consecutive contracts, the agency worker reaches phase C. In phase C the agency employee receives a contract for an indefinite period of time with the agency. The period of notice is now one month for both the agency and the worker. However, before giving notice, the temp agency is obliged to look for suitable replacing jobs for a couple of months in case the user firm has ended the contract for a worker in stage C with the agency. Meanwhile, the worker is entitled to continued pay. Moreover, the

---

39. *Ibid.*; W. Plessen & A. Muntz, *Rechtspraak in Uitzendland, over complexe regels en immanente discussiethema's*, SMA 203-213 (2003).
40. See Art. 13 of the recently concluded (at the time of writing not yet extended) ABU-CLA 2012-2017.

temp agency, like any regular employer in the Netherlands, needs a permit to fire the worker.

§7.07 EQUAL TREATMENT CLAUSE IN LAW AND COLLECTIVE AGREEMENTS

As mentioned above, the law on temporary work agencies, WAADI, contains an equal treatment clause, establishing the principle of equal treatment with comparable workers in the user firm (Article 8). According to this provision the agency has to offer the agency worker the same wage and other working conditions as the employees of the user enterprise with the same or a comparable type of job. Thus, in the Netherlands, there is a basic principle of equal treatment between agency workers and workers in the user enterprise. However, this rule does not apply if either the collective agreement for agency workers of TEAs (ABU-CLA) provides to the contrary, or if the CLA applicable to the user firm requires remuneration (and other working conditions) of agency workers to conform with this CLA. These two rules thus allow the social partners to depart from the basic principle of equal treatment between agency workers and comparable workers in the user firm. In this way a balance has been struck between, on the one hand the rule of equal treatment for work of equal value and on the other hand the contractual freedom and autonomy of the collective bargaining partners, which is limited by the equal treatment rule.[41]

It is exactly this seeking for a balance between potentially conflicting fundamental rules which has led to the possibility to deviate from the statutory equal treatment clause by collective agreement.[42] At the collective bargaining table, the parties concerned have made a more refined deal concerning equal pay, taking into account all work related factors before the comparable worker can be determined. With respect to agency workers, the comparable worker may either be the colleague agency worker or the user company worker. The representatives of the TAW-employers associations tend to emphasize their role as 'genuine' employers, which should be a reason to enable them to apply first and foremost their own collective agreements to agency workers. The unions stress the fact that the interest of TAW-employers in collective bargaining is positive only if the agency workers profit from it, meaning their labour conditions should be more favourable under the ABU-CLA. If not, the unions prefer to arrange agreements on pay and other working conditions for agency workers with their counterparts at the bargaining table in the different sectors where agency workers are performing their jobs in the user firms.[43]

Thus, behind the innovative 'flexicurity deal' at legislative level, in the TAW-employers associations and amongst the unions it is an ongoing debate whether an agency worker should be remunerated according to the wage of the user firm as laid down in its collective agreement (or according to another agreement on labour

---

41. C. Passchier, *supra* n. 25, 2002; E. Sol, *supra* n. 26, 2001.
42. This makes (or better: 'made', since Germany has introduced this method as well, and, also the EU Directive 104/2008 on Temporary Agency Work is based on this method) the Dutch system unique.
43. R. Knegt et al., *supra* n. 32, 2007.

conditions applied in the user firm), or according to the wage as laid down in the collective agreement for agency workers. In order to prevent unfair competition between agency workers and a sector's permanent employees and to deal with the problem of overlap between the collective agreements for TAW and the other sector agreements, several solutions were tried out. From 2004 on, this led to specific regulation in the ABU-CLA on the remuneration of agency workers: after having worked for more than twenty-six weeks at the same company, agency workers will be paid on the same level as the employees of the hiring company. For the first twenty-six weeks of employment, it was stipulated that in principle an agency worker is paid according to the remuneration scheme of the ABU-CLA unless otherwise stipulated by the parties to the CLA covering the specific sector. Thus, currently, for workers in phase A the wages are in most cases determined by the TAW sector's collective agreements.[44] If an employee has worked twenty-six weeks for the same user company, the user firm has to pay the agency worker the same wage (and overtime and costs) as the regular employees in the company.

In phase A the employee receives only wages for the hours he has worked. In phase B and C he also receives wage for the hours he is not able to work (e.g., in case of idle time, sickness etc.). In the period between two contracts the employee also receives wage, when it is not his fault that he cannot work. Pay levels in the ABU-CLA are based on the average of fifty other collective agreements. This means that in practice the wages in the user firms and TWA firms will not necessarily be equal for the same work. For pay purposes, the ABU-CLA further distinguishes between two groups of workers. The first includes holiday workers, and so-called target groups: school-leavers, persons reentering the labour market and the long-term unemployed. Workers in the first group earn a low starting salary. The idea behind this is their lower productivity because they have to be (re)integrated into the labour market.[45] All other employees are in the second group and earn a higher salary. To prevent abuse, one may remain for only a maximum of twelve months in the first group.[46]

In some collective agreements for user firms, social partners have bargained over the use of agency workers in that specific company or sector. Several extended CLAs stipulate that the provisions (especially regarding wages and allowances) also apply to agency workers who are placed at the disposal of the employer by a TEA.[47] Sometimes the user firm is explicitly obliged to check the compliance with the CLA-provisions (by the TEA) as regards the hired temp agency workers.[48] One of these CLA-provisions states that the recipient should irrevocably agree in the commission contract with the

---

44. However, according to the ABU-CLA 2012-2017, this will change from 2015 on. Then, the main rule will be that agency workers will receive the same CLA-wage as their comparable colleagues at the user company in the first twenty-six weeks. Nevertheless, the TAW-CLA wage will still be paid to specific groups of workers.
45. According to the Eurociett 2012 report, an average of 31% of all temporary agency workers in the Netherlands in 2008 belonged to these special target groups.
46. See E. Sol & S. Engelsman, *Temporary Agency Work Country Report: The Netherlands* (EIRO 2008); Wilthagen et al., *supra* n. 31, 2008.
47. For example Art. 2B CLA Finishing Work (construction industry).
48. Article 5 extended CLA (Window-)Cleaning; Art. 3 extended CLA Carpentry Industry; Art. 1 (3.1) extended CLA for the Travel Branch.

TEA that the latter shall comply with the CLA-provisions regarding wages/allowances and other employment conditions towards the borrowed agency workers. If the recipient fails to do so, he is liable for the non-compliance with these CLA-obligations, as if the agency worker is his own employee.[49]

§7.08 CROSS-BORDER SUPPLY OF AGENCY WORKERS

Non-compliance is currently a key issue of concern also for the social partners of the TAW sector itself. Starting at the beginning of this century, the Dutch TAW sector has been plagued by a considerable increase in dubious temporary agencies, using illegal employees and/or evading the payment of taxes and premiums. This may partly be due to the abolishment of the permit system in the WAADI Act of 1998, but that is not the only reason. Part of the problem also stems from the increased demand for and supply of workers from other EU Member States, in particular from the new Member States, with Poland as the main supplier of 'cheap labour'. According to an investigation of the ABU, in 2004 the number of organized branches (companies) was 3,000, whereas the number of mala fide branches was 6,600. The number of agency workers through bona fide placement was 650,000, whereas from an estimated number of 210,000 illegal workers in the total Dutch workforce, 100,000 of them were temporary workers through mala fide placement.[50] Apart from TAW, all kinds of other creative constructions are used to offer labour from 'low wage regimes' in 'high wage' countries, such as subcontracting and (bogus) self-employment.

In particular, since the transitional regime for the free movement of workers was abolished for most CEE countries from May 2007 on (not including workers from the newest Member States, Bulgaria and Romania), the attention of policymakers and public opinion turned to unsafe and illegal housing of migrant workers and tackling circumvention of the applicable labour conditions.[51] The social partners in the TAW sector have been very active in recent years in making agreements with municipalities on the housing of foreign temp agency workers. Especially for group-based deployment the TAW sector has developed a standard concerning decent accommodation of foreign temporary workers in the Netherlands at a reasonable price. Moreover, TEAs are obliged by (partly self-)regulatory measures to give proper information and where necessary assistance concerning transport from and to the country of origin and on transport to and from the place of employment; concerning possibilities to complete tax refund forms, and guaranteeing that the refund must be credited to a bank account of the temporary worker; next to this, TEAs are obliged to offer health insurance, without the agency worker being obliged to accept the offer. The TEA is also obliged to inform the agency worker of the benefits and necessity of taking out Health Insurance. Finally, some special provisions are included in the ABU-CLA for agency workers not permanently resident in the Netherlands, in order to bring the working conditions and labour

---

49. Article 1 (3.5) extended CLA for the Travel Branche.
50. The ABU investigation, *Illegal Practices in the Temporary Work Agency Industry*, is available in English at: http://www.abu.nl/abu/pagina.asp?pagkey=37892&mode=read.
51. See Regioplan 2005.

standards of this group more in line with their needs as a result of their specific working and living pattern (consisting often of circular migration).[52]

Upon concluding the temporary employment contract, the TEA is therefore obliged to enter into consultations with each agency worker who is not permanently resident in the Netherlands about the provisions of this article on the alternative shape given to the working conditions concerned. The financial value of the working conditions for this group should be the same as that of the other agency workers.

Another special provision in the ABU-CLA concerns the agency workers with a foreign employment contract. For this group of cross-border posted agency workers, it is stipulated which provisions of the ABU-CLA have been decreed to be compulsorily applicable also to agency workers who are deployed from abroad by a foreign TEA to a user firm in the Netherlands, and whose employment contract is governed by the law of a country other than the Netherlands. This provision is in accordance with the Terms of Employment (Cross-border Work) Act (Waga), which is an implementation of the EU Directive on the Posting of Workers (Directive 96/71/EC).[53] Actually, the ABU-CLA contains a special matrix stipulating which (parts of) provisions apply to posted agency workers (with reference to the WAGA).[54] Regarding several applicable (parts of) provisions the text has been rewritten to adapt it to the specific situation of posted workers (this implies particularly the deletion of references to Dutch provisions and situations). The parties to the CLA Construction Industry and the ABU-CLA have agreed on a specific regime for temp agency workers in construction, which also applies (as is explicitly stated) to posted temp agency workers. This regime is laid down in both CLAs.[55]

§7.09 ENFORCEMENT OF CLA AND LEGISLATION: ACHILLES HEEL

As for most countries, for the Netherlands non-compliance and (lack of) enforcement of labour law is an Achilles heel.[56] With regard to the enforcement of collective agreement provisions social partners do not have a very active tradition. Until some years ago, the sense of urgency for a very active approach was lacking. However, since it became clear that undeclared work[57] and creative constructions are on the rise, the call for tackling these practices has been growing ever stronger.

In this context, social partners in TAW did create self-regulation for monitoring compliance to the ABU-CLA, such as the establishment of the Compliance Office of the

---

52. See Houwerzijl & Sol, *supra* n. 31, 2009.
53. See Mijke Houwerzijl, *The Dutch Understanding of Posting of Workers in the Context of Free Services Provision and Enlargement: A Neutral Approach?*, FORMULA working (and conference) paper 32 (Oslo 2010). See: http://www.jus.uio.no/ifp/english/research/projects/freemov/publications/papers/2010/september/.
54. Article 46 of the ABU-CLA in conjunction with Annex IV.
55. Article 91 in conjunction with Annex 15 CLA Construction Industry; Art. 21 in conjunction with Annex II, Art. 8-16 ABU-CLA. NB The same specific regime is laid down in Art. 37 in conjunction with Annex 10 of the not extended NBBU-CLA.
56. See Guy Davidov, *The Enforcement Crisis in Labour Law and the Fallacy of Voluntarist Solutions*, ICLLIR 61 (2010).
57. See, for example, C. Bosse & M. Houwerzijl CLR National Report Undeclared Work (2006).

social partners (SNCU) to combat illegal employment and unfair competition by migrant workers.[58] The aim is to actively monitor compliance of the rules by (foreign) TEAs and (foreign) agency workers. The Compliance Office SNCU aims to be a central point of contact and registration for firms and employees. Moreover, the SNCU is actively searching cooperation with the Labour Inspectorate and other enforcement authorities. Actually, the TAW sector is a trendsetter in providing information on working conditions laid down in legislation and collective agreements in other languages than Dutch. Currently, information is made available in English, Polish and some other languages as well.[59]

Next to this, social partners developed a so-called norm against illegal activities. This norm (NEN 4400) regulates for the whole sector on what conditions a TEA is considered a bona fide enterprise.[60] When agencies have shown to fulfil requirements concerning the payment of statutory minimum wages, taxes and social insurance and the legitimacy of employment in the Netherlands, they will be certified.[61] The assessment is made by private certifying companies. After certification, the temporary work agency will be registered by the Foundation for Employment Standards (Stichting Normering Arbeid, SNA). Regular monitoring of the registered agencies on compliance with the applicable law and regulations and on their payment record must ensure that the agencies stay on the right track. Otherwise, a non-compliant agency will be removed from the register.[62] TEAs are under no obligation to acquire the quality label 'NEN-norm 4400', nor are user firms obliged to hire workers from a certified TEA. However, in order to encourage certification of agencies as well as the use of certified TEAs, several generally applicable CLAs oblige undertakings to hire agency workers exclusively from NEN-norm certificated Dutch and foreign TEAs.[63]

Notwithstanding these self-regulating initiatives, evasion of the rules still remains a serious problem, especially in sectors with much cross-border labour mobility. Though hard figures are not available, it follows from research of 2010 that the extent

---

58. Foundation for monitoring compliance with the Collective Labour Agreement for Temporary Agency Workers (*Stichting Naleving CAO voor Uitzendkrachten* (SNCU)). See http://www.sncu.nl/EN/AboutSNCU.aspx.
59. See website www.abu.nl.
60. C.C.A.M. Sol & E. Schram, *'Naming and Praising' als nieuwste methodiek in de regulering van de uitzendbranche*, 4 SMA (2007).
61. Recently, the social partners who concluded the new ABU-CLA 2012-2017 have decided that the NEN-norm will be enhanced by including also abidance to the ABU-CLA-provisions on wages etc.
62. See M.S. Houwerzijl & S.S.M. Peters, *Liability in Subcontracting Processes in the European Construction Sector – Netherlands*, http://www.eurofound.europa.eu/publications/htmlfiles/ef08877.htm (research commissioned by the European Foundation for the Improvement of Living and Working Conditions (Eurofound), published January 2009), 10. See also parts on the Netherlands in Yves Jorens, Saskia Peters & Mijke Houwerzijl, Study on the Protection of Workers' Rights in Subcontracting Processes in the European Union: Final Study (Research Commissioned by the European Commission), June 2012, based on the Dutch country study of Lucy van den Berg and Saskia Peters: http://ec.europa.eu/social/main.jsp?catId=471.
63. This is for instance stipulated in the extended CLA for the construction industry (Art. 96b), CLA Finishing Work (Construction Industry) (Art. 2B), CLA Road transport and haulage (...) (Art. 9) and CLA for the painting, finishing and glass business (Art. 7).

of the mala fide practices in the TAW, construction, transport, cleaning and meat-processing sector, did not decrease in recent years, but on the contrary has probably increased.[64] The use of all kinds of legal constructions makes it sometimes hard for user undertakings and inspection entities to distinguish between mala fide and reliable partners. The real business partner may be concealed by means of non-transparent company constructions with interrelated firms; the user thinks he is dealing with a bona fide partner, but in fact this is just the 'front' agency, the actual employment is organized by mala fide entrepreneurs.[65] It also occurs that a NEN 4400 certified TEA – being the formal business partner of the user – actually supplies workers via a non-certified sister company.[66]

Hence, as time passed by, both employees and employers associations agreed that their self-regulation needed to be backed up by the government in order to be effective. After consultation of the social partners, the government proposed to introduce a user firm liability for payment of the statutory minimum wage and minimum holiday allowance to the hired agency workers. This statutory liability scheme is meant to further the use by user companies of certificated TEAs. Therefore this regulation is considered as a (at least in the Netherlands) unique mix of public and private measures.[67] The Act entered into force on 1 January 2010. The liability is laid down in Article 7:692 of the Dutch Civil Code (CC). The user company and the TEA are jointly and severally liable. However, the liability does not apply in case the user firm makes use of a certificated TEA. Article 7:692 CC applies irrespective of the law that is applicable to the employment contract and the contract between the employer and the user company. Hence, the law also applies to users of foreign TEAs and may be seen as a tool to further compliance with the host labour standards – i.e., the Dutch statutory minimum wage and holiday allowance[68] – by foreign service providers (including foreign TEAs).[69]

Very recently, in July 2012, another measure entered into force which may substantively improve the efficiency of the voluntary and private NEN-norm 4400 certificate in combination with the statutory liability scheme of Article 7:692 CC. The

---

64. Report Mala fide practices in the temp agency sector 2010, 17.
65. A general trend is that fraudulent practices in the temp agency sector have become more 'refined' (often pushing the boundaries of the law or just crossing it). For instance: instead of paying below the Dutch minimum wage, mala fide TWAs withhold – especially as regards foreign workers temporarily working and residing in the Netherlands – excessive percentages of the wages for transport, accommodation, fines etc. Such abuses are obviously much harder to trace for the inspection institutes Report Mala fide practices in the temp agency sector 2010, 27–29.
66. Report Mala fide practices in the temp agency sector 2010, 28.
67. See Guy Mundlak, Els Sol & Eva Schram, *Hard Law/ Soft Law Hybrids as a Conceptual and Policy Framework: A Look at the Regulation of Temp Agency Work in Highly Regulated Countries*. Hugo Sinzheimer Institute, University of Amsterdam, Working Papers Series 10 (2012).
68. Applicable ex Art. 3 (1) (c) Posting of Workers Directive in conjunction with Art. 9 Rome I regulation.
69. Mijke Houwerzijl (2010), *supra* n. 54.

'Act Obligation to register for intermediaries who assign temporary workers'[70] introduces an obligation to register at the Chamber of Commerce in the WAADI. In the past, companies established abroad and so-called mobile TEAs (without a place of business, in practice: minibuses picking up foreign workers in the morning and paying them in cash at the end of the day)[71] could not register. Companies established in the Netherlands were already under obligation to register, but not yet obliged to mention that they supply manpower. In the new Act, recipients (user undertakings) are also addressed: it is forbidden to hire manpower from non-registered TEAs/labour suppliers. In case a recipient makes use of workers hired from a non-registered labour supplier, both the recipient and the supplier will be sanctioned. The sanction consists of an administrative fine of maximum Euros (EUR) 76,000. This amount will be doubled in case of recidivism. If the recipient assigns the hired workers to another recipient (which makes the first recipient also a supplier), all the parties in the chain are liable and will be fined.[72] The 'Inspectorate SZW'[73] is responsible for the enforcement of these rules. Non-registered TEAs cannot obtain the NEN 4400 certificate. The Inspectorate SZW and the Tax Administration have gained legal authority to provide information to, for instance, the Compliance organization SNCU about companies which where penalized.[74]

The idea is that this mix of (public) hard law measures – liability of recipient for payment of the statutory minimum wage to the hired agency workers and obligation to register – and (private) 'soft law' measures – certification – of the TAW sector itself, will effectively combat mala fide practices in the TAW sector.[75]

§7.10 FINAL REMARKS

Compared to most other countries, TAW is already for a long time a more or less accepted phenomenon in the Netherlands, and is not considered inferior to so-called normal work. All in all, in the Netherlands the protection of agency workers at statutory level and especially at sector level through CLAs and other forms of self-regulation, is relatively well developed. This does not mean that agency workers have an enviable position in the labour market, but considerable groups of employees actually seem to be content with and may even benefit from working through TEAs.[76] Although difficult to assess, there are studies which suggest that TAW may indeed be a stepping stone for workers entering or reintegrating in the Dutch labour market. Together, Dutch

---

70. *Wet registratieplicht intermediairs die arbeidskrachten ter beschikking stellen*, Kamerstukken II 2010/11, 32 872.
71. These 'TEAs' only have a mobile phone number and are therefore often called '*06-busjes*'.
72. New Art. 15 Waadi. See Kamerstukken II 2010/11, 32 872, no. 3, 12.
73. A merger of the Labour Inspectorate and related Inspectorates, such as for social security contributions and benefits fraud.
74. Annex to Kamerstukken II 2010/11, 17 050, no. 402.
75. Some observers cast doubt on this optimistic view. See R.S. Ferouge & E.J.A. Franssen, *Inlenersaansprakelijkheid verder uitgebreid door registratieplicht in nieuwe WAADI*, 2 TAP 69-74 (2012).
76. See Sol (2001), *supra* n. 26; Knegt (2007), *supra* n. 32. See also joint report commissioned by EuroCiett and Uni Europa, The role of temporary agency work and labour market transitions in Europe, 2012.

employer associations and trade unions involved in TAW have come up with sometimes innovative solutions for classical problems like (lack of) equal treatment and self-regulation of irreproachable behaviour and compliance as alternative for a licensing system in the fight against fraud and undeclared or illegal labour. The Dutch creation of a possibility to deviate from the legal equal pay clause (only) by collective agreement, attracted international attention and was followed first by Germany and later on by the EU as a whole, since it is now incorporated (as an option) in the EU Directive 2008/104 on Temporary Agency Work. Although the role of social partners should not be underestimated, also the Dutch government has recently taken numerous practical and legal measures with a view to enhancing the public and private enforcement of labour law provisions in the context of TAW, especially under the influence of the influx of (agency) workers from the new EU Member States into the Dutch labour and services markets.[77]

As noted above, in the last ten to fifteen years, the regulatory and legislative activity by social partners and government was triggered by two major driving forces:

First of all, the pursuit of a right balance between flexibility and security on the national labour market. This 'flexicurity' agenda has also reached the European stage and is especially manifest within the EES. Both in the Netherlands and on a European level, TAW is seen as one of the means of achieving flexicurity.

Second, a 'Europeanisation' of the national labour markets as a result of increasing cross-border mobility of (agency) workers in the gradually expanding internal market of goods and services. This development was clearly accelerated by the recent enlargements of the EU.

Interestingly, policy papers, legislative documents and academic literature usually treat the two topics separate from each other, as if there would not be any overlap or interplay.[78] However, it appears that opportunities for flexicurity policies are affected by the growing use of 'cheap' cross-border (agency) workers. Especially in situations where intermediairies do not (fully) abide by legal standards in the host state, this leads to undercutting of statutory and collectively bargained wage standards and limits employment opportunities for (vulnerable groups of) domestic (agency) workers.[79]

Perhaps the stance of EuroCiett on the draft Enforcement Directive of the Posting of Workers Directive[80] may be seen as a first step of acknowledging the interconnection

---

77. Kamerstukken II 2010/11, 17 050, no. 403; Kamerstukken II 2010/11, 29 407, no. 118.
78. See for an exception Monika Schlachter (2012), Equal Treatment for Transnational Temporary Agency Workers? FORMULA working (and conference) paper, Oslo, WP 32. See: http://www.jus.uio.no/ifp/english/research/projects/freemov/publications/.
79. See examples *supra* n. 23 and compare with similar 'anecdotical evidence' in for instance Sweden, Belgium, the UK, collected in the study of Aukje van Hoek and Mijke Houwerzijl on behalf of the EC 2011, *supra* n. 18, Annex I.
80. See: Proposal for a Directive on the enforcement of Directive 96/71/EC concerning the posting of workers in the framework of the provision of services, Brussels 21 Mar. 2012, COM(2012) 131 final. See also Aukje van Hoek & Mijke Houwerzijl, *'Posting' and 'Posted Workers' – The Need for Clear Definitions of Two Key Concepts of the Posting of Workers Directive*, in Cambridge Yearbook of European Legal Studies (CYELS) 14, 2011-2012, in particular 443-451 (Catherine Barnard, Markus Gehring eds., 2012) (on workers hired for the purpose of posting only).

between both topics. In its position paper on a job-rich recovery of European labour markets in which it emphasizes the crucial role of TAW as a stepping stone, Eurociett also states that 'to secure well-regulated work mobility, it strongly supports a more appropriate and better implementation of the EU Directive 1996/71 on the Posting of Workers'.[81] Moreover, in one of its recommendations it is put that: 'Labour market reforms to reach a job-rich recovery should secure progress in implementing Flexicurity policies, especially by removing existing, unjustified restrictions on private employment services and by *reducing undeclared work.*' In my view, it is high time for a bolder acknowledgement by all stakeholders of the need for an integrated and mutually reinforcing approach to the two topics discussed above.

Within such a comprehensive approach elimination of abuses by proper enforcement of rules on transnational TAW should play a key role. Interestingly, the Dutch historical development towards a flourishing bona fide TAW sector, highlights the key role of appropriate regulation and enforcement. Arguably, where enforcement is weak, the goodies in TAW will suffer from the bad image of their mala fide colleagues and from their unfair competition. In fact, without strict rules to distinguish the goodies from the baddies, the positive side of TAW would probably never have gotten a chance to prove itself in the Netherlands in the first place.[82] Also at European level, the first policy documents on TAW in the 1970s emphasized the need to eliminate the abuses characterizing at that time the activities of TEAs.[83] It is no coincidence that the EU has been able to adopt the Directive 2008/104 on the facilitation of TAW and the recognition of a basic protection of agency workers at a time when the problems concerning TEAs (at national level) have been solved in most of the Member States.

In a similar vein, fostering and facilitating the stepping stone function of TAW in the context of flexicurity on national labour markets may benefit from a focus on effectively combating abuse (and hence unfair competition) of cross-border agency workers. Moreover, the remaining scope for bona fide use of cross-border (agency) workers may also result in a 'stepping stone' function of TAW for this particular group of workers itself, enhancing their employment opportunities and career prospects. Hence, a comprehensive approach to both topics would be mutually reinforcing and may even be envisaged as advancing a cross-border layer of flexicurity by promoting (only) 'quality' labour mobility across borders with a view to creating a fair and genuine European labour market.[84]

---

81. Eurociett, Position Paper Towards a job-rich recovery Private employment services drive job creation and strengthen dynamics of the labour markets 4 Sep. 2012, section 5.6, 12.
82. See Passchier, 2002, *supra* n. 25.
83. As pointed out by Massimiliano Delfino, *Interpretation and Enforcement Questions in the EU Temporary Agency Work Regulation. An Italian Point of View*, 2 European Lab. L. J. 297-298 (2011), referring to Council Resolution of 21 Jan. 1974, concerning a social action programme, which was the first EC document that referred to temporary agency work among the measures to attain a full and better employment in the Community.
84. See Council of the EU, Background note on Labour Mobility – Towards a European Labour Market, Brussels, 28 Sep. 2012, 14323/12, SOC 783, 3, where it was stipulated that labour mobility between the Member States should be fostered in a way that respects the free movement principles and does not create phenomena of unfair competition, exploitation of workers and poor working conditions as well as imbalances in national labour markets.

CHAPTER 8
Regulating Temporary Work in Poland

Andrzej Marian Świątkowski & Marcin Wujczyk

§8.01 INTRODUCTORY NOTE

Temporary agency work is a brand new legal institution in Poland. It was introduced by the statutory act of the Polish parliament (Sejm) of 9 July 2003.[1] The act on the Employment of Temporary Workers (ETW) became active (went into the force) 1 January 2004. It was introduced for the sole purpose of overcome the legal effects of Article 25[1] of the Polish Labour Code (PLC) of 26 June 1974[2] which automatically transformed each fixed term contract concluded by the very same parties to employment relationship without any break into a contract of employment for indefinite period of time. Therefore, in our article we will not deal with any type of a temporary employment contract regulated by the legal provision of the PLC due to clear and precise division introduced by Article 21 of the Act on ETW according to which fixed term employment contracts concluded by temporary work's agencies and their employees – temporary workers within the meaning of the ETW shall not be regulated by Article 25[1] of the PLC.[3] Therefore, the act on the ETW introduces into the Polish individual labour law an ultimate priority of an employment contract for indefinite period. With the exception of a period between 2 August 2009–31 December 2011, during which the statutory Act of 1 July 2009 on moderation of the effect of economic

---

1. Journal of Laws, No. 166, item 1608 as amended. See, M. Paluszkiewicz, *Zatrudnienie tymczasowe w polskim prawie pracy. Konstrukcja i charakter prawny* (*Temporary Employment in Polish Labour Law. Legal Construction and Legal Nature*). (Warsaw: Wolters Kluwer, 2011), passim; *Z problematyki zatrudnienia tymczasowego* (*Some Problems of Temporary Work*) (A. Sobczyk ed., Warsaw: Wolters Kluwer, 2011), passim.
2. Journal of Laws of 1998, No. 1998, item 21 as numerously amended. See, A.M. Świątkowski, *Kodeks pracy. Komentarz* (*Commentary to Labour Code – PLC*) (4th ed., Warsaw: C.H. Beck, 2012).
3. A.M. Świątkowski, *Commentary to the PLC, supra*, 152 ff.

crisis[4] (the anti-crisis act)[5] was in force, the legal effect of above mentioned priority of an employment contract concluded for indefinite period over a fixed term contract was and still is prevailing. Despite intents displayed in the Polish labour law literature the threat of economic crisis was not used by the government as a chance to liberate rigid, overprotective PLC.

According to Article 2 section 3 of the Act of 9 July 2003 'temporary work' means the performance of a task listed in items 'a'-'c' for a given user employer for a term no longer than thirty-six consecutive months during which temporary agency work (TAW) may post temporary worker at the same user employer for twelve months (Article 20 section 1). Temporary work utilized by the same employer can be extended for the total period of thirty-six months during which TAW may post temporary worker at one user employer in case of a replacement of a permanent employee absent from work (Article 20 section 1). The other causes which may be used as legal grounds for utilization by user employer of temporary work furnished by TAW are:

- seasonal, periodic, or ad hoc tasks;
- tasks which timely performance by the workers employed by user employer would not be possible – temporary increase of the workload (Article 2 section 3).

As far as legal construction of employment relationship regulated by the PLC is concerned (in general this construction is based on the Roman law principle *do ut des* which means equitable obligation of both parties of an employment contract: an employee is obliged to provide work for an employer with whom an employment contract was concluded and, in exchange, an employer is under legal obligation to pay wages) the temporary work is structured as triangular relationship[6] between three parties:

(1) TAW and its employee – temporary worker (TW).
(2) TAW and user employer.
(3) TW and user employer.

---

4. Journal of Laws, No. 125, item 1035.
5. A.M. Świątkowski, *Ustawa antykryzysowa z komentarzem* (*Commentary to Anti-crisis Act*), (Warsaw: C.H. Beck, 2010), passim.
6. M. Paluszkiewicz, *supra*, 76 ff; A. Patulski, *Doktrynalne aspekty zatrudnienia tymczasowego. Wybrane aspekty* (*Theoretical Aspects of Temporary Work. Selected Issues*) in *Some Problems of Temporary Work*, *supra*, 84 ff; J. Stelina, *Tradycyjna koncepcja stosunku pracy a stosunek pracy tymczasowej – potrzeba redefinicji?* (*Traditional Notion of Employment Relationship and Temporary Work – Need for Recodification?*), in *Some Problems of Temporary Work*, *supra*, 103 ff.

§8.02 TEMPORARY WORK

[A] Notion of Temporary Work

The exhaustive catalogue of reasons a which may be used to employ TW's is listed in Article 2 section 3 of the act on ETW. There is no legal explanation of seasonal, periodic, or occasional (ad hoc) tasks which ought to be dealt with as an excuse of necessity to hire TW. The first two legal grounds listed under items 'a' and 'b' of Article 3 section 3 of the ETW depend entirely on an employer's estimation of factual situation in a given enterprise. However, the third ground listed in item 'c' of above mentioned provision of the ETW requires further legal explanation. A prospective user employer may enter into a legal contract with TAW concerning employment of TW only to fulfil tasks normally falling within the ambit of an absent worker employed by him. It leads to conclusion according to which the temporary replacement of permanent employee is allowed only if an employment contract between a user employer to be and absent permanent employee is still valid and – due to the absence of permanent employee (PE) to be temporarily replaced – suspended.

[B] Temporary Work Through TAW

All TW should be engaged exclusively *via* TAW. The act on ETW limits the rights of a prospective user employer to employ TW's. Situations in which an employer may not act as user employer is stated in Article 4 of the ETW. He may not act in dual role: as a regular employer employing at the same time the very same individuals as PE and TW.

Another obstacle introduced by the ETW deals with the type of jobs in which TW's may not be posted by a user employer. Article 8 of the ETW provides an exclusive list of posts which may not be entrusted to TW during his/period of performance of work provided in favour of the user employer. That catalogue includes:

- particularly dangerous jobs and tasks listed in Article 237^{15} PLC. Detailed list of such jobs and tasks is regulated in a resolution issued by the Minister of Labour and Social Policy of 26 September 1997 on general rules of health and safety at work;[7]
- positions occupied by the PE during his/her participation in strike;
- any position previously occupied by PE whose employment contract was terminated by a prospective user employer due to the reasons stated in Article 1 of the statutory act of 13 March 2003 related to collective redundancy[8] during the three months prior to the expected commencement of temporary work to be performed by TW.

---

7. Journal of Laws of 2003, No. 169, item 1650. See, A.M. Świątkowski, *Commentary to the PLC, supra*, 1067 ff.
8. Journal of Laws, No. 90, item 844.

As a matter of the principle all adult TW's employed by TAW are employed by user employers on the basis of fixed term contracts. That includes also the contracts concluded for the purpose to replace an absent PE's. TAW may also post within a user employer adult individuals performing work on civil type contracts. In such a case, protective regulations listed in Article 8 of the ETW act applies to non-workers in the meaning of Article 2 PLC.[9] A user employer is obliged to respect terms and conditions stated in Article 9 section 1 ETW which should be mentioned in the written contract concluded with TAW. A user employer to be has to inform the most representative trade union organization as defined in Article 241^{25a} PLC[10] about his intention to entrust the performance for a period shorter than six months of temporary work to TW to be posted at his enterprise by TAW. If the user employer intends to entrust the performance of work to a TAW worker for a period longer than six months he shall be obliged to take legal steps to obtain an approval of such idea by the representative trade union organization (Article 23 section 1 ETW). The user employer shall be obliged to pass to the above mentioned trade union organization an information listed in Article 9 ETW concerning: type of work, qualification required for the performance of temporary work, anticipated period of temporary work, working hours of TW, place of temporary work, remuneration of TW, occupational health and safety conditions for performing the temporary work (Article 23 sec ETW).

To adolescents aged 16–18 years posted by TAW, performing temporary work under a civil law type of contract, engaged for the sole purpose of getting practical training under the PLC provision concerning the employment of youth workers, Article 190–Article 205[11] must be applied by the user employer.

§8.03 THE TEMPORARY WORKER (TW)

[A] Legal Qualifications Relationship Worker: Agency

Article 2 item 2 of TAW provides that 'temporary worker' means a worker employed by a temporary agency work exclusively for the purposes of performing temporary work for and under the management of the user employer. For the purpose of the TAW directive, a worker is any person who enjoys legal protection guaranteed by national labour law (Article 3.1a). Although the basic contract which constitutes the legal ground for the relationship between TW and TAW is the employment contract, ETW does not exclude posting workers to perform temporary work under a civil (service) work contract (Article 26 item 2 with connection of Article 1 TAW). In this situation only part of ETW provisions apply (i.e., Article 8 – prohibition of TW, Article 9 – conditions of performing TW, Article 23 – information of trade unions about intention to employ TW). An individual performing TAW on the bases of civil (service) contract

---

9. A.M. Świątkowski, *Commentary to PLC, supra*, 10 ff.
10. *Ibid.*, 1194 ff.
11. *Ibid.*, 878 ff.

is entitled to claim employment relationship governed by Article 22 § 1[1] of the PLC[12] because regardless of the type of contract concluded by the parties (employment or civil) work performed under employer's supervision is treated by PLC as employment relationship.

[1] Object and Nature of the Employment Contract

Article 7 of ETW states that the temporary agency work shall employ temporary workers on the basis of an employment contract for a fixed term or for the duration of the performance of specified work. That means that it is prohibited to employ TW under an employment contract for an indefinite or a trial period.

The only permitted object of the contract is to perform temporary work (see §8.02 above). Therefore, employing by the TAW worker to perform non-temporary work constitutes a violation of ETW. The Polish doctrine indicates that such violation entitles a worker to demand to establish the existence of an employment relationship directly between TW and user employer.[13]

[2] Form of the Employment Contract

The employment contract between TW and TAW must be concluded in writing. An employment contract which has not been concluded in writing is invalid. However, the temporary agency work shall provide written confirmation to the temporary worker of the type of employment contract that has been concluded and its terms not later than the second day of temporary work (Article 13 section 4 ETW). This regulation is more liberal that the provisions of PLC which require that the employee be provided with a written statement of the settlements in relation to the parties to the contract, the type of the contract as well as its conditions at the latest on the date when the employee commences work.[14]

Failure to notify TW about conditions of temporary employment contract is punishable with a fine.[15]

[3] Contents of the Employment Contract

The employment contract between TW and TAW shall define:

- the parties to the contract;
- the type and date of contract;
- the user employer;
- the agreed period in which temporary work is to be performed.

---

12. The ruling of the Supreme Court of 12th Dec. 2011, Ref. Act I UZP 6/11, Monitor Prawa Pracy (Monitor of Labour Law), No. 10/2012, 544.
13. A. Sobczyk, *Zatrudnienie tymczasowe. Komentarz* (*Temporary Employment. Commentary*) 24 (Warsaw: Wolters Kluwer, 2009).
14. Article 29¹ § 2 PLC.
15. E. Drzewiecka, *Agencja pracy tymczasowej – trójstronny charakter zatrudnienia* (*Temporary Agency Work – Three Partial Employment*), 4 Monitor Prawa Pracy (Lab. L. J.) (2002).

The contract shall also lay down the terms of employment for the temporary worker during the period of work for the user employer, in particular:

- the type of work to be entrusted to the temporary worker;
- the working hours of the temporary worker;
- the place of temporary work;
- the pay for work;
- the date and method of payment remuneration by the TAW.

It is sufficient to determine the type of work for the validity of the employment contract. The Polish labour law judiciary recognizes that the lack of indication of the other elements (mentioned above) in the contract does not affect its validity. It is considered that they may be determined through the interpretation of the circumstances in which the contract was concluded as well as on the basis of the analysis of the intentions of the parties.[16] It should be noted that Article 29^1 paragraph 3 of Polish Labour Code applies to the employment contract concluded between TAW and TW. According to the said provision of PLC the employer must inform an employee, in writing, not later than within seven days of date of concluding the employment contract about: (i) the standard daily and weekly working time binding an employee; (ii) the frequency of the remuneration payments, (iii) the length of annual leave to which the employee is entitled, (iv) the length of notice period binding upon the termination of the employee's employment contract, (v) any collective labour agreement that covers the employee.

[B] Equal Treatment and Holiday Leave

Article 15 of ETW clearly provides that during the period of employment with the user employer, the TW may not be treated less favourably as regards the working conditions and other employment conditions than the user employer's workers employed in the same or similar position.[17] This provision considers especially the right to equal treatment in relation to health and safety at work as well as remuneration. In legal literature it has been noted that this provision forbids using a different wage system for the temporary and not-temporary workers.[18] The exception from the rule derived from Article 15 was made with respect to access to training organized by the user employer to improve worker qualifications. In this situation, non-discrimination rule does not apply to temporary workers performing work for the user employer for a period shorter than six weeks.

The temporary worker with respect to whom the user employer has violated the principle of equal treatment regarding the conditions specified in Article 15 ETW shall be entitled to seek damages from the temporary agency work in the amount stipulated

---

16. The ruling of the Supreme Court of 20 Sep. 1977 Ref. Act I PR 67/77 (not published).
17. *Introduction to Polish Law* 288 (S. Frankowski (ed.), Kluwer L. Intl. 2005).
18. K. Walczak, *Zakaz dyskryminacji w stosunku do osób wykonujących pracę na podstawie atypowych form zatrudnienia* (*Prohibition of Discrimination of Workers Performing Work on the Basis of Atypical Form of Employment*), 3 Monitor Prawa Pracy (Labour Law Journal) (2012).

by the provisions of the PLC on damages due to the worker from the employer for the violation of the principle of equal treatment of workers in an employment relationship.[19] This means that TW has the right to compensation of at least the amount of the minimum remuneration for work established in Poland.[20]

Apart from ETW, another regulation, which imposes the obligation to equal treatment of TWs is the Act on Employment Promotion and Labour Market Institutions.[21] It states that TAW shall not discriminate TWs with regard to sex, age, disability, race, religion, nationality, political beliefs, trade union membership, ethnic origin, creed and sexual orientation.[22] A breach of this rule is punishable with a fine up to Polish Zloty (PLN) 3,000 (around Euros (EUR) 750).

Another aspect of the TWs' equal treatment is the right of TWs to use the social facilities of the user employer on the terms applicable to workers employed by such the user employer during the period of temporary work for the user employer.[23] This regulation is consistent with the provisions of the Directive 2008/104/EC on temporary agency work (TAW).

According to the Polish legislation, the annual leave rules for TWs are less favourable than the ones for regular workers. Pursuant to Article 15 section 1 of the ETW the temporary worker shall be entitled to two days of vacation leave for each month of being at the disposal of one or more than one user employer. In most cases TWs will be entitled to use fewer days of annual leave than regular worker as, according to PLC, the length of leave amounts to twenty-six days if an employee has been employed at least ten years.[24] To make temporary work more attractive the Polish legislator decided that the temporary agency work and the user employer may, but do not have to, agree that the temporary worker uses his annual leave entitlement in whole or in part during the period in which he performs temporary work for the user employer, setting also the terms for granting such annual leave. However, in the event that the period of work for a given user employer is six months or more than six months, the user employer is obliged to allow the TW to take his annual leave during this period by granting time off to the worker based on his vacation leave entitlement and on the dates agreed with the worker.[25] In our opinion, regulation of the leave of TW included in ETW is not consistent with Article 5(1) of the Directive 2008/104/EC on temporary agency work and required amendment.

---

19. Article 16 of ETW.
20. Article 183d PLC.
21. Journal of Laws 2004, No. 99, item 1001 as amended.
22. Article 19 c of the Act on Employment Promotion and Labour Market Institutions.
23. Article 22 of ETW.
24. Article 154 § 1 PLC also provides that if an employee has been employed for less than ten years the length of leave amounts to twenty days. Most employees are entitled to twenty-six days of leave as graduating from the majority of Polish schools resulted in counting additional periods into the total length of employment e.g., graduating from schools of higher education adds eight years to the period of employment.
25. A. Daszczyńska, *Prawo pracownika tymczasowego do wypoczynku* (*Temporary Worker Right to Holiday Leave*, in *Some Problems of Temporary Work*, supra, 198 ff.

[C] Termination of the Contract

In principle, the general rules which apply to the termination of an individual employment contract also apply in case of temporary work. An employment contract concluded with the TW shall be terminated upon the expiry of the period of temporary work for a given user employer. However, in an employment contract concluded for a fixed term, the parties (TW and TAW) may envisage the possibility of early termination of the contract by either of the parties giving:

- three days' notice if the employment contract has been concluded for a period that does not exceed two weeks;
- one week's notice if the employment contract has been concluded for a period of more than two weeks.[26]

With respect to the rules of termination of the employment relationship with TW it is worth mentioning that Article 6 ETW excludes temporary workers from the application of the Act of 13 March 2003 on specific terms and conditions for terminating employment relationship with employees for reasons not related to the employees.[27]

In case the termination of employment contract concluded with TW violates the provision of law, general rules set forth in PLC apply.

[D] Employment with the User Employer

Very often in Polish reality contracts between ETW and the user employer include a provision according to which the user employer shall not employ TW after he or she has completed TW. However, this kind of provision is invalid according to Article 12 of ETW. Sometimes both parties agree that the user employer will be obliged to pay TAW a compensation in case he employs TW after the completion of the temporary work. This practice is consistent with the Directive 2008/104/EC only if TW receives a reasonable level of compensation for the services rendered to the user employer's undertakings for the assignment, recruitment and training of temporary agency workers (Article 6(2) of the Directive 2008/104/EC).

§8.04 THE TEMPORARY AGENCY WORK (TAW)

[A] Establishing TAW

The rules of establishing TAW are regulated by the Act on Employment Promotion and Labour Market Institutions. The activity of TAW in Poland is a law-regulated activity and requires an entry into the register of subjects running employment agencies. The register shall be maintained by the marshal of a voivodeship (chairman of the local governmental authority) competent for the seat of the subject applying for an entry.[28]

---

26. D. Makowski, *Praca tymczasowa jako nietypowa forma zatrudnienia* (*Temporary Work as Atypical Form of Employment*), 122 ff. (Warsaw: Difin 2006).
27. Journal of Laws 2003, No. 90, item 884 as amended.
28. Article 18d of the Act on Employment Promotion and Labour Market Institutions.

The marshal of a voivodeship shall make an entry into the register based on a written application for entry in the register submitted by a subject intending to run an employment agency containing the following data:

- the designation of the subject applying for an entry in the register;
- the address of residence or seat of the subject and addresses at which the activity will be carried out, including the name of the *gmina* (local administrative unit) and voivodeship, as well as the phone number;
- designation of the legal form of the activity being carried out;
- the tax identification number NIP, if one has been assigned;
- the number in the National Court Register or the number in the economic activity records, if one has been assigned, as well as the name and address of the records-keeping authority;
- electronic mail address.

Together with the application, the subject which wants to be TAW shall submit a declaration saying:

> I hereby declare that the data contained in the application for entry in the register are complete and true. I am aware of and fulfil the conditions of running an employment agency in the field of job brokerage, personnel consultancy, occupational guidance or temporary work, respectively – the conditions being specified in the Act of 20 April 2004 on Employment Promotion and Labour Market Institutions.

The declaration shall also contain:

- the designation of the subject running the employment agency and address of his or her place of residence or seat;
- the designation of the place and date of making the declaration;
- the signature of the person entitled to represent the subject, indicating his or her forename and surname as well as the function he or she fulfils.

The marshal of a voivodeship issues a certificate on making an entry of the subject into the register, which contains the following particulars: (1) the name of the subject; (2) the address of the subject's seat; (3) the number in the register; (4) the date of making an entry in the register; (5) the date of making the first entry in the register in the case of issuing a certificate due to the change of the subject's designation or address of the subject's seat.[29]

[B] Obligations of TAW as an Entrepreneur

Obtaining a certificate confirming the registration of TAW does not mean the end of contacts with local authorities. Under Article 19e of the Act on Employment Promotion

---

29. Z. Goral (ed.), *Ustawa o promocji zatrudnienia i instytucjach rynku pracy. Praktyczny komentarz* (*Act on Employment Promotion and Labour Market Institutions. Practical Commentary*) 152–183 (Warsaw: Wolters Kluwer 2011).

and Labour Market Institutions, TAW shall inform the marshal of a voivodeship of any change to the data entered into register as well as of discontinuation of its activity.

Each year, by 31 January TAW is obliged to provide the marshal of a voivodeship with the information about the employment agency's activity in the preceding year, in particular including the number of:

- persons who started work through an employment agency, as divided into basic profession groups, in accordance with the applicable classification of professions and specialities for labour market needs, together with the states of their employment;
- employers and persons making use of services of personnel consultancy and occupational guidance;
- persons seconded by an employment agency to carry out temporary work, as divided into basic profession groups, in accordance with the applicable classification of professions and specialities for labour market needs, together with the states of their employment.[30]

[C] Removal from the Register

The marshal of a voivodeship removes, by decision, TAW entered into the register, in particular, where:

- TAW has filed a written application.
- TAW has been put into liquidation or bankruptcy.
- TAW has not been run in the field of temporary work in two years period.
- TAW has violated the conditions for running an employment agency.
- the data in the register does not correspond to the state of fact, after having summoned TAW to provide explanations on this matter within seven days after the day of receipt of the summons.[31]

[D] The Agency as an Employer

TAW is the employer to TW. This was clearly confirmed by the Polish Supreme Court, which claimed that 'temporary worker does not have two employers, because his or her employer is only a temporary agency work and he or she is not bound any contractual relationship with the user employer'.[32] This means that the agency is obliged to fulfil all the obligations imposed on employers by labour and employment law. In particular, TAW employs TW, pays remuneration, terminates employment

---

30. Article 19f of the Act on Employment Promotion and Labour Market Institutions.
31. Article 18m of the Act on Employment Promotion and Labour Market Institutions.
32. The ruling of the Supreme Court of 12 Dec. 2011 Ref. Act I UZP 6/11, OSNP 2012. No. 9-10, pos. 122.

contracts with TW, recalls TW assigned to the user employer, e.g., in case when the user employer does not obey the working time regulations.[33]

The consequences of having the status of the employer by TAW is its responsibility for any damage caused by TW. TAW is obliged to redress the damage caused to the user employer by the TW while performing temporary work on the terms and within the limits that are binding upon the worker in accordance with the provisions on the financial liability of the worker (Article 19 ETW). Nevertheless, TAW has the right to seek reimbursement by the temporary worker for the equivalent of the damages paid to the user employer (Article 19 ETW). It should be noted that TAW is responsible only for the damage caused by TW through performing his or her work duties and not for the damage caused only on the occasion of performing these duties.[34]

§8.05 THE USER EMPLOYER

[A] The Relationship User Employer: TAW

The relationship between the user employer and TAW is based on service contract considered by the act on ETW as a necessary precondition of a temporary employment contract signed later by TAW and TW. Before an employment contract is concluded between TAW and TW, the TAW and the user employer shall conclude in writing a service contract concerning:

- the extent of information regarding the performance of the temporary work that influences the level of pay for the temporary worker's work, as well as the method and deadlines for submitting such information by the user employer to TAW for the purpose of correct calculation of TW pay;
- the extent to which the user employer assumes the obligation of the employer with respect to TW's occupational health and safety, in particular, by providing TW with working clothes and footwear, personal protection equipment, drinks and preventive meals, as well as providing occupational health and safety training, establishing the circumstances and causes of industrial accidents, and assessing and disclosing occupational risk;
- the extent to which user employer assumes the obligations of the employer with respect to payments to cover business travel expenses (Article 9 section 3 ETW).

The TAW and the user employer may agree that TW uses his/her vacation leave entitlement in whole or in part during the period in which TW performs temporary work for the user employer. They are entitled to set the terms for granting such vacation leave (Article 10 section 1 ETW). In case the period of work for particular user employer exceeds six months, the user employer shall be obliged by the TAW to allow

---

33. L. Wisniewski. *Prawne aspekty pracy tymczasowej* (*Legal Aspects of Temporary Work*). Dom Organizatora, Bydgoszcz-Toruń 94 (2007).
34. The ruling of the Supreme Court of 28 May 1976 Ref. Act IV PR 49/76, Praca i Zabezpieczenie Spoleczne (Labour and Social Security), No. 8-9/1977, 90.

TW to take vacation leave during that period by granting him/her time off based on his/her entitlement to such acquired right on particular dates agreed upon with TW (Article 10 section 2 ETW).

Damages caused to the user employer by TW while performing temporary work ought to be remunerated by TAW.[35] General PLC regulations applies to the scope and conditions of such obligation of TAW (Article 19 section 1).[36]

[B] The Relationship User Employer: TW

The user employer is not considered by the act on ETW the employer of TW. The ETW act obliges him to perform the duties and enjoy the rights of an employer to the extent necessary to organize work at his enterprise performed by TW (Article 14 section 1 ETW). The user employer is obliged to:

- provide TW with safe and healthy working conditions at the place assigned for the performance of temporary work;
- keep record of TW working time to the extent and on the terms applicable to his PE's;
- not to change TW's the terms and conditions of temporary work neither on the legal ground regulated by Article 42 section 4 PLC[37] (by order), or entrust him/her with work for and under the supervision of another entity (Article 14 section 2 ETW).

During the period of employment with the user employer, TW may not be treated less favourably as regards the working conditions and other conditions of work employed by the user employer vis a vis PE's performing the same or similar tasks (Article 15 section 1 ETW).[38] This provision is not applied with respect to access to training organized by the user employer to TW's performing work for the user employer for period shorter than six weeks (Article 15 section 2 ETW). TW whose right to equal treatment was violated by the user employer is entitled to seek damages from his/her legal employer – TAW (Article 16 section 1 ETW) in the amount stipulated by Article 18^{3d} PLC[39] (at least at the level of the national minimal monthly salary).

§8.06 COLLECTIVE LABOUR RELATIONS ASPECTS

There are no particular regulations concerning collective relations aspects of employment of temporary workers.[40] They are entitled to general rights guaranteed by the

---

35. Ł. Pisarczyk, *Praca tymczasowa a ryzyko pracodawcy* (*Temporary Work and Employers Risks*), in *Some Problems of Temporary Work*, supra, 129 ff.
36. A.M. Świątkowski, *Commentary to PLC*, supra, 601 ff.
37. *Ibid.*, 233 ff.
38. D. Dörre-Nowak, *Zatrudnienie tymczasowe a regulacje dyskryminacyjne* (*Temporary Work and Antidiscrimination Law*), in *Some Problems of Temporary Work*, supra, 168 ff.
39. A.M. Świątkowski, *Commentary to PLC*, supra, 104-105.
40. K.W. Baran *Zatrudnienie tymczasowe a zbiorowe prawo pracy* (*Temporary Work and Collective Labour Law*), in *Some Problems of Temporary Work*, supra, 35 ff.

Trade Union Act of 23 May 1991,[41] i.d. the right to bargain with the aim to conclude collective agreement, as well as the right to start collective labour disputes, and, eventually, a strike (according to the provisions of the act on collective labour disputes of 23 May 1991).[42] All above mentioned rights TW may use only within the legal relationship regulated by the act of ETW – an employment relationship into which they entered with their real employer – TAW.

§8.07 THE ROLE OF THE GOVERNMENT

As has been indicated in section §8.04[D] above, the supervision under TAW is exercised by local authorities. The Marshal of a voivodeship exercises control in the scope of the compliance with the conditions for carrying out the activity of TAW (Article 18o of the Act on Employment Promotion and Labour Market Institutions).

The Labour Inspection also has the right to control TAW; it may impose financial penalties up to PLN 30,000 (around EUR 7,500)[43] on TAW

In case of severe breach of TW's rights, TAW as well as the user employer may be subject to legal sanctions imposed by the Polish criminal law.

---

41. Journal of Laws of 2001, No. 79, item 854 as amended.
42. Journal of Laws, No. 55, item 236 as amended.
43. Article 37 of the Act on State Labour Inspection of 13th Apr. 2007, Journal of Laws of 2007, No. 89, item 589 as amended.

CHAPTER 9
Regulating Temporary Work in Sweden*

Birgitta Nyström

§9.01 INTRODUCTION

In the beginning of the 1990s temporary agency work was deregulated in Sweden. The situation before had been that temporary agency work in principle was forbidden. After the deregulation process temporary-work agencies are treated in the same way as other businesses in Sweden. There are no requirements of any kind of permission, license, registration or any obligation to notify the authorities about the type of business that is going to be conducted. Regular labour legislation, social law and tax law is applicable to temporary agency workers in the same way as to any other kind of workers. The temporary employees' rights are towards the employer, i.e., the temporary employment agency. Collective agreements adapted to temporary agency work covers over 90% of the agency workers.[1]

---

*   This chapter was finished in October 2012. Swedish developments have then been very fast. It has not been possible to rewrite the article considering that the 2012 Act on Agency Work has replaced older legislation. The author although hopes that the small changes that were possible to make will clarify the present situation to the reader.
1. The notions temporary work or agency work has no direct correspondence in Swedish legislation. Instead, the Swedish terminology is hiring out of employees or staffing (*bemanning*). In this article the terminology of the Directive 2008/04/EC is generally used, besides in situations where a more direct translation from Swedish terminology is preferred. See further, A. Adlercretuz & B. Nyström. *Sweden. International Encyclopaedia of Labour Law and Indusrial Relations* (R. Blanpain ed., Kluwer 2009); R. Eklund, *A Look at Contract Labour in the Nordic Countries*, 3 Juridisk Tidskrift 625–654 (1995/96); R. Fahlbeck, *Employment Exchange and Hiring Out of Manpower in Sweden: From Rigid State Planning to Freedom of the Market*. Y.B. Polish Lab. L. Soc. Policy, vol. 7, 247–267 (1995); R. Fahlbeck, *Employment Exchange and Hiring Out of Employees in Sweden*. 4 Tidskrift for Rettsvitenskap 589–622 (1995); B. Nyström, *Sweden. Private Employment Agencies*. Bulletin of Comparative Labour Relations 36 (R. Blanpain ed., Kluwer 1999); B. Nyström, *The Legal Regulation of Employment Agencies and Employment Leasing Companies in Sweden*, 23 Intl. Lab. L. & Policy J. (2003); B. Nyström, *Sweden*, in *Temporary Work and the Information Society*. Bulletin of Comparative Labour

An Inquiry Chair was appointed by the Swedish Government in 2009 in order to implement the Directive 2008/104/EC on temporary agency work (the Temporary Agency Work Inquiry). The Inquiry Chair was also to consider whether there were any prohibitions or restrictions on the use of temporary agency work in national legislation and practice, and if such restrictions were found, to verify if they are compatible with the provisions of the Directive. The Inquiry should also suggest a form of implementation of the Directive with the least interference with the Swedish model for labour relations. The Temporary Agency Work Inquiry presented its report in January 2011.

The Directive should be implemented in the Member States on 5 December 2011. Since Sweden not yet had transposed the Directive into Swedish law by that date the European Commission sent a reasoned opinion to the Swedish Government. Hereafter, in September 2012 the Government presented a proposal to the Parliament (*Riksdagen*) about the implementation of the Directive in a new Act on Temporary Agency Work[2] which was approved and entered into force 1 January 2013.

§9.02   TEMPORARY AGENCY WORK IN SWEDEN

[A]   Background

[1]   Temporary Agency Work: Illegal

Public employment service enjoyed a monopoly in Sweden in the years between 1935 and 1993. The 1935 Swedish Act on employment agencies was adopted to comply with the 1933 International Labour Organization (ILO) Convention No. 34 concerning Fee-Charging Employment Agencies. The 1935 Act outlawed profit-orientated employment exchange. In 1942 the Act was amended so that hiring-out of labour was considered a form of employment exchange. Under certain circumstances hiring-out of labour was regarded as employment exchange undertaken as a gainful occupation, which was prohibited; even under circumstances that allowed hiring-out of labour it was looked upon with disapproval, almost not tolerated. The legislation was also adjusted to the 1949 ILO Convention No. 96 concerning Fee-Charging Employment Agencies. In 1976, the Act was amended and profit-oriented international exchange of musicians and stage artists was allowed under certain conditions. Other profit-oriented employment exchange was considered a crime and so was employing or hiring employees assigned by a profit-aiming employment agency.

In spite of the restrictions in the 1935 Act, temporary-work agencies had to some extent been in operation for a long time in Sweden. That was especially the case in the typewriting business, the so-called ambulatory typewriting firms, but also in areas like transportation, printing and cultural work. Their legality was questionable, and sometimes they were found to be in contravention of the ban of hiring-out of labour,

---

Relations 50 (R. Blanpain & Graham eds., Kluwer 2003); B. Nyström, *SOU 2011:5 Bemanningsdirektivets genomförande i svensk rätt* (Summary in English).

2. Prop. 2011/12:178 *Lag om uthyrning av arbetstagare* (Law on Hiring Out of Employees).

but the line of demarcation between legal and illegal was difficult to ascertain. Developments in the labour market gradually led to a situation where the notion of employment exchange was difficult to interpret. A large amount of small companies offering different kinds of services emerged, for instance in the cleaning, account- and computer businesses. Regarding many of these companies' activities it was uncertain if they were contract work or hiring-out of labour. Temporary-work agencies in the office staff sector were not entirely uncommon and could operate quite openly. Users could be found even in the public sector. Some of the temporary-work agencies even concluded collective agreements with trade unions already in the 1980s, which of course was a confirmation of their seriousness. The number of cases brought to court was very small. One reason for this was a rather well-spread notion that some temporary-work agencies (i.e., the ambulatory typewriting firms) was in fact acceptable, even more or less desirable, although illegal.

The trade union head organizations LO (the Swedish Trade Union Confederation) and TCO (the Central Organisation of Salaried Employees) have traditionally been opposed to temporary work. During the 1980s the private employers in SAF (the Swedish Employers' Federation, nowadays the Confederation of Swedish Enterprise, SN) and the head organization SACO (the Swedish Federation of Professional Associations) instead supported deregulation.

[2]   Deregulation

In 1991, the Job Placement and Hiring-Out of Labour Act was enacted. The Act introduced an entirely new approach to temporary work. There were still rather strict limitations on temporary-work: The user had to show that there was a temporary need of extra manpower and the possibilities for temporary-work agencies to use employees under fixed-term employment contracts were limited compared to the generally applicable rules in the Employment Protection Act. Further, it was not possible to assign an employee to a user undertaking for a time-period longer than four months.

A social democratic Government introduced the 1991 Act. The explicit aim was to achieve a better functioning labour market. In 1993, the deregulation process was completed under a non-socialist Government in a new act on private employment agencies and hiring-out of employees, the Private Employment Agencies and Temporary Work Act (1993:440). The monopoly on employment exchange was abolished. Sweden had to denounce the ILO Convention No. 96 in order to enact the 1993 Act. The 1993 Act applies both to labour exchange and hiring-out of manpower.[3] Both LO and TCO opposed the changes and wanted to keep the restrictions from the 1991 Act.

Also ILO changed its attitude towards private employment agencies and temporary work and in 1997 the ILO Private Employment Agencies Convention, No. 181, was enacted. Sweden has not ratified Convention 181.

---

3. Lag 1993:440 om privat arbetsförmedling och uthyrning av arbetskraft. (A direct translation would be the 1993:440 Employment Agencies and Hiring-Out of Labour Act.)

After the deregulation process agency work is treated as any other form of economic activity. General legislation on association is applicable to the agency firm. There are no requirements for registration, licensing or certification, no limits concerning how large part of the workforce could be agency workers, no time limits regarding how long an employer could hire in temporary agency workers etc. Since the deregulation process started the sector has expanded very quickly. In 1994 there were about 5,000 people employed by temporary-work agencies, to be compared with 42,300 in 2000. Temporary work still includes only a small number of employees. Just below 1.5% of the Swedish labour forces are agency workers.

Collective agreements regarding agency work started to be concluded in the 1980s – before agency work was legalized! Today, collective agreements cover about 92% of the agency workers. (To be compared with about 90% on the Swedish labour market as a whole.) Temporary employees working under a collective agreement have some kind of wage guarantee when they not are assigned to a user undertaking (see further below §9.02[D]).[4]

Generally, trade unions are more or less opposed, or at least reluctant, to agency work, but when agency work was legalized in the 1990s trade unions instead of fighting something already legalized, concentrated on regulating temporary agency work in collective agreements. There also has been a gradual change of attitude towards temporary work. Nowadays it is not considered unserious to use temporary workers.

The business organizations are so in shape today that the need for supply in case of illness, maternity leave or peak-periods is not possible to provide for by transfer among the ordinary workforce. To hire manpower is one way to handle this situation. Employers also occasionally seem to use temporary employees as a recruitment tool. Hiring in labour is also a way of testing the employee without considering the limitations on fixed-term contracts and probationary employment in the 1982 Employment Protection Act.

[B] Agency Work in Practice

A few very large companies dominate the temporary agency business in Sweden. The three largest companies are Manpower, Proffice and Adecco. The users of temporary employees are found in all kinds of businesses; private and public sector, big and small companies, even trade unions.

In terms of turnover the largest occupational areas for temporary agency work are industry/manufacturing, office/administration, warehousing/logistics and accounting/finance; these four areas together account for almost two-thirds of the total turnover. The smallest occupational areas are hotel/restaurant/tourism and pedagogy.[5]

---

4. To be compared with 1996 when about 35% of the temporary employees had some kind of wage guarantee, often 50% of normal pay if they were not assigned to a user.
5. Figures from the Swedish Staffing Agencies' Annual Report 2010.

Many surveys have been conducted regarding the working conditions for temporary employees in Sweden; trade unions, employers' organizations and academic research projects have dealt with temporary work.

The agency workers are of a relatively low average age, most of them stay in the agency work sector for a rather short period of time. However, there is a group of employees who choose to stay in this line of business for many years. Most temporary workers who quit agency work become employed by a user undertaking instead. There are more immigrants employed in temporary agency work than on the Swedish labour market as a whole. Women still dominate this group of employees, but during the last years when traditionally male areas of the sector have expanded the male share has increased.

Studies indicate that the average pay for temporary employees is comparatively low, but certain groups, e.g., medical doctors, nurses, dentists, and some categories of teachers, often can raise their salary if they do the same work as agency workers instead of being directly employed by the user undertaking, for example a hospital.

[C]   The Legislative Framework

The employment contract is between the temporary worker and the temporary-work agency. The temporary-work agency is always considered to be the employer and has all employer's responsibilities, except for a division of responsibility between the agency and the user undertaking regarding work environment and non-discrimination, see further below. There is no contractual relationship between the user and the temporary worker. The 1993 Act on Private Employment Agencies and Temporary Work did not deal with this relationship at all. This is changed in the new 2012 Agency Work Act which replaces the 1993 Act, because according to the Agency Work Directive the agency worker should have the right to access certain amenities at the user undertaking and temporary agency workers must be informed of vacant permanent positions at the user undertaking, see further §9.03 below. The relationship between the temporary employment agency and the user undertaking is a contract under standard contract and commercial law and neither the 1993 Act nor the new 2012 Act deals with this relationship. There are not any demands for a written contract or any particulars. The user has not to show a special need for hiring in employees, and there are no restrictions regarding the length of the hiring arrangement.

The now abolished 1993 Act contained a few rules regulating employment for agency employees. Temporary employment was here defined as a legal relationship between a client and a temporary employment agency whereby the agency in return for a fee, places its own employees at the disposal of the client (the user) to perform work in the latter's business (section 2).[6] Temporary-work agencies must not in any way prevent employees from accepting employment by a user undertaking for which the employee presently or previously has been working (section 4, subsection 1). An

---

6. The Swedish Staffing Agencies has this definition of 'staffing': Staffing refers to operations in which the staffing company supplies employees to perform work in the customer company. A contract employee is supervised by the customer company.

employee who has terminated an employment relationship and then accepts a job with a temporary-work agency must not be hired out to his/her previous employer sooner than six months after the employment relationship ended (section 4, subsection 2). This provisionwas intended to prevent circumvention of labour law and socially unwanted recruiting techniques by temporary-work agencies. In practice, the provision prevented employees in profession where there was a need for manpower, i.e., in health care, to change employer. The provision in question is removed from the new 2012 Act, see further below §9.03. Temporary-work agencies may not request, agree or receive payment from employees to assign them work (section 6 of the 1993 Act).

There are no special rules regarding fixed-term contracts, neither in the 1993 Act nor in the new 2012 Act. The (1982:80) Employment Protection Act is fully applicable, which means that employment contracts of an indefinite period are the main rule. It must be underlined that, although a permanent employment contract exists, the employer is not obliged to provide paid work all the time. (See further below about rules regarding guarantee payment in collective agreements for situations where the temporary-work agency is not able to assign the temporary worker to any user undertaking.)

Labour and social security legislation is generally applicable also to temporary employees and the responsibilities are towards the employer in the employment contract, not towards the user undertaking.

Unemployment benefits have nevertheless caused problems for temporary employees. Courts have in their interpretation regarding legislation on unemployment benefits stated that those regularly employed by a temporary-work agency – although on fixed-term contracts – should be considered as employed for an indefinite period; to be at the disposal of the agency, and not unemployed. This very strict interpretation, with the aim that unemployment benefits should not – in a way – subsidize temporary-work agencies' staff-expenses, has led to problems and unequal treatment of temporary employees compared to other workers. The Temporary Agency Work Inquiry established that there was unequal treatment of temporary workers, and also that some unemployment agencies did not seem to follow new court practice.[7] It also seemed like the instructions from the Swedish Unemployment Insurance Board (IAF),[8] the public authority exercising supervision over unemployment insurance funds, was unclear.[9] The High Administrative Court declared in a decision 2007[10] that a temporary worker with repeated fixed-term contracts with the same agency, in accordance with the Security of Employment Act and the applicable collective agreement was considered to be unemployed between the fixed-term contracts and entitled to unemployment benefits during these periods. Further, there has been a problem regarding unemployment benefits for temporary workers working part-time. Contrary to other employees,

---

7. Sweden has a system of union unemployment funds with close links between unions and unemployment funds.
8. IAF is a public authority subject of the Swedish Government that exercises supervision over unemployment insurance funds and the Swedish Public Employment Service's handling of matters that relate to unemployment insurance.
9. SOU 2011:5 pp. 132–141.
10. RÅ 2007 ref. 20 I-II.

temporary employees have not been able to take up a part-time work, when searching for full-time work, and then be entitled to part-time unemployment benefits. The temporary worker has been considered to be at the temporary-work agency's full-time disposal and not part-time unemployed, except in rare cases where the temporary employee has been able to show that there is a strict schedule with the temporary-work agency which enables the temporary employee to search for other jobs under a defined time schedule. In a recent judgment from the Administrative Court of Appeal an employee working as temporary worker one day a week for a temporary-work agency was considered to be at the labour market's disposal the rest of the time and thereby entitled to part-time unemployment benefits.[11] After these two judgments from the Administrative Courts the unequal treatment of temporary workers is removed in court practice. The government has commissioned the IAF to examine the situation and make sure that all unemployment insurance funds follow established court practice and that temporary workers are not treated unequally.

The temporary worker is a part of the user's business organization during the period he/she is assigned there, and subject to the managerial authority of the user, e.g., follow orders, safety regulations etc. The user has to follow good labour market practice regarding the treatment of temporary employees. The user's authority is however, restricted to the employee's professional qualifications. The special task the employee has to perform is designated by the employment relationship with the temporary employment agency and the contract between the temporary employment agency and the user undertaking.

The 1977 Work Environment Act (1977:1160) was amended in 1994 in order to transpose the Council Directive 91/383/EEC supplementing the measures to encourage improvements in the safety and health at work of workers with a fixed-duration employment relationship or a temporary employment relationship into Swedish law. The temporary agency firm is responsible as employer, but cannot easily influence or control working conditions at the user undertaking. Chapter 3 section 12 subsection 2 of the Work Environment Act prescribes that 'A person hiring temporary labour to work in his activity shall take the safety measures which are needed in that work.' Thus, the user has a far-reaching obligation to provide safe working conditions for temporary workers. The user's responsibility for the working environment for temporary employees is, in principle, the same as for his/her own employees. He/she is obliged to take the same safety precautions as he/she would have taken for his/her own employees. However, the responsibility for the user is limited to the specific work conducted on his/her premises and does not include long-term measures such as rehabilitation, which is the sole responsibility for the agency. The employee safety representatives of the agency are allowed to enter the premises of the user if it is necessary in order to fulfil their task. If the user undertaking tries to hamper the safety representatives from the temporary-work agency in any way it may be liable to damages.

---

11. Kammarrätten i Stockholm, mål nr. 7348-11, 4 Apr. 2012.

The employer's obligations regarding consultation, negotiations, information etc. according to the Co-determination Act (1976:580) rest with the temporary-work agency. The temporary employees' trade unions have no rights of negotiation, information etc. towards the user undertaking. These rights are carried out towards the own employer, the temporary-work agency. It is considered to be difficult though, for trade unions to work when their members are assigned to many different workplaces and far away from their employer.

The Co-determination Act gives the trade unions in the user undertaking special rights, the so-called trade union veto. If an employer intends to use a contractor for the performance of a certain task or otherwise to allow non-employed persons to perform work in his/her business the employer is, according to the Co-determination Act (section 38), obliged to initiate negotiations in advance with the trade union to which he/she is bound by a collective agreement for such work. The employer must give all information that the trade union might need and have to postpone his/her decision until the negotiations have been concluded. If the measure planned by the employer can be presumed to involve the setting-aside of law or of a collective agreement for the work, or of what is otherwise generally approved within the industry concerned, the union has the right to block (veto) the proposed decision (section 39). This is very rarely the case. Nevertheless, the employers' duty to initiate negotiations gives the trade union information about the situation and a possibility to influence the employers' decision. The right of veto is not to be used for the purpose of reserve jobs for the employees in the own undertaking and does not authorize the union to veto contract work or temporary-work situations. It merely confers upon the unions the authority to veto illegal practices.

The employer is not obliged, according to the Co-determination Act section 38, to initiate negotiations if the planned arrangement essentially corresponds to what earlier has been approved by the trade union. Still, in this situation it is possible for the trade union to request negotiations with the employer. Another general exemption from the duty to initiate negotiations regarding short-term and temporary agreements, or for work for which special expert-knowledge is required, is not applicable in a temporary agency work situation; the employer has to initiate negotiations. It is possible for the labour market parties to conclude collective agreements and deviate from the veto rules.

A controversial situation is where the employer dismisses employees because of redundancy and soon thereafter engages temporary employees. According to section 25 of the Employment Protection Act, employees who have been dismissed due to redundancy have priority to re-employment in the activities in which they were previously employed (priority to re-employment). The right of priority applies (nowadays) for a period of nine months. The question is if the employer by hiring temporary employees in reality has circumvented the rules on priority to re-employment. In the case before the Labour Court AD 1980 No. 54 an employer had dismissed employees because of redundancy. During the period when former employees had priority to re-employment the employer leased employees from another employer instead of re-employing the dismissed employees. The Labour Court decided that this was not a circumvention of the Employment Protection Act. The main reason for this was that the lease of workers was for a limited period, not aimed to be permanent. In the case AD 2003 No. 4 an employer had engaged temporary employees instead of re-employing dismissed employees who still enjoyed a preferential right of re-employment. Also in this case the Labour Court found it not to be a circumvention of the Employment Protection Act. The Court referred to the 1980 case and stated that since temporary work is permitted under Swedish law since 1992, there was no reason for a more restrictive interpretation than adopted by the Court in its 1980 judgment. In the present case, there was nothing indicating that the employer used temporary employees for other reasons than difficulties in planning the work. The boundaries here are not quite clear. The cases indicate that there is no general prohibition against the use of temporary workers during the period of time when previously dismissed workers have the right of priority to re-employment. Only practices which must be considered as improper in the individual case, where there is reason to believe that the employer has acted in bad faith, can be regarded as instances of the circumvention of the right of priority and the Security of Employment Act.

The Labour Court's decisions in the cases mentioned above have been widely discussed and demands have been raised from the trade union side that legislation should be changed in order to make it illegal to engage employees from temporary-work agencies when there are dismissed employees still enjoying priority to re-employment. (About collective agreements regarding this question, see below §9.03[D].) In January 2013 the Swedish Government appointed an Inquiry Chair which should investigate if such situations are frequent and if the right to re-employment is affected in practice.

Both the employer and the user are responsible according to the Discrimination Act (2008:567). In Chapter 2 section 1 it is prescribed that an employer may not discriminate against a person on grounds of sex, transgender identity or expression, ethnicity, religion or other belief, sexual orientation or age, who, with respect to the employer is an employee or is performing work as temporary labour.

[D] The Social Partners and Collective Agreements

One reason for the smooth deregulation of private employment agencies and temporary work in Sweden is the existence of strong labour unions and well-organized employers covering virtually the whole labour market. Although a decreasing number of employees join trade unions the Swedish labour market still is highly organized. About 70% of the employees belong to a trade union. The figures are lower for younger than for older employees. This means that the unionization degree probably is lower than 70% for agency workers. Industry-wide collective agreements cover every sector of the Swedish labour market. Legally binding agreements can be concluded at all levels of bargaining. Collective agreements cover about 90% of the Swedish workforce, and in the temporary work area the collective agreement coverage is about 92% due to the high rate of organization on the employers' side.

Swedish collective agreements also have an impact on working conditions of non-unionized employees according to labour market practice and case law. It is a general principle that the employer is considered to be obliged to apply a collective agreement provision also to non-unionized employees and employees belonging to a different union than the signatory union to the collective agreement, unless anything contrary has been agreed with the signatory union. It is important to underline that it is not possible to make Swedish collective agreement universally applicable or an *erga omnes* effect.

There were employers and trade institutions working with the aim of supporting seriousness in the agency business when it was legalized. The most important was SPUR (the Swedish Association of Temporary-Employment Business and Staffing Service) which was entirely a trade and not an employers' organization. The main aim was to work for high quality, ethics and sound staff policy in the business. SPUR built up a self-regulating system and adopted rules of ethics. In 2003, a merger between SPUR and Almega Services Employer's Association (for staff agencies) founded *Bemanningsföretagen* (the Swedish Staff Agencies) which today is the employer and trade federation for staffing, outplacement and recruitment companies. The Swedish Staff Agencies is a member of the Confederation of Swedish Enterprise (SN). The Swedish Staffing Agencies have a voluntary accreditation system. There is also a Code of Conduct which serves as ethical and moral support for member companies in their daily activities. Over 400 companies are members, and over 340 of these are accredited staffing agencies and/or outplacement companies.[12]

The Staff Agencies' accreditation is a form of a voluntary authorization system. There are a range of conditions which an authorized member must fulfil. The requirements are for example: The member must fulfil the Staff Agencies' statutes, their Code of Conduct, have collective agreement and insurances, and have a plan for equal treatment. There are also economic requirements and several business requirements. An Accreditation Board has been set up, consisting of an independent chairman (a former member of Government) and representatives from the Staff Agencies, the LO and other trade unions concerned.[13]

Collective agreements adapted to temporary work emerged in the mid-1980s while hiring-out of employees still was unlawful. This first so-called ambulatory agreement was an appendix to the regular collective agreement for white-collar workers in the service area regulating some aspects of the working conditions for temporary employees. This agreement was for a long while the dominating as well as pattern agreement for temporary work. Today there are special industry-wide collective agreements totally adapted to temporary work for both white-collar and blue-collar temporary work employees.

The two most important agreements is the agreement for blue-collar workers belonging to a union affiliated to the LO, the LO-agreement, and the agreement for white-collar workers belonging to Unionen (affiliated to TCO) and the Union for Professionals (affiliated to SACO), the white-collar agreement. There is also a large agreement for the health care area.

---

12. Figures from the Swedish Staffing Agencies' Annual Report 2010.
13. Unionen (affiliated to TCO)/Akademikerförbundet (the Union for Professionals affiliated to TCO).

The collective agreements regarding temporary agency workers stipulate wage guarantees in different forms. This means that the temporary employees are guaranteed some wages although the employer is not able to assign the employee to a user undertaking. Early agreements had a guarantee of twenty working hours weekly on average per month. The 1998 white-collar agreement had a guarantee of 75% of full-time work (which normally meant a thirty hours wage guarantee). The first blue-collar agreement 2000 stipulated a wage guarantee of 85%, and from 2002 of 90%. According to the 2001 white-collar agreement the wage guarantee for employees with more than eighteen months of employment was 100%.

According to current agreement (5 May 2012–30 April 2013) between the Swedish Staff Agencies, Unionen and the Union for Professionals the white-collar temporary employee has an individual monthly salary and a wage guarantee for 133 hours work per month for the first 18 months of employment, and for 150 hours per month for those employed for at least 18 months. There is a special agreement on training of temporary employees.

The collective agreement 2010-2012 in the blue-collar area between the Swedish Staff Agencies and thirteen unions affiliated to the LO stipulates that the temporary worker shall, when assigned to a user, receive the average wages for comparable workers at the user undertaking. Guarantee wages are 90% of the average wages for the employee during the last three months. Also in this agreement there are special rules about training.

It follows from the forgoing that wages for temporary employees are determined in different ways. The white-collar agreement and the collective agreement in the health care business are based upon the notion that temporary employment is a special profession with a wage system of its own. This means that wages per month are set individually for each employee in relation to other employees in the temporary-work agency, not in relation to the same category of workers in the user undertaking. The collective agreement in the blue-collar sector, however, sets wages in accordance with a kind of equality principle. The agreement stipulates that the temporary employee shall earn the same salary per hour/per month corresponding to the average salary for the comparable group of employees in the user undertaking. This way to set wages could mean that a young inexperienced temporary employee who is hired out to a user undertaking where comparable employees are older and more experienced get higher wages than if he/she would be employed directly by the user.

On 17 October 2012 the Swedish Staffing Agencies concluded a collective agreement on terms and conditions of employment with all the fourteen trade unions affiliated to LO. It is a three-year agreement, which is a very long period for Swedish circumstances. The agreement changes the way to estimate wages for time when the employee is not assigned to a user undertaking. Earlier wages per hour not hired out were estimated on the ground of the average wage for the last three months, this is now changed to a fixed hourly wage (Swedish Krona (SEK) 108 (EUR 13) for skilled workers, and SEK 100 (EUR 12) for others).

§9.03 THE 2012 AGENCY WORK ACT

As mentioned above, the Agency Work Directive was not implemented in time in Sweden. The Swedish Government presented a proposal on 13 September 2012 regarding an entirely new law; the Act on Temporary Agency Work/or the Act on Hiring-Out of Employees (hereinafter called the Agency Work Act).[14] The Act was approved by the Parliament in December 2012 and entered into force on 1 January 2013.

The aim in Sweden is to implement the Agency Work Directive with the least possible interference in the Swedish model. Since implementation through collective agreements would mean that employees not covered by collective agreements would not enjoy the rights afforded by the Directive it was decided that the Directive had to be transposed through legislation. Nevertheless, it is considered important to uphold the basic labour market principle that the primary responsibility for setting salary and employment conditions lies with the social partners. The Act therefore takes the form of a regulatory framework.

The Act applies only to temporary agency work, not to contract work or labour lending. It applies to all temporary workers, blue-collar or white-collar, and also both to private and public sector. The 2012 Act begins: 'This Act concerns employees that are employed by a temporary-work agency with a view to being assigned to a user undertaking to work under its supervision and direction.' (section 1 of the Act). (This definition is in accordance with the Directive, but slightly different from the definition in the 1995 Act.)

The principle of equal treatment, Article 5(1) of the Directive, is transposed into the Act, section 6, which entitle temporary workers to the same basic working and employment conditions as if they had been recruited directly by the user undertaking to occupy the same job. The right to equal treatment arises on a temporary agency worker's very first day.

The equal treatment principle is not absolute, the Directive allows the Member States to make exceptions in accordance with Article 5(2)–5(4) of the Directive. Since Sweden applies equal treatment from day one there are not any specific measures in the Act to avoid the circumvention of the Directive (Article 5(5)). The possibility to allow exceptions to the principle of equal treatment with regard to pay is, however, used in section 6 on the condition that the temporary employee is permanently employed by the temporary-work agency and paid between assignments. This exception is supposed to be in accordance with the Swedish labour market traditions that it is the social partners that in the first instance are responsible for the regulation of wages and other working conditions. It is also possible that this exception may increase the willingness to join a trade union. Further, the equal treatment principle should not apply to workers who are employed through special employment support, in sheltered employment or in development employment. (section 7).[15]

---

14. Prop. 2011/12:178.
15. Other obligations for the temporary-work agency or the user undertaking according to the Act applies also to workers employed through these special labour market provisions.

The possibility to allow the social partners to enter into collective agreements concerning working and employment conditions that deviate from the principle of equal treatment provided that the overall protection for workers according to the Agency Work Directive is respected is used in the Act section 3. (That this is the only possibility to deviate from the Act by an agreement follows from section 2.) The possibility to deviate from the Act by collective agreement is very important considering that collective agreements cover about 92% of temporary employees in Sweden today. It is a requirement according to section 3 that the collective agreement is entered into or approved by a nation-wide trade union. It is explicitly prescribed that an employer bound by a collective agreement which allows exceptions from the equal treatment principle is allowed to apply the collective agreement also to employees that do not belong to the trade union (section 4). It has not been questioned that the nation-wide collective agreements concerning temporary work should not provide the overall protection according to the Directive.

'Temporary work agency', 'user undertaking' and 'basic working and employment conditions' are defined in section 5 of the Act in accordance with the Directive.

Section 6 from the 1993 Act which forbade agency firms to request, agree or receive payment from employees to assign them work (see above section §9.02[C].) is transferred to the 2012 Act, section 10. According to Article 9 of the Directive, Member States may adopt more favourable conditions for temporary workers than those laid down in the Directive, and this provision seems to be in line with the Directive's approach.

The provision in the 1993 Act, which forbade agency firms to prevent workers from taking employment with a user company, is moved over to the 2012 Act section 9. The prohibition is without prejudice to agreements under which temporary-work agencies receive a reasonable level of recompense for services rendered by user undertakings for the assignment, recruiting and training of agency workers. Temporary-work agencies may not charge workers any compensation for taking employment with a user undertaking (section 10). This prohibition was also to be found in the 1993 Act and is in accordance with Article 6(3) of the Directive.

The 2012 Act also includes provisions on the right of temporary employees to access certain amenities at the user undertaking (section 11) and also rules to the effect that temporary agency workers must be informed of vacant permanent positions at the user undertaking (section 12).

Article 6(4) of the Directive is transposed into section 11 of the 2012 Act. The amenities particularly mentioned in the Directive are canteen, childcare facilities and transport services. Other amenities could, for example, be sport halls and other rooms for employees like rest rooms etc. The amenities or facilities should be of a general nature and temporary employees cannot claim equal treatment regarding for example, the right to have a company car. According to the Directive difference in treatment could be justified by objective reasons. This must be assessed in each individual case taking into regard the amenity or facility in question, in some cases the length of assignment with the user, and what measures the user undertaking have to take in order to give the temporary worker access to these amenities or facilities.

Article 6(1) of the Directive is transposed into section 12 of the 2012 Act. All vacant permanent positions, including probation positions, in the user undertaking are included, not only positions which could be of interest for the temporary worker in question. Information about vacant positions could be provided over internet or by general announcement at the user undertaking.

Article 6(5) of the Directive, according to which Member States are to take suitable measures or promote dialogue between the social partners in order to improve temporary worker's access to training and childcare facilities, is not transposed into the new Act. Childcare is only provided by Swedish employers in very exceptional cases (this is a task for Swedish municipalities) and regarding training for agency workers it is considered more appropriate for the social partners to regulate this matter. Swedish legislation already fulfilled the requirements in Article 7 of the Directive regarding representation of temporary employees and information of workers' representatives in Article 8 (provisions mainly in the Co-determination Act).

Non-compliance with the obligations for the temporary-work agency under the Act (as well as for the user undertaking regarding access to amenities and information about vacant positions) can result in damages (section 13-15). Disputes under the Act should be dealt with in accordance with the Labour Disputes (Judicial Procedure) Act (1974:37).

[A]   The Equal Treatment Principle in Detail

It must be underlined that collective agreements cover about 92% of Swedish temporary agency workers. These collective agreements are considered to respect the overall protections of workers. Further, Sweden intends to use the possibility to deviate from the equal treatment principle regarding pay for temporary workers with permanent employment contracts and paid between assignments. Thus, only a very small amount of temporary agency workers are encompassed by the equal treatment principle, even less by equal treatment regarding pay. Nevertheless, the transposition of the equal treatment principle into Swedish law causes some problems. The temporary agency worker shall receive at least those basic working and employment conditions that would apply as if he/she had been recruited directly by the user undertaking to occupy the same job. How is it possible to determine pay for the temporary employee? Here, it is important to underline that there is a consensus in Sweden that wages is a subject for the social partners and collective agreements and/or employment contracts only. There is no legislation in Sweden regarding wages or minimum-wages, and no definition of 'pay'.

It is possible to argue that the nation-wide collective agreement for the trade in question is some kind of custom for this part of the labour market. From this follows that pay should be determined according to the nation-wide agreement. Beside the fact that this could cause problems if the nation-wide agreement does not say anything about pay (according to some sectoral agreements this is something entirely up to local/company negotiations), this should indirectly constitute an *erga omnes* effect of the collective agreement (make the collective agreement universally applicable). Since there is no intention to introduce collective agreements *erga omnes* on the Swedish labour market, this line of reasoning was rejected.

If there is an applicable collective agreement in the user undertaking pay and other basic working and employment conditions within the equal treatment area it should be determined in accordance with this collective agreement. It is possible that this agreement only determines minimum levels of pay. According to the Swedish interpretation of the equal treatment principle minimum pay is not enough. A temporary worker assigned to the user undertaking is entitled to the same pay as a worker who has been recruited by that undertaking to occupy the same job. If the user undertaking according to the collective agreement or other binding general provisions in the user undertaking determines the pay level taking into account qualifications, professional experience and seniority, the same circumstances shall be taken into account when determining the temporary employees' wages.

If there neither is an applicable collective agreement at the temporary-work agency nor at the user undertaking the basic working and employment conditions, except pay, follows from legislation. The user may have binding general provisions or some formalized way of determining wages taking different circumstances into account. Then the same way should be applied when determining the temporary employees' wages.

In the absence of any general provisions in relation to pay in the user undertaking there is nothing that could help in the process of determining the temporary employees' wages. According to the Swedish interpretation the only protection for equal treatment the individual temporary employee has in this situation is the possibility to apply the general law of contracts to the employment agreement. The 1915 Contracts Act stipulates in section 36 that a contract term or condition can be modified or set aside if it is found to be unfair. In application of this provision, special consideration shall be given to the need of protection of a person who has an inferior position in the contractual relationship.[16]

[B] Posted Temporary Agency Workers

Following the ECJ's decision in the Laval-case[17] it is only possible to demand that a foreign service provider posting workers to another country should apply some national minimum provisions within the 'hard core' laid down in the Posting of Workers Directive 96/71/EC Article 3(1). The decision in the Laval-case has led to restrictions in the possibilities for national trade unions to use industrial action in order to force the foreign employer to conclude collective agreements. Following the Court's decision a new provision was added to the Swedish Posting of Workers Act (1999:678) in 2010 narrowing the conditions under which Swedish trade unions can demand,

---

16. In AD 1982 No. 142 s. 36 of the Contracts Act was invoked to modify wages stipulated by a contract of employment not regulated by collective agreement. The wages in the case amounted to roughly one-half of the standard wages stipulated by the national collective agreement for the trade in question. The Court found the collectively agreed wage level to be a reasonable standard. See also AD 1991 No. 81.
17. Case C-341/05 *Laval un Partneri Ltd/Svenska Byggnadsarbetareförbundet and others*.

ultimately through industrial action, the application of a Swedish collective agreement on workers posted to Sweden. Industrial action can only be taken to demand minimum conditions within the 'hard core' of the Posting of Workers Directive. The outcome in the Laval-case has caused a lot of criticism in Sweden (and in other Nordic countries).

The preamble (clause 22) to the Agency Work Directive stipulates that the Directive should be implemented without prejudice to the Posting of Workers Directive. According to Article 3(9) of the Posting of Workers Directive it is possible for Member States to apply the entirety of their national terms and conditions to temporary agency workers posted to their territory. The Temporary Agency Work Inquiry proposed that the equal treatment principle as a whole in the Agency Work Act should apply to posted temporary agency workers. The Government considered this to be too wide and contrary to the interpretation of the Posting of Workers Directive in the Laval-case. However, some parts of the Agency Work Act apply also to posted agency workers, mainly the rules that forbids the agency to receive payment from the employee for the job or assignment, forbids the agency to prevent the employee to take employment at the user firm, and rules about damages.[18] Further, there are some new rules that in practice will have the consequence that posted temporary agency workers can claim more favourable terms than other posted workers regarding the area habitually referred to as the 'hard core' of the Posting of Workers Directive. An important condition here is wages where the posted temporary agency workers will be entitled to equal wages, not as other posted workers only minimum-wages.

This has required new regulation about the extent to which Swedish trade unions have the right to take industrial action in order to bring about collective agreement for posted workers. This issue is regulated in the Posting of Workers Act from 1 January 2013. Industrial action may only be undertaken in order to guarantee posted temporary agency workers equal treatment regarding pay or other conditions referred to as the hard core. Further, if the employees already enjoy conditions that at least equal the conditions that the intended collective agreement would afford, it should not be possible to take industrial action. However, if the conditions in practice correspond to the principle of equal treatment but are less favourable than those required by the collective agreement that workers want to force through, it should be possible to take industrial action, even if equal treatment is in fact practiced. In a situation where the posted temporary workers' basic working and employment conditions do not correspond to the collective agreement the workers want to force through, but do correspond to the collective agreement at the user undertaking it should not be possible to take industrial action.[19]

In other words, it has been commissioned to the trade unions to secure better conditions for posted temporary workers than the minimum conditions that follow from the Posting of Workers Directive.

---

18. Sections 2, 9, 10, 13 and 15 of the 2012 Act shall apply also to posted agency workers.
19. Also the other Nordic countries have discussed implementing or has implemented the Directive in a way that privileges posted temporary employees compared to other posted workers.

The Swedish Work Environment Agency (*Arbetsmiljöverket*) is the competent body (liaison office) for information about working conditions in collective agreements than can be forced through by industrial action.

[C] Prohibitions and Restrictions

Article 4(1) of the Agency Work Directive stipulates that prohibitions and restrictions on the use of temporary agency work are justified only on grounds of general interest relating in particular to the protection of temporary agency workers, the requirements of health and safety at work or the need to ensure that the labour market functions properly and abuses are prevented. The Temporary Agency Work Inquiry also had the task to review whether there are any restrictions or prohibitions in Swedish legislation and practice in order to verify if they are justified.

According to the Co-determination Act, the employer is obliged to take initiative to negotiate with the trade union when the employer intends to engage a non-employed person to perform work (see above §9.02[C].). Section 38 of the Co-determination Act allows the employer the exception to negotiate in situations regarding short-term and temporary arrangements, or for expert-knowledge work. This exception does not apply however, if the employer intends to use temporary agency workers. Thus, temporary agency work is treated stricter than other situations where an employer intends to use non-employed persons to perform work for him/her, for example a contractor. No changes are suggested in this regard, it is considered to be justified by the need to guarantee that the labour market functions properly.

In the 2012 Act there is no correspondence to the stipulation in the 1993 Act that a worker who has terminated his/her employment and takes employment with at temporary agency may not be assigned to work for the previous employer until at least six months after the employment there ended. This has been considered to be a non-justified restriction. There has been evidence that individuals who have been employed by a temporary-work agency are treated different with regard to benefits from unemployment insurance funds. There has also been evidence that individuals who are part-time employed by a temporary-work agency are not treated equally with other part-time employees. There have not been any proposals for legislative amendments here, but after a couple of court decisions the situation has changed in practice and in the future there should not be any obstacle for temporary workers in this area (see above §9.02[C]).

According to the Directive, restrictions and prohibitions in collective agreements shall also be reviewed in order to verify whether they are justified (Article 4(2)). This review may be carried out by the social partners who have negotiated the relevant agreement (Article 4(3)). The Swedish social partners have, on the Government's initiative, conducted such a review, and the Government has informed the Commission about this.

There are restrictions to temporary agency work laid down in Swedish collective agreements. Collective agreements stipulating that only a small part of the workforce can be temporary workers are not entirely uncommon. There are even company collective agreements where the parties have agreed that the employers should not use temporary agency workers at all. It seems not possible to justify such an agreement on the grounds mentioned in the Directive, Article 4(1).

After the above mentioned decisions (see §9.02[C]) by the Labour Court enabling employers to engage temporary agency workers instead of re-employing dismissed redundant employees that still enjoy a priority to re-employment a discussion started within some of the unions affiliated to the LO if it would be possible to regulate this situation in collective agreements. In the 2010 wage rounds this became an important question and resulted in varied solutions in collective agreements. One approach was to strengthen the right to re-employment and introduce supplementary rules concerning temporary agency work. Another was to strengthen the unions' negotiating rights and use an arbitration board to decide whether a given procedure conflicts with the right to re-employment. In some areas, the parties found there was no need to introduce rules into their agreements, and in such cases none were included. In other areas, rules were introduced but it was stated in the agreements that temporary work did not present a problem.[20]

The Swedish Staff Agencies have criticized the new Agency Work Act, because there is no rule about unjustified restrictions and prohibitions.

§9.04 COMMENTS AND CONCLUSIONS

LO and TCO have not entirely accepted hiring-out of employees, but the trade unions have gradually recognized that there could be a need for temporary work. Instead, they have tried by means of collective agreements to secure working conditions and terms of employment at the same level as other employees. During the deregulation period in the early 1990s both LO and TCO wanted some kind of registration where consideration was given to whether personal qualifications or personal suitability of the person(s) in charge of the agency was required. This was rejected with reference to the trade organizations and the development of a voluntary accreditation system. Both LO and TCO wanted the Temporary Agency Work Inquiry to propose provisions prohibiting the permanent use of temporary employees. This was rejected both by the Inquiry and by the Government.

Instead of fighting employment agencies and agency work they have more and more been integrated in the normal system of labour relations and collective agreements. Still, LO and TCO are in favour of restricting the possibilities to use temporary workers. At the LO congress 2012 the following statement was made: Temporary workers shall not be used on a more permanent basis. Temporary workers are nevertheless a part of the Swedish labour market and the same rules applies as concerns other parts of the labour market. Therefore organization and influence is the line that LO will follow, not demands on prohibition, although LO will work for stricter rules on authorization.

The transposition of the Agency Work Directive will probably not result in large changes in practice, except for posted temporary work. Posted temporary workers are

---

20. SOU 2011:5 61–65, see also the Mediation Office's yearly report 2010 (summary in English, www.mi.se).

not many in Sweden but this is a particularly vulnerable group. The result of the Swedish solution is that it will be cheaper to use contract work with posted workers than to hire in posted agency workers. At first sight, this may be considered inconsistent but considering the protection of both posted workers and agency workers, and the outcome in the Laval-case this is a suitable way to protect a particularly vulnerable group.

The trade federations affiliated to the LO have commissioned the LO to develop an agreement aimed to be a so-called application agreement which foreign service providers hiring-out employees to Swedish user companies shall be presented to sign. The planned agreement is supposed to consist of the 'hard core' regarding wages and employment conditions in the current collective agreement regarding agency work.

It is essential to respect the social partners' independence and concluded agreements. The temporary agency work sector in Sweden is a prominent example of how the social partners by collective agreements have combined the demand for flexibility at the same time as the demand for security. Also the voluntary accreditation system should be mentioned here. Nevertheless, it is desirable that the parties conduct a serious review of restrictions in collective agreements according to Article 4 of the Agency Work Directive.

CHAPTER 10
Regulating Temporary Work in the United Kingdom

Alan Neal

§10.01 THE NATURE OF THE BEAST

For an area in relation to which so much comment and controversy are aired, there is a remarkable absence of reliable data on the extent of, and conditions relating to, temporary agency work in the UK. Thus, for example, while a figure of 1.4 million is commonly tossed around,[1] the basis for that quantification derives from strongly contrasting research, relying upon sharply differing methodologies and survey groups.

Little by way of statistical evidence emerges from the trade union side, whose general approach to the growing phenomenon of temporary agency work was made clear in a 2005 TUC report prepared in the context of developments at the level of the EU,[2] although a 2007 report from the TUC repeats the figure of 1.4 million.[3]

There is some recent data emanating from the employer side, in the shape of the most recent report prepared by CIETT (the International Confederation of Private Employment Agencies), which, however, only offers statistics from 2009.[4] This

---

1. See, for example, TUC, *Counting the Cost of Flexibility* (London, February 2007); BBC News, *Agency Workers Get Greater Work Rights from 1 October* (30 Sep. 2011).
2. TUC, *The EU Temp Trade: Temporary Agency Work across the European Union* (London, June 2005). For a comparative framework within which to place the situation of the UK, see *inter alia* European Foundation for the Improvement of Living and Working Conditions, *Temporary agency work in the European Union* (Dublin 2007); ILO, *Final Report of the Discussion at the Global Dialogue Forum on the Role of Private Employment Agencies in Promoting Decent Work and Improving the Functioning of Labour Markets in Private Services Sectors* (18–19 Oct. 2011), (ILO, Sectoral Activities Department GDFPSS/2011/10, Geneva 2012); and ILO, *From Precarious Work to Decent Work* (Outcome Document to the Workers' Symposium on Policies and Regulations to combat Precarious Employment, Geneva 2012).
3. TUC, *Counting the Cost of Flexibility, supra*, 39.
4. CIETT, *The Agency Work Industry Around the World* (Brussels 2011), 18.

suggests that in 2009 there were some 1,068,197 agency workers, hired through the 17,000 branches of around 11,500 private employment agencies.[5] Of particular interest in that set of data is the indication that, of the just over 1 million workers, some 95,865 are 'internal' employees – leading the CIETT report to comment that:

> The UK has the lowest 'branch to PrEA ratio' and the highest 'internal staff to branch ratio'. This can be explained by the high level of fragmentation of the UK agency work market, characterised by a majority of small private employment agencies that operate locally.

Commenting in 2008, a report prepared for the UK government's Department for Business, Enterprise and Regulatory Reform suggested that:[6]

> The best estimate for the number of agency workers comes from the REC 'ensus' and SORA business surveys of the agency sector. These figures show there are between 1.1 and 1.5 million agency workers, with the mid-point being 1.3 million. The high turnover, the seasonality and the flexibility of agency work make it difficult to come to a definitive figure.

That same source opined that:

> there are an estimated 16,000 recruitment sites (branches and offices). A number of large well-known agency businesses operate in this sector but there are also significant proportions (just under 60 per cent) of small single site agency businesses with between one and five employees who match agency workers with assignments.

On the basis of SORA data, the number of agency workers rose from 550,000 in 1999 to 1,523,000 by 2007. Turning to other data, between 1997 and 2006, according to the REC Census, the number rose from 879,000 to 1,080,000. However, if one looks at the UK government's own Labour Force Survey statistics, the rise between 1998 and 2007 was in a totally different range, from 259,000 to 264,000.[7]

---

5. It is reported that 'there were 6,500 UK recruitment businesses registered for VAT in 1994 and by 2005 this had risen to 16,800'. See European Foundation for the Improvement of Living and Working Conditions, *Temporary Agency Work and Collective Bargaining in the EU* (Dublin 2008), 6.
6. EMAR, *Agency Working in the UK: A Review of the Evidence* (Employment Relations Research Series No. 93) (London, October 2008). The report proceeds on the basis of a definition for the group in terms that: 'In this report, the term "agency" will be used for all types of businesses involved in providing employers with temporary workers. In this context "agency workers" mean those workers supplied to a client – where the agency continues to pay the agency worker. It excludes those people who obtain work through agents in the entertainment and modelling sectors (including writers and professional sports persons).', and makes the more general point that: 'Agency workers are a category within overall temporary work which is a wider group of workers including those on fixed-term contacts, casual or seasonal work contracts.'
7. EMAR 2008, *supra*, para. 1.2. The authors of the report observe that: 'As sources, we recognise the REC and SORA business surveys have their limitations but they are preferable to the Labour Force Survey (LFS) because of strong evidence this source underestimates the number of agency workers for the following reasons: §§ The LFS interviews people and there is a lack of

The most recent available *Labour Force Survey* (LFS) statistics for the UK (which relate to the period July–September 2012) indicate a total number of temporary employees standing at some 1,646,000, of which just under half are employed part-time (784,000). Within that overall figure, the number employed under 'agency temping' arrangements is put at 303,000 (of which 73,000 are part-time). Other categories of temporary work are broken down into those working under fixed-period contracts, casual workers, seasonal workers, and a 'catch-all' category of 'others'.[8]

A government-commissioned 'review of the evidence' (published in 2008) indicated that, on the basis of the available data, agency workers are 'more likely to be younger, from an ethnic minority group but with broadly similar qualifications compared with all employees'. It was further suggested that 'the proportion of agency workers who are female is lower than the proportion of all employees who are female', while there are more agency workers aged under 35 compared with all those who are employees'. These findings, which reinforced earlier research undertaken on the basis of LFS data,[9] also found there to be 'significantly more agency workers who are from a minority group (including Eastern Europeans) compared with all employees', while – perhaps again unsurprisingly – there are 'fewer people with disabilities who are agency workers compared with all employees', and 'agency workers have broadly similar qualifications compared with all employees'.

In respect of the sectors in which work was undertaken by these workers, it appeared that the more frequently listed occupations were 'professional, administrative, secretarial, personal services (e.g. social carers, class room assistants and workers in hospitality) and process/plant/machine operations'. The government's 2008 survey also suggested (on the basis of evidence which was acknowledged to be less than comprehensive) that 'the duration of assignment is less than three months for around 55% of agency workers who knew the length of time they had been on their current assignment', while, on the basis of LFS data for the final quarter of 2007, 'overall hourly earnings of agency workers were 94% of the level for all employees with less than two years' service in their company'.

---

  awareness by people who are employed by agency workers of their employment status; §§ SORA 2007 found a significant number of assignments lasted less than a week – just 15 minutes in some cases. This indicates the extent to which high turnover and flexibility is present in this sector and the difficulties a household survey like the LFS will come cross when identifying respondents as agency workers (i.e. especially where such short assignments count as a second or even third job); §§ The LFS does not directly target agency workers but tries to capture them in the 60,000 households surveyed each month; and §§ With a turnover of £29.3 billion and between 200,000 and 225,000 individuals employed by the labour recruitment and provision of personnel sector, it is likely that there is a larger agency worker population supporting this sector than current LFS estimates suggest.'

8. Office for National Statistics (ONS), Table EMP07, published 23 Jan. 2013.
9. C. Ford & G. Slater, *Agency Working in the UK: Character, What Do We Know?* (Centre for Employment Relations Innovation and Change, University of Leeds May 2008). See also the earlier work of these authors, published as C. Ford & G. Slater, *Agency Working in Britain: Character, Consequences and Regulation*, 43 British J. Indus. Rel. 249 (2005), and C. Ford & G .Slater, *The Nature and Experience of Agency Working in Britain: What Are the Challenges for Human Resource Management?*, 35 Personnel Rev. 141 (2006).

That 2008 survey also discovered that approximately 57% of temporary assignments were full-time compared to 43% part-time, and that, according to the LFS, 25% of agency workers were part-time, which was the same proportion as for all employees.

§10.02 ATTITUDES TO TEMPORARY AGENCY WORK[10]

The UK has not historically been a labour market in which strong ideological resistance has been experienced to agency work placement or associated forms of 'private labour exchange'. Unlike countries in which this function has been regarded as a matter properly for 'the State', and in relation to which 'private profit-making' activity has been frowned upon, or even outlawed, a relative freedom has been given to actors within the UK system to develop various forms of staffing arrangements on the basis of commercial contracting undertakings between labour suppliers and 'end-users' of that labour. The totemic declaration in the International Labour Organization's (ILO's) Declaration of Philadelphia, to the effect that 'Labour is not a commodity' has, consequently, not been a driving motivation for or against activity in this sector of the economy.[11]

Indeed, although an ILO survey of 'regulation, monitoring and enforcement' in 2007 makes mention of 'typologies' in this context, the frame of reference is weak, and the treatment of the UK does little more than provide a superficial sketch of some contemporary arrangements in this part of the labour market.[12]

Not surprisingly, therefore, the supra-national manoeuvrings which led to the adoption by the ILO's Private Employment Agencies Convention, 1997 (No. 181) hardly gave rise to a murmur in the UK, while even the developments at the level of the

---

10. For recent rehearsal of some of the arguments deployed for and against the utilization of temporary agency work arrangements, see *inter alia*, R. Böheim & M. Zweimüller, *The Employment of Temporary Agency Workers in the UK: For or against the Trade Unions?*, 80 Economica 65 (2013); A. Bryson, *Do Temporary Agency Workers Affect Workplace Performance?*, J. Productivity Analysis (2012) (published online 22 Apr. 2012); and for broader treatment, see the contributions of C. Ford & G. Slater, *supra*; together with the material cited in E. Markova & S. Mckay, *Agency and Migrant Workers: Literature Review* (TUC Commission on Vulnerable Employment (CoVE), Working Lives Research Institute, London Metropolitan University, 30 Jul. 2008) – especially in Part 5 of their presentation.
11. The original ILO Constitution was to be found as Part XIII of the Treaty of Versailles (1919), although, over time, it became a separate instrument, and has subsequently been amended on a number of occasions. In 1944, the Conference adopted the *Declaration of Philadelphia*, which re-stated the fundamental aims and purposes of the ILO. That Declaration is annexed to, and forms an integral part of, the current ILO Constitution. Part I of the Declaration provides that: 'The Conference re-affirms the fundamental principles on which the Organisation is based and, in particular, that: (a) labour is not a commodity; (b) freedom of expression and of association are essential to sustained progress; (c) poverty anywhere constitutes a danger to prosperity everywhere; (d) the war against want requires to be carried on with unrelenting vigour within each nation, and by continuous and concerted international effort in which the representatives of workers and employers, enjoying equal status with those of governments, join with them in free discussion and democratic decision with a view to the promotion of the common welfare.'
12. ILO, *Guide to Private Employment Agencies – Regulation, Monitoring and Enforcement* (ILO Skills and Employability Special Action Programme Department 2007). See also the earlier report *The Role of Private Employment Agencies in the Functioning of the Labour Market* (ILO 1994).

EU which resulted in the adoption of Directive 2008/104/EC of the European Parliament and of the Council of 19 November 2008 on temporary agency work have not had much of the dramatic whiff of controversy which some lobbyists or commentators would have one believe.[13]

Rather, the relatively deregulated framework for the UK labour market had been well established during a period of successive Conservative governments under the leadership of Prime Minister Margaret Thatcher, and the reality of so-called New Labour administrations following electoral success by Tony Blair in 1997 turned out to be a remarkable unwillingness to 'tinker' with the established regulatory status quo. Only with the advent of a 'Coalition government' in 2010 has one been able to discern clear evidence of a more ideologically driven approach to labour market and employment regulation – but this comes well in the wake of the confirmation of current arrangements for temporary work and agency placement activity, and is substantially driven by 'the business case' for the perceived 'flexibility' which this form of engagement can bring to the UK labour market.

A commonly presented position from the trade union perspective is reflected in comments by Böheim & Zweimüller,[14] to the effect that, 'British trade unions are known for their resistance to temporary work agencies ...', although 'their stance in a given firm on hiring agency workers is not clear *a priori* ...'. That ambivalence is, however, very much a modern phenomenon, marking a clear shift from the old historical position adopted in 1928 by the TUC which favoured what Heery describes as the *exclusion* of 'fee-charging employment agencies' in the labour market.[15] Indeed, that antagonistic position was expressly continued after the Second World War, and can be seen in the TUC's enthusiasm that the UK government should ratify the ILO's Fee-Charging Employment Agencies Convention (Revised), 1949,[16] which called, in its Part II, for 'the progressive abolition of fee-charging employment agencies conducted with a view to profit'.[17]

Although that 'abolitionist' stance of the UK labour movement was maintained for a further three decades, the TUC eventually began to change its position during the 1980s. Faced with a rapidly changing world of work, where a combination of new technology, increasing globalization, disappearance of traditional patterns such as 'lifetime employment' or rigid working routines (whether by reference to location, tasks, or hours worked), and an increasingly hostile regulatory environment, the TUC adjusted its approach to one of calling for 'improved regulation' in relation to the

---

13. See, for example, N. Countouris & R. Horton, *The Temporary Agency Work Directive: Another Broken Promise?*, 38 Indus. L. J. 329 (2009).
14. R. Böheim & M. Zweimüller, *The Employment of Temporary Agency Workers in the UK: For or against the Trade Unions?*, 80 Economica 65 (2013).
15. E. Heery, *The Trade Union Response to Agency Labour in Britain*, 35 Indus. Rel. J. 434, at 437 (2004). The author puts forward a spectrum of trade union responses, ranging from 'exclusion', through 'replacement', to 'regulation', and, finally, 'engagement'.
16. Convention No. 96. This instrument was introduced to take over from the provisions of ILO Convention No. 34, concerning Fee-Charging Employment Agencies (1933).
17. Article 3(1) of the 1949 Convention provided that 'Fee-charging employment agencies conducted with a view to profit ... shall be abolished within a limited period of time determined by the competent authority.'

activity of labour placement. Notwithstanding that gradual shift, however, it has been suggested that '… agencies were still considered "parasitic" and agency workers were seen as workers with no legitimate interest in obtaining employment through an agency'.[18]

Thus, by the time of a 'survey of legislation on temporary agency work', prepared by the European Trade Union Institute in 2000,[19] the TUC's reaction to proposals for reforming the private recruitment industry put forward by the recently elected 'New Labour' government in a consultation document published the previous year was reported in terms that:[20]

> The TUC welcomes the Government's proposals to better regulate the operation of the private recruitment industry. In particular, the TUC welcomes the proposals to: enforce the distinction between an employment business and an employment agency, so that agency workers know who their employer is; ban introducers' fees; ensure that agency workers are paid on time; provide more clarity over contractual terms; ensure that agency workers are not being supplied to do jobs for which they are not qualified, or where there are health and safety hazards – with the caveat that separate measures must be taken to deal with any employer whose workplace does not comply with health and safety laws; enforce the general prohibition on charging a fee for finding work; tighten up protection for workers in the entertainment industry.

That confirmation of a willingness (however much tinged with 'reluctance') on the part of the TUC to engage in the development of a regulatory framework for this sector was supplemented by a number of specific calls for additional measures to be introduced, in order to:

> re-introduce a licensing system for agencies, with minimal criteria for registration and a 3-yearly re-application system; produce more detailed guidelines for agencies on compliance with the Working Time Regulations, in particular in relation to record-keeping obligations; give workers in the entertainment industry the right to inspect their client account; limit the extent of charging to clients in the entertainment industry, so that fees are limited to the work actually negotiated by the agent; ensure that performers are paid on the day or night of their performance and remove the opt-out clause (Regulation 25(10)); set up a working group covering relevant Government departments to solve the problem of bogus self-employment, contracts 'for' services, tax problems for freelancers and other areas where workers fall outside employment protection; and provide better resources for the DTI enforcement operation.

The UK labour movement's modern stance in this field was further clarified during the period leading up to adoption at the level of the EU of the 2008 Directive on temporary

---

18. R. Böheim & M. Zweimüller, *supra* n. 13, at 65.
19. See S. Clauwaert, *Survey of Legislation on Temporary Agency Work* 100-101 (ETUI 2000).
20. Employment Agency Standards, Employment Relations Directorate, Department of Trade and Industry, *Regulation of the Private Recruitment Industry: A Consultation Document* (May 1999). The thrust of that reform proposal was summarized by Clauwaert such that: 'The objective of the new proposed regulation is fourfold: to increase clarity, to promote labour market flexibility, to give proper protection to the clients and general public, to curb payment abuses and to safeguard clients' money.'

agency work, in documents such as the TUC's 2007 report on *'Agency Workers: Counting the Cost of Flexibility'*. In particular, the report of the TUC's 'Commission on Vulnerable Employment', published in the following year, identified temporary agency work arrangements as constituting one element in the 'context of vulnerable employment', noting that:[21]

> The number of employment agencies in the UK is likely to be rising, and the UK also has the most fragmented agency labour market in Europe. As a proportion of all temporary work, agency work is showing steep increases, comprising 17.1 per cent of all temporary work in Autumn 2007 compared to 13 per cent in 1997. The European Foundation estimates that in 1998 the top five agencies controlled between 75 per cent and 80 per cent of the market in France, Belgium and the Netherlands, compared with only 16 per cent in the UK. We also have the highest agency work penetration rate (defined as the average daily number of agency workers as a percentage of total employment) – 4.3 per cent in 2006, compared to 2.1 per cent in the USA and the Netherlands, 1.3 per cent in Ireland and 0.9 per cent in Germany.

While acknowledging that 'many employment agencies operate within the law, and good employers agree with us that more needs to be done to prevent rogue operators from exploiting vulnerable workers', the TUC concluded that: 'being placed in work by an employment agency can in many cases place workers at considerable risk of vulnerable employment'. Indeed, the authors of the TUC Commission's report maintained that 'some of the worst abuses we heard of during our work were experienced by workers whose jobs had been supplied by an agency, a complex employment relationship that currently reduces the employment rights to which a worker is entitled, and can create uncertainty as to whether the supplying agency or the user organisation has responsibility for their treatment'.[22]

§10.03 REGULATING THE LABOUR SUPPLIER SIDE

The UK approach adopted for dealing with regulatory issues concerning temporary labour placement reflects a primary focus upon the 'governance' and administrative supervision of undertakings acting in that particular sector of the labour market. The existence or otherwise of formal 'employer-like' obligations on the parts of end-users has, by and large, not been dealt with directly by way of statutory interference, outside the (nonetheless quite broadly conceived) field of 'health and safety at work'. Meanwhile, consequential and complementary issues arising in relation to the nature and content of the relationship between the worker and the labour supplier have been left as a continuing conundrum for the judiciary to 'resolve', using the traditional tools of the Common Law (particularly as these relate to contractual analysis).

Thus, for a long time, the UK authorities have been content to regulate the business of temporary agency work provision through regulations designed to cover

---

21. TUC, *Hard Work, Hidden Lives* 15 (The full Report of the Commission on Vulnerable Employment, London, May 2008).
22. *Ibid.*, 154.

either what are described as 'employment agencies' or 'employment businesses'. Both have been the subject of regulation since the enactment of the Employment Agencies Act 1973, and are additionally subject to the provisions of the Conduct of Employment Agencies and Employment Business Regulations, which were introduced in 2003.[23] This latter instrument was subjected to amendment by 2007 Regulations, which came into force in the Spring of 2008.[24] The technical scope and form of that regulation is currently under discussion as part of the UK government's strategies to reform labour market mechanisms in the name of 'growth, competitiveness and employment'.[25]

Section 13 of the 1973 Act defined an 'employment agency' as 'the business (whether or not carried on with a view to profit and whether or not carried on in conjunction with any other business) of providing services (whether by the provision of information or otherwise) for the purpose of finding workers employment with employers or of supplying employers with workers for employment by them', while an 'employment business' was defined as 'the business (whether or not carried on with a view to profit and whether or not carried on in conjunction with any other business) of supplying persons in the employment of the person carrying on the business, to act for, and under the control of, other persons in any capacity'. Notwithstanding subsequent minor amendment – whereby the expression 'workers' in the definition of an 'employment agency' was replaced by the term 'persons' – those definitions have been retained in the current versions of the statutory rules dealing with this activity.[26]

Thus, in short, the 'employment agency' is seen by the 1973 Act as an organization providing 'services', whereas the 'employment business' is identified as an organization which supplies its own employed persons to a controlling end-user.

The same distinction is utilized in the Conduct of Employment Agencies and Employment Business Regulations 2003. There, the term 'agency' is used, defined by reference to the definition in section 13 of the 1973 Act, and 'includes a person carrying on an agency, and in the case of a person who carries on both an agency and an employment business means such a person in his capacity in carrying on the agency'. The expression 'employment business' features in both instruments, and is similarly defined in the 2003 Regulations by reference to the 1973 Act, while it also 'includes a person carrying on an employment business, and in the case of a person who carries on both an employment business and an agency means such a person in his capacity in carrying on the employment business'.[27]

---

23. See also the DTI, *Guidance on the Conduct of Employment Agencies and Employment Businesses Regulations 2003* (January 2004).
24. See the Conduct of Employment Agencies and Employment Businesses (Amendment) Regulations 2007.
25. The mantra in common use since the publication of the European Commission's White Paper, *Growth, competitiveness, employment: The Challenges and Ways Forward into the 21st Century*, COM (93) 700 (Brussels, 5 Dec. 1993). See the UK government's Department for Business Innovation & Skills, *Recruitment Sector Legislation: Consultation on Reforming the Regulatory Framework for Employment Agencies and Employment Businesses* (January 2013), together with its associated *Impact assessment*.
26. The amendment was effected by the Employment Relations Act 1999 – see Schedule 7, s. 7.
27. See the Conduct of Employment Agencies and Employment Businesses Regulations 2003, s. 2.

Mention should also be made of a specific regime which operates under the Gangmasters (Licensing) Act 2004 – a regulatory framework introduced in the wake of a tragedy involving cockle pickers off the North-West coast of England.[28] 'Gangmasters' are individuals or businesses who supply labour to, or who use labour to provide a service in, one of the regulated sectors to which the Act extends, and the protected class of 'workers' comprises individuals who do work to which the Act applies.[29] The 2004 statute set up a 'Gangmasters Licensing Authority' to regulate labour providers in the regulated industries, and, with effect from the Autumn of 2006, made it a criminal offence to operate as, or to use, a gangmaster without a license. This regime operates to the exclusion of the 1973 Act and the 2003 Regulations.[30]

Where the regulatory framework under the 1973 Act and the 2003 Regulations applies, the approach is essentially 'administrative', insofar as monitoring and enforcement is carried out through an Employment Agencies Standards Inspectorate (EAS), with additional sanctioning arrangements being made available under the criminal law. Although the government is keen to present the arrangements as including 'protection for workers' and 'protection for vulnerable people',[31] the nature of the 'protection' reflects a number of prohibitions upon employment businesses resorting to certain types of activity, rather than 'employment rights' enforceable at the instigation of the individual. This 'administrative monitoring' approach contrasts with the provision of employment protections such as the right not to be unfairly dismissed, the right not to have unauthorized deductions made from pay, or the right to holiday pay, which are constituted as statutory 'employment rights' enforceable through the system of Employment Tribunals.[32]

The key elements of the 1973 Act's regulatory regime may be presented as:

- The establishment of a licensing system, whereby a current license is required before any person undertakes activity as an employment agency or an employment business.

---

28. That event cost the lives of twenty-three (mainly Chinese) workers on the night of 5–6 Feb. 2004, when they were cut off by the tide after dark. See *Cocklers Tragedy Highlights Need for High Safety Standards* (HSE press release C005:06 24 Mar. 2006). Subsequent criminal prosecutions resulted in the conviction of the main 'gangmaster' (Lin Liang Ren) on twenty-one counts of manslaughter, and two further defendants being found guilty with him of various offences relating to the facilitation of illegal immigrants to work in the UK.
29. See the Gangmasters (Licensing) Act 2004, s. 26(1). The scope of the work covered by the Act is set out in s. 3, and covers: '(a) agricultural work, (b) gathering shellfish, and (c) processing or packaging — (i) any produce derived from agricultural work, or (ii) shellfish, fish or products derived from shellfish or fish'.
30. See s. 27(1).
31. See, for example, Department for Business Innovation & Skills, *Recruitment Sector Legislation: Consultation on Reforming the Regulatory Framework for Employment Agencies and Employment Businesses* 12 (January 2013).
32. It should also be noted that where protective arrangements relate to the health, safety and hygiene of the worker, the UK utilizes a framework of enforcement which relies predominantly upon criminal law sanctions (including fines, imprisonment, and – where appropriate – disqualification from the right to hold the position of a director of a company). The basis for these arrangements can be found in the Health and Safety at Work Act 1974.

- Within that licensed system, powers for the responsible Minister to make 'general regulations' in order to 'to secure the proper conduct' of those bodies and 'to protect the interests of persons availing themselves of the services of such agencies and businesses'.[33]
- A general prohibition (subject only to prescribed exceptions) against the making of a demand for, or the receipt of, any payment (fee) for finding employment or for seeking to find employment for any person.[34]

The 2003 Regulations, which were made under powers contained in the 1973 Act, introduce a variety of additional restrictions as part of the framework within which labour placement activity can proceed in the UK. In particular:

- There are general prohibitions against charging fees for the service of labour placement (work finding services), and a broad range of associated provisions which endeavour to ensure that labour placement organizations cannot disguise other charges or services in order to circumvent that fee-charging prohibition.[35]
- Of particular note is the prohibition in Regulation 7 upon providing labour in the context of industrial disputes – although it may be noted that this does not apply in situations where the action consists of 'an unofficial strike or other unofficial industrial action'.[36]
- As well as dealing with the keeping of accounts, the Regulations also make detailed provision in relation to advertising, record-keeping, and the confidentiality of any information held about work-seekers.

The arrangements established by the 1973 Act and the 2003 Regulations have been described as 'complicated and difficult to understand', while it has further been suggested that they place 'a burden on business' and are 'potentially acting as a barrier to growth'.[37] Indeed, this underlying judgment is driving a newly-announced political commitment to reform of the existing provisions 'to ensure it is fit for purpose in today's labour market'.[38]

In consequence of such concerns, recent proposals have been put forward for consultation during the Spring of 2013. Those proposals, which start out from the

---

33. Employment Agencies Act 1973, s. 5.
34. Section 6.
35. These are set out in Part II of the Act, in the form of 'restrictions', and are complemented by provisions in Part III of the Act, which cover a variety of requirements to be satisfied before the organization can undertake such activities. The latter include various items of information which have to be furnished in relation to terms and conditions of both the work placement service and the eventual hiring into which the worker may be directed.
36. This notion of 'unofficial' industrial action forms part of a wider restrictive framework touching the regulation of strikes and other industrial action in the UK, and is dealt with in detail by provisions contained in the Trade Union and Labour Relations (Consolidation) Act 1992.
37. See Department for Business Innovation & Skills, *Recruitment Sector Legislation: Consultation on Reforming the Regulatory Framework for Employment Agencies and Employment Businesses – Impact Assessment* 2 (January 2013).
38. Jo Swinson MP, Minister for Employment Relations and Consumer Affairs, in the Foreword to the government's consultation document of January 2013, at 5.

proposition that 'The UK has a labour market that is flexible, efficient and fair but some of our laws are still outdated' – with express reference to the Employment Agencies Act 1973 and the Conduct of Employment Agencies and Employment Businesses Regulations 2003 – are given the stated purpose of establishing 'a new, fit for purpose regulatory framework with minimum regulation' which can enable the sector 'to take a more active role in developing its own methods of maintaining standards so that it has the confidence of hiring companies and people seeking work'. At the same time, the UK government is seeking views on the current enforcement regime and 'whether individuals should be able to enforce their own rights at Employment Tribunals, bringing the recruitment sector in line with other areas of employment law'.[39]

The government's proposals have a distinct 'light touch' ethos to them – perhaps unsurprisingly, given that the reform stimulus derived from a so-called employment law Red Tape Challenge in 2011[40] – and can be seen as broadly consistent in approach to reform currently being undertaken in relation to health and safety at work, in the wake of a major report into that area of regulation.[41]

Thus, having made clear that 'complete deregulation of the recruitment sector is not considered to be viable or desirable',[42] the government has declared that:[43]

> We believe that legislation should be minimised and, for the most part, focussed where work-seekers are most at risk of exploitation. Our vision for the recruitment sector is that it will be regulated by the simplest regulatory framework possible, reducing the regulatory burden and allowing businesses to play an active role in developing their own methods of maintaining standards so they can compete for work-seekers and hiring companies.

In order to deliver that vision, the proposed reform sets out 'four outcomes', which are said to be 'important to ensure that the recruitment sector operates fairly and flexibly'.

---

39. See Department for Business Innovation & Skills, *Recruitment Sector Legislation: Consultation on Reforming the Regulatory Framework for Employment Agencies and Employment Businesses* (January 2013), 11–12.
40. The phenomenon of the so-called red tape challenge has been driven through the Cabinet Office, and – at least in relation to the field of employment law and regulation – has seen a remarkable premium placed upon opinion-based propositions, at the expense of evidence-based research. A three-week online 'window' for public responses in relation to employment law was launched with the publication of the Department for Business Innovation & Skills document, *Flexible, Effective Fair: Promoting Economic Growth through a Strong and Efficient Labour Market* (October 2011) – a naked statement of preference for the 'economic dimension' as opposed to the 'social dimension' in this area! Subsequent proposals for regulatory reform of the area – most significantly, those contained in an *Enterprise and Regulatory Reform Bill 2012-13*, currently making its way through the United Kingdom Parliament – take the weight of opinion-based propositions as support for 'the voice of business' and as self-evident and conclusive.
41. See the report prepared for the UK government by Professor Ragnar E. Löfstedt, *Reclaiming Health and Safety for All: An Independent Review of Health and Safety Legislation* (Cm 8219, November 2011).
42. Department for Business Innovation & Skills, *Recruitment Sector Legislation: Consultation on Reforming the Regulatory Framework for Employment Agencies and Employment Businesses* (January 2013), at para. 6.5, 10.
43. *Ibid.*, para. 6.10.

Those outcomes are described in terms that: (1) employment businesses and employment agencies are restricted from charging fees to work-seekers; (2) there is clarity on who is responsible for paying temporary workers for the work they have done; (3) the contracts people have with recruitment firms should not hinder their movement between jobs and temp-to-perm transfer fees are reasonable; and (4) work-seekers have the confidence to use the recruitment sector and are able to assert their rights.

The method suggested for achieving those outcomes is to replace the existing Employment Agencies Act 1973 and the 2003 Regulations with new legislation, in order 'to free employment agencies and businesses from unnecessary regulation and allow them more scope to operate in the way that is best for them'.[44]

§10.04 REGULATING THE COMMERCIAL RELATIONSHIP BETWEEN LABOUR SUPPLIER AND END-USER

The position in the UK as regards this part of the complex agency work arrangements is, essentially, to leave matters to the normal (contractual and otherwise) rules for commercial contracting. Indeed, given the homage paid by successive governments (of all political hues) to the perceived need for ensuring that the UK 'maintains labour market flexibility which is important for the creation of jobs',[45] and the most recently expressed commitment of the current Coalition government 'to establish a new, fit for purpose regulatory framework with minimum regulation',[46] this comes as little surprise. The 'market-centric' legacy of 'the Thatcher years', combined with a new ascendency in modern Coalition government policies for 'the business case' (however anecdotal) over concerns for social protection, renders this a particularly fertile field for advocates of 'deregulation' and 'the rolling back of the State'.

However, when considering the commercial practices which manifest themselves in this area, it is noteworthy that the pattern of temporary agency work provision is characterized by the existence of 'approximately 16,000 agencies across the UK' which, according to background research undertaken for the Department for Business Enterprise and Regulatory Reform, 'employ a combined workforce of approximately 225,000 people to match agency workers with assignments'.[47] This heavily fragmented characteristic presents various challenges in terms of monitoring, reporting, and other administrative supervision arrangements. It is not, therefore, surprising that the main thrust for regulatory reform in this area has been in relation to precisely those issues.

Notwithstanding this (broadly) *laissez-faire* attitude of seeking to leave 'business' unfettered by 'red tape', however, certain limitations upon the unbridled freedom to

---

44. *Ibid.*, para. 6.11.
45. See, for example, the 'Ministerial Foreword' in Department for Business Innovation & Skills, *Implementation of the Agency Workers Directive: Response to Consultation on Draft Regulations* (January 2010), 4.
46. Department for Business Innovation & Skills, *Recruitment Sector Legislation: Consultation on Reforming the Regulatory Framework for Employment Agencies and Employment Businesses* (January 2013), 6.
47. The *Survey of Recruitment Agencies* (SORA) was undertaken in the Autumn of 2007. This was a follow-up to a first *Survey of Recruitment Agencies*, conducted in 1999 for the then Department of Trade and Industry (DTI).

conduct business on 'Wild West lines' are to be found. These reflect, by and large, matters encompassed by the international standards applicable to temporary agency work – notably, the ILO Private Employment Agencies Convention, 1997 (No. 181) and the accompanying ILO Private Employment Agencies Recommendation, 1997 (No. 188).

Thus, the general UK 'Labour Law' protections in relation to exercise of the right to freedom of association apply to this field of business activity, as they apply elsewhere in the labour market, while the general framework of protections against discrimination (on specified grounds) also applies here. So, too, do the established protections to ensure compliance with the ILO's 'core conventions' – the subject-matter of which receives mention in both the 1997 Convention and Recommendation.

Going somewhat beyond those formal restrictive provisions, the express prohibition in the 2003 Regulations against provision of 'strike-breakers' has already been mentioned.[48] Indeed, this issue (along with related matters of workforce organization) became a focus for comment during an industrial dispute at a Lincolnshire oil refinery in January 2009, when local contractors embarked on strike action following the appointment by an Italian construction contractor (IREM) of several hundred (mainly Italian and Portuguese) contractors on the site at a time of high unemployment in the local economy.[49] It also featured in the course of a 2009 dispute in the UK's Royal Mail business, when the main trade union representing workers participating in a strike sought to challenge the use by management of some 30,000 agency staff to handle a backlog of letters caused by the industrial action.[50]

The proposed recourse to the prohibition against 'strike-breakers' being supplied through employment businesses in the context of the Royal Mail dispute, and subsequent comment in the national media, served to highlight a number of practical shortcomings associated with the operation of the 2003 Regulations in this area. In particular, the law firm representing the Communication Workers Union (CWU) maintained that there had, to date, been no prosecutions under the relevant regulation (Regulation 7), which, it was said, was partly due to the fact that '… the business department is first required to conduct an inquiry into whether agency staff are being improperly used, a process that might take many months'.

---

48. *Supra.* See Regulation 7 of the 2003 Regulations.
49. See, for example, 'Britons walk out in foreign jobs protest', *Daily Express*, 29 Jan. 2009. The dispute was perceived as being more to do with the operation of the EU Posted Workers Directive than an immediate problem in relation to the provision of temporary agency workers, although many of the same kinds of concerns on the parts of trade unions representing the striking workers were to be seen in this context as are voiced in relation to the use of temporary agency labour provision. For broader discussion of some of the legal issues arising in the context of this dispute, see C. Barnard, *'British Jobs for British Workers': The Lindsey Oil Refinery Dispute and the Future of Local Labour Clauses in an Integrated EU Market*, 38 Indus. L. J. 245 (2009).
50. See 'Postal Union to Take Legal Action over Royal Mail's 30,000 Agency Staff', *The Guardian* (2 Nov. 2009).

§10.05 SAFEGUARDING THE WORKER: IN SEARCH OF 'THE EMPLOYER'

One of the most significant problems posed in the context of identifying the recipient of various employment protections in the UK has been the enthusiasm to approach identification of the 'employer' party to employment relationships in terms of 'Common Law tests' which look for particular features (some of which might be positive in that quest, others of which may tend to detract from such status) as a 'package'. A basic version of that approach can be seen in analysis of the so-called wage-work bargain,[51] while judicial susceptibility to the same approach can be discerned at the level of the Privy Council, underlying its decision in the 1990 case of *Lee v. Chung & Shun Shing Construction & Engineering Co. Ltd.*[52]

The search for 'the employer' in the context of temporary work placement arrangements is commonly referred to in terms of analysing 'the triangular relationship',[53] said to exist between the worker, the labour supplier, and the end-user ('hirer' or 'client'). For the UK, this particular quest constitutes part of a broader framework within which a variety of statutory employment protections are bestowed upon 'employees' or 'workers', so that 'qualification' within the definitions of one of those classifications becomes a pre-requisite for protected status on the part of the individual performing work.[54]

Success in achieving the sought-after protected status in relation to key employment protections is, normally, by way of satisfying the statutory definition of 'employee' – to be found in section 295(1) of the Trade Union and Labour Relations (Consolidation) Act 1992 and (in identical terms) in section 230 of the Employment Rights Act 1996, such that:

> 'employee' means an individual who has entered into or works under (or, where the employment has ceased, worked under) a contract of employment.

A further group of protections is afforded to the (wider) group who satisfy the definition of 'worker', to be found in section 296(1) of the Trade Union and Labour Relations (Consolidation) Act 1992 – mirrored by section 230(3) of the Employment Rights Act 1996 (which is in the same terms) – such that:

> 'worker' (subject to the following provisions of this section) means an individual regarded in whichever (if any) of the following capacities is applicable to him, that is to say, as a person who works or normally works or seeks to work – (a) under

---

51. See, for example, the presentation by P. Davies & M. Freedland, *Labour Law: Text and Materials* (1st ed., Weidenfeld & Nicolson 1979), drawing upon the work of M. Freedland, *The Obligation to Work and to Pay for Work*, 30 Current Leg. Problems 175 (1977). See also the much broader treatment by B. Napier, *Aspects of the Wage-Work Bargain*, 43 Cambridge L. J. 337 (1984).
52. *Lee v. Chung & Shun Shing Construction & Engineering Co. Ltd*, [1990] I.R.L.R. 236.
53. See, for example, the discussion in G. Davidov, *Joint Employer Status in Triangular Employment Relationships*, 42 British J. Indus. Rel. 727 (2004). More generally, see S. Deakin, *The Changing Concept of the 'Employer' in British Labour Law*, 30 Indus. L. J. 72 (2001).
54. The following is drawn from A. Neal, *The Protection of Working Relationships under United Kingdom Law*, in *The Protection of Working Relationships: A Comparative Study*, Ch. 10 (F. Pennings & C. Bosse eds., Kluwer, 2011).

a contract of employment, or (b) under any other contract (whether express or implied, and, if express, whether oral or in writing) whereby he undertakes to do or perform personally any work or services for another party to the contract who is not a professional client of his; or (c) in employment under or for the purposes of a government department (otherwise than as a member of the naval, military or air forces of the Crown) in so far as any such employment does not fall within paragraph (a) or (b) above.

Central to the eventual categorizing of persons performing work is the analysis of whether the individual can be found to be working under what is described in the legislation as a 'contract of employment' – a phenomenon which is additionally defined as meaning 'a contract of service or of apprenticeship'. However, apart from the situation of apprentices, there is no further statutory elucidation of what is required to satisfy the criteria for establishing the existence of 'a contract of service'. In consequence, the judiciary, when called upon to determine issues involving this 'employee status', have resorted to a set of 'Common Law tests', developed through case-law over decades – at the heart of which lie the need to establish 'control' on the part of 'the employer',[55] and what is described as 'an irreducible minimum of obligation' between the parties.[56]

Before moving on, however, it must be noted that there has been mention of the object for protection in temporary agency work placement arrangements in two statutes dating from the late 1990s. Thus, arguably reflecting the need to recognize explicitly the presence in the labour market of various categories of 'atypical' workers,[57] both the National Minimum Wage Act 1998 and the Working Time Regulations 1998 contain a definition of 'agency worker' in terms of an individual who:[58]

(a) is supplied by a person ('the agent') to do work for another ('the principal') under a contract or other arrangements made between the agent and principal; but (b) is not, as respects that work, a worker, because of the absence of a worker's contract between the individual and the agent or the principal; and (c) is not a party to a contract under which he undertakes to do the work for another party to the contract whose status is, by virtue of the contract, that of a client or customer of any profession or business undertaking carried on by the individual.

In passing, and also within the context of the National Minimum Wage Act 1998 provisions, we can also find a (rare) example of how modern UK legislative draughtsmanship has begun to take a more particularized approach to the actors in the modern

---

55. Flowing from the old-established case of *Yewens v. Noakes* (1880) 6 Q.B.D. 530.
56. Deriving from the observations in relation to this issue by the House of Lords in *Carmichael and Another v. National Power Plc.*, [2000] I.R.L.R. 43 – *per* Lord Irvine, drawing upon earlier propositions in *Nethermere (St. Neots) Ltd. v. Gardiner*, [1984] I.C.R. 612, and in *Clark v. Oxfordshire Health Authority*, [1998] I.R.L.R. 125. The phrase itself was in use during the period of the Second World War – see, for example, *Chadwick v. Pioneer Private Telephone Co. Ltd.*, [1941] 1 All E.R. 522 (per Stable J.).
57. For a contemporary consideration of the problem of what was coming to be regarded as 'atypical' in the developing context of globalized labour markets, see A. Neal, *Atypical Workforms and European Labour Law*, 45 Recht der Arbeit 115 (1995).
58. See National Minimum Wage Act 1998, s. 34, and Working Time Regulations 1998, Regulation 36.

world of work, since that statute also deals with the notion of what are described as 'superior employers', by providing that:[59]

> Where – (a) the immediate employer of a worker is himself in the employment of some other person, and (b) the worker is employed on the premises of that other person, that other person shall be deemed for the purposes of this Act to be the employer of the worker jointly with the immediate employer.

However, such 'rarities' apart, the judicial approach to identifying the 'contract of service' under the umbrella of which the participants in an employment relationship undertake their respective obligations has tended to consist of a 'weighing' exercise – much along the lines indicated by the Privy Council in *Lee*.[60] This leads to a significant practical problem where the search for a 'classical' bundle of 'employer obligations' is addressed in the context of 'the triangular relationship'.

As has been described by various commentators,[61] a relationship between the worker and a labour supplier (such as an employment business under the UK arrangements) may involve the labour supplier taking on responsibility for payment of 'wages' and the administration of deductions to provide for tax liabilities and social contributions, but will not involve the worker actually undertaking labour directly for the benefit of that labour supplier. At the same time, the worker may be sent to the end-user/client, where work will be undertaken under the supervision and 'control' of that end-user, and where obligations in respect of matters such as health, safety and hygiene at work can only effectively be discharged by that end-user. A number of instances may be offered in which the 'classical bundle of employer obligations' is allocated between the labour supplier and the end-user.

If the judicial search for 'protected employee' status confines itself to the formalistic contractual analysis approach of applying the historical 'Common Law tests' against the background of a fundamental need to establish 'control' and some 'irreducible minimum of mutual obligation' between the parties, the danger swiftly becomes apparent that neither the worker's relationship with the labour supplier nor his relationship with the end-user has all of the requisite components to lead to a conclusion that there exists the requisite 'contract of employment' for enjoyment of related employment protections.

Some of the frustration to which this can lead has been illustrated sharply in the context of cases brought before the UK's Court of Appeal during the mid-1990s. Thus, in *Dacas v. Brook Street Bureau (UK) Ltd*,[62] Mummery LJ, endorsed the evaluation of Professor Mark Freedland that:[63]

> Our analysis of the current state of the law of personal employment contracts showed that there was a complex of serious functional problems with regard to

---

59. National Minimum Wage Act 1998, s. 48.
60. *Supra* n. 44.
61. See, *inter alia*, M. Wynn & P. Leighton, *Will the Real Employer Please Stand Up? Agencies, Client Companies and the Employment Status of the Temporary Agency Worker*, 35 Indus. L.J. 301 (2006).
62. *Dacas v. Brook Street Bureau (UK) Ltd*, [2004] EWCA Civ 217.
63. See M. Freedland, *The Personal Contract of Employment* (2nd ed. Oxford U. Press 2003), at 55.

employment arrangements or relations involving an end-user of services and an intermediary entity such as an employment agency having some kind of employing role between that end-user and the worker. The problems were firstly, that there is great resistance to the construction of triangular personal employment contracts, secondly, that there may be great difficulty in deciding whether the worker's bilateral personal employment contract is with the end-user or the intermediary, but thirdly and most fundamentally that the triangular nature of the arrangement may have the effect that the worker fails to qualify as having a contract of employment or even as having a personal work or employment contract of any kind.

In his subsequent search for 'employee' status in order to determine whether the claimant in the case was entitled to statutory protection against unfair dismissal, Mummery LJ, having recognized the need to find an 'irreducible minimum of mutual obligation', expressed the view that:

> I approach the question posed by this kind of case on the basis that the outcome, which would accord with practical reality and common sense, would be that, if it is legally and factually permissible to do so, the applicant has a contract, which is not a contract of service, with the employment agency, and that the applicant works under an implied contract, which is a contract of service, with the end-user and is therefore an employee of the end-user with a right not to be unfairly dismissed;

but then went on to find (for technical reasons relating to the way in which the appeal proceedings had been brought) in favour of the arguments put forward by the agency.

The prospect of discovering 'an implied contract, which is a contract of service' between the worker and the end-user served to raise hopes unrealistically high that 'protective cover' might be available, after all, to persons performing work for end-users in the kinds of circumstance addressed by the Court of Appeal – until the same court (again including Mummery LJ) returned to the issue in *James v. London Borough of Greenwich*, four years later.[64] On this occasion, having set out the challenge for the judiciary in this area such that:

> the correct legal question is not whether the claimant was 'an agency worker' (whether working for an employment agency or for an end-user under an employment agency agreement) but whether the claimant was employed by the respondent end-user under a contract of employment,

Mummery LJ observed that:

> The two types of contract – agency agreement and contract of employment – are not necessarily mutually exclusive. It is legally possible for a worker to have one kind of contract with an employment agency and another kind of contract with the end user to whom he renders services.

However, while acknowledging that this called for 'an exercise in legal classification', the learned judge eventually found himself driven almost to the point of despair at the formal inability of the judiciary to achieve appropriate practical results through the

---

64. *James v. London Borough of Greenwich*, [2008] I.R.L.R. 302.

legal analysis of the employment status of persons working within the increasing temporary agency work sector.[65]

In particular, the Court of Appeal in *James* made clear that there was no inevitable step to be taken in the direction of finding 'an implied contract' of the kind envisaged in *Dacas*, although the point was stressed that it would constitute an error of law for a judge or a tribunal in a fact-finding instance to fail to ask itself the question whether the evidence contained sufficient to constitute such an 'implied contract'.

The practical challenges arising out of what evidently appeared to the Court of Appeal to be an unsatisfactory state of the UK law, given trends in the composition of the modern labour market, were perceptively and succinctly spelled out by Mummery LJ, who demonstrated a commendable appreciation of some of the pragmatic issues facing the actors on the modern UK labour market stage. Underlining the fundamental point that:

> The distinction between workers who are employees and those who are not is crucial for the determination of statutory rights, principally the right not to be unfairly dismissed,

it was made clear that:

> The courts and tribunals are fully aware of the current controversy about the absence of job protection for agency workers, who do not have an express or implied contract of employment.

Furthermore, however, while courts and tribunals 'are also well aware of the nature of the arguments for and against a change in the law', it was emphatically stressed that, within the constraints of the UK's Common Law system, 'it is not for them to express views about a change or to initiate change'.[66]

---

65. For contrasting perspectives on the 'Common Law approach' to this analysis (and, in particular, the permissibility of resort to the notion of an 'implied contract') in order to locate obligations on the basis of employer-like duties, compare the 2006 views of M. Wynn & P. Leighton, *supra* n. 53 (reiterated by the same authors in *Temporary Agency Working: Is the Law on the Turn?*, 29 Co. Law. 7 (2008)) and the comments in F. Reynold, *The Status of Agency Workers: A Question of Legal Principle*, 35 Indus. L. J. 320 (2006).

66. The judgment then proceeded to set out contrasting perspectives in terms that: 'On the one hand, there are arguments for a flexible labour market in the interests of a competitive economy and of full employment. There is a real need to hire temporary workers from agencies at short notice for extra busy periods or special projects. If this is made less attractive or more costly, job losses may follow and more work may be added to the burden borne by long term employees', but 'On the other hand, a significant move in the direction of the casualisation of labour and the growth of a two tier workforce, one tier enjoying significant statutory protection, the other tier in a legal no man's land being neither employed nor self-employed, vulnerable, but enjoying little or no protection, may create social injustice and a festering sense of grievance which would not be satisfactory in the interests of an efficient workforce, a competitive economy, a healthy society or anything else. There is, however, nothing to prevent wise employers from recognising that their long term interests may be better served by treating their entire workforce in a responsible and considerate way than by insisting on the strict letter of the law.' Nevertheless, with a clear tone of exasperation, it was concluded that: 'Policy decisions have to be taken by others about what changes (if any) to make, what rights to confer on whom, what qualifying periods to set and so on. The increasing amounts of money, time and effort

Since the observations of the Court of Appeal nearly two decades ago, however, it has to be said that little sign of progress along the lines indicated by Mummery LJ has been witnessed.

§10.06 IMPACT OF THE EU DIRECTIVE ON TEMPORARY WORK

In the lead-up to adoption of Directive 2008/104/EC of the European Parliament and of the Council of 19 November 2008 on temporary agency work, what pass in the UK as the 'social partners' – in the shape of the Confederation of British Industry (CBI) and the Trades Union Congress (TUC) – entered into discussions with the (then Labour) government over some of the basic issues arising in the context of future implementation. The outcome of that 'social dialogue' was a 'Joint Declaration', which was issued on 20 May 2008.[67] That document purported to express 'agreement on how fairer treatment for agency workers in the United Kingdom should be promoted, while not removing the important flexibility that agency work can offer both employers and workers' – further evidence of the continuing move on the part of the trade union movement towards 'accepting the inevitable' in relation to the established role of temporary agency work in the modern 'flexible' labour market.

More specifically, with an eye to the status of negotiations at the level of the EU Member States over the eventual final wording for the Directive, the parties agreed that, so far as the UK was concerned: (a) after twelve weeks in a given job there will be an entitlement to equal treatment; and that (b) equal treatment will be defined to mean at least the basic working and employment conditions that would apply to the workers concerned if they had been recruited directly by that undertaking to occupy the same job. It will not cover occupational social security schemes.

For their part, it was agreed that the Government would consult the social partners regarding the implementation of the Directive more generally, and in particular: (i) mechanisms for resolving disputes regarding the definition of equal treatment and compliance with the new rules that avoid undue delays for workers and unnecessary administrative burdens for business; (ii) appropriate arrangements to enable the two sides of industry and also public services to reach appropriate agreements on the treatment of agency workers, while respecting the overall protection of agency workers; and (iii) appropriate anti-avoidance measures reflecting Article 9(2), in particular relating to the treatment of repeat contracts for the same worker and the position of workers with permanent contracts of employment with agencies who continue to be paid between assignments; it is not intended that Article 5(2) will be used to evade the aims of the Directive.

---

spent on litigating this issue in tribunals and on appeals might in some cases be invested more productively in making representations to and through bodies which can pursue the debate on policy or even reform the law.'

67. See *Agency Workers Joint Declaration by Government, the CBI and the TUC*, set out in Annex C to the Department for Business Enterprise & Regulatory Reform document *Employment Agencies – Implementation of the Agency Workers Directive: A Consultation Paper* (May 2009), at 81.

Finally, it was agreed that the new arrangements were to be reviewed 'at an appropriate point in the light of experience'.

With the declared commitment of the 'social partners' to the national strategy for dealing with the proposed Directive, therefore, the Labour government felt able to 'engage with its European partners to seek agreement on the terms of the Agency Workers Directive that will enable this agreement to be brought into legal effect in the United Kingdom' – expressing, too, the aspiration that 'the Government hopes that EU agreement will be obtained in time for the necessary UK implementing legislation to be introduced in the next parliamentary session'.

The eventual implementation of the Directive's provisions into domestic UK law was undertaken through the enactment of the Agency Workers Regulations 2010, which came into force on 1 October 2011.[68] That implementing instrument reflects – as is normally the case with UK implementation of EU Directive provisions – an attempt to integrate the requirements of the Directive – which has application both in the private sector and across much of the public sector[69] – within the 'natural shape' of existing domestic labour market regulation.

Thus, the definitions included in Article 3 of the Directive find their way into the domestic statutory terminology through Regulations 2, 3 and 4, which, in particular, include a definition of 'worker', for the purposes of the Regulations, to mean:

> an individual who is not an agency worker but who has entered into or works under (or where the employment has ceased, worked under) — (a) a contract of employment, or (b) any other contract, whether express or implied and (if it is express) whether oral or in writing, whereby the individual undertakes to do or perform personally any work or services for another party to the contract whose status is not by virtue of the contract that of a client or customer of any profession or business undertaking carried on by the individual.

This has the consequence that the notion of 'agency worker' (which is defined in Regulation 3) applies, for the purposes of the 2010 regulatory arrangements, without interference from any notion of 'the worker' elsewhere in UK labour law. By the same token, the notion of the 'temporary work agency' is defined by Regulation 4 as the object of regulation under these implementing provisions.

Regulation 5 sets out the rights of agency workers in relation to 'basic working and employment conditions' – although with adjustment of the notions contained in Article 3(1)(f) of the Directive, to take account of the particular UK legal position in respect of 'collective agreements' and 'other binding general provisions'.[70] In that context, the 'relevant terms and conditions' are further described in Regulation 6,

---

68. S.I. 2010 No. 93.
69. See, in particular, Regulation 21, together with the 'special' provisions in relation to House of Lords staff (Regulation 22), House of Commons staff (Regulation 23), and police service (Regulation 24).
70. For the nature and legal effect of the 'collective agreement' under UK law, see *inter alia* F. Schmidt & A. Neal, *Collective Agreements and Collective Bargaining* (International Encyclopedia of Comparative Law, vol. XV, ch. 12, Tübingen 1984); A. Neal, *The Collective Agreement as a Public Law Instrument*, in *United Kingdom Law in the 1980s* (E. Banakas ed., J.C.B. Mohr 1988).

while the enjoyment of the Regulation 5 rights is made subject to a qualifying period – requiring the agency worker to 'work in the same role with the same hirer for 12 continuous calendar weeks, during one or more assignments'.[71] That latter provision reflects the terms of the *Agency workers joint declaration by government, the CBI and the TUC*, reached between the UK 'social partners' in May 2008,[72] and derives its legitimacy from the finally negotiated wording of Article 5(4) of the Directive, which expressly provides that such arrangements 'may include a qualifying period for equal treatment'.

Of particular note is the formulation in Regulation 10 of the 2010 Regulations, which introduces into the UK arrangements the so-called 'Swedish derogation' – contained in Article 5(2) of the Directive.[73] This provision, which excludes the operation of the principle of equal treatment in relation to 'an agency worker who has a permanent contract of employment with a temporary work agency', comes into play where such an agency worker receives pay between assignments at a level not less than 50% of the pay paid to the agency worker in a 'relevant pay reference period' – itself defined in detail by Regulation 11.

The rights of agency workers in relation to accessing 'collective facilities and amenities' – as provided for in Article 6 of the Directive – are dealt with by Regulation 12 of the domestic Regulations, while rights in relation to 'access to employment' are contained in Regulation 13.

Meanwhile, various rights to receive information – particularly where contravention of rights provided for by Regulation 5 is believed to have taken place – are set out in Regulation 16, which also contains the 'implicit sanction' that, where there has been a failure by a temporary work agency or a hirer to furnish such information on request, and that failure has been done 'deliberately, and without reasonable excuse' – or if any written statement supplied is 'evasive or equivocal' – then an Employment Tribunal dealing with any subsequent claim against that agency or hirer 'may draw any inference which it considers it just and equitable to draw, including an inference that that temporary work agency or hirer (as the case may be) has infringed the right in question'.[74]

In addition to a prohibition on 'contracting out' of the provisions of the Regulations (contained in Regulation 15)[75] – something common across UK labour law in general – there are also some interesting provisions set out in relation to what is described as 'liability, protections and remedies', with a view to making clear where the formal responsibility for certain 'employer-like' duties is located. These arrangements, contained in Regulation 14, bear a faint resemblance to the approach adopted in the context of the UK's regime for the criminal enforcement of employer duties in respect of the health, safety and hygiene of workers – so that an attempt is made to

---

71. Regulation 7(2).
72. *Supra* n. 66.
73. So named by reason of having been sought by the Swedish government during the course of negotiations between the Member States over the final wording of the Directive.
74. See Regulation 16(9).
75. This makes cross-reference to s. 203 of the Employment Rights Act 1996 (as amended), which is the general provision applicable to domestic labour law rights.

ensure that liability for the discharge of such duties does not 'fall between two stools' where there is more than one potential party bearing the duty.[76]

Closely associated with these enforcement provisions are the protective arrangements contained in Regulation 17, which seek to ensure that an agency worker is not victimized or subjected to 'any detriment' by reason of having relied upon rights contained in the 2010 Regulations – once again, bringing this area into line with commonly found protective provisions applicable to UK labour law at large. Indeed, if the treatment of an agency worker on the basis of having sought to rely upon rights set out in the Regulations reaches the stage of dismissal of the worker, that dismissal will be 'automatically unfair',[77] and subject to enhanced judicial remedies. As with the majority of individual employment rights granted by statute in the UK, provision is made for complaints alleging infringement of the Regulation to be presented to an Employment Tribunal,[78] from which appeal (on a point of law only) lies further to the Employment Appeal Tribunal, the Court of Appeal (Civil Division), and eventually to the United Kingdom Supreme Court.

In terms of the immediate impact of the implementing Regulations, key findings from a survey of the first six months' impact of those Regulations – undertaken for the UK employers' confederation, the CBI, – reflected that:

> almost half of firms (46%) report that their business has been affected; with new bureaucratic burdens increasing the costs and complexity of using agency staff, the most common response of businesses has been reduced use of agency workers (57%) and one in twelve firms (8%) have stopped using agency workers altogether; Companies have had to adapt their resourcing plans, with over a third using more fixed-term contracts (36%) while others are adopting alternative models of temp use, such as the 'Swedish derogation' model of paying between assignments in return for no equal treatment or managed service contracts (27%); and the regulations are having a detrimental impact on work opportunities, with more than one in ten firms (12%) reporting a lower overall headcount and one in six (17%) increasing overtime amongst existing staff rather than use agency temps.[79]

In addition to the business voices complaining about the 'bureaucratic burdens' and the 'red tape' alleged to have been created by the 2010 Regulations, some degree of disappointment has also been expressed on the parts of trade unions, both that the eventual implementation measures are not generous enough and that too many 'loopholes' have been left to enable employers to organize their businesses free from constraints beyond those already in place before October 2011.

One of the areas in which high hopes had been expressed that 'assistance' might be forthcoming through implementation of the 2008 Directive was in relation to the

---

76. Cf. the arrangements for allocating liability in respect of duties contained in the Health and Safety at Work Act 1974, together with the enforcement provisions made in respect of subordinate legislation introduced under powers contained in that Act. See generally, the 'classic' work on this area, *Redgrave's Health and Safety* (8th ed., Butterworths 2012).
77. Regulation 17(1).
78. Regulation 18.
79. CBI, *Facing the Future – The CBI/Harvey Nash Employment Trends Survey 2012* Ch. 8, at 34 (London, July 2012).

identification of 'employee status' within the 'triangular relationship'. Such hopes, indeed, were not confined to the area of activity of temporary work agencies, but extended to clarification of some of the problems raised by senior judges in the Court of Appeal over the past two decades.[80] However, perhaps unsurprisingly, given the definitional provisions in the Directive itself, this has not proved to be the case. Indeed, it has to be recognized that any changes required to UK law in consequence of the adoption of the 2008 Directive do not deal directly with the analytical problem raised by the Court of Appeal in relation to the treatment of 'triangular relationships' – nor was this ever the intention.

With just over a year's experience of the provisions in operation, the first reported testing of the 2010 Regulations has also been taking place before the Employment Tribunals, as litigation begins to address perceived areas of uncertainty or shortcoming. One early clarification has already been forthcoming in a judgment delivered in December 2012 by an Employment Tribunal sitting in Watford, dealing with the obligation to furnish information (including information concerning agency workers) in a public sector 'transfer of undertaking' situation involving the outsourcing of services originally provided by a local authority in the London area.[81] Meanwhile, the judgment of an Employment Tribunal sitting in Hull to hear a group of cases challenging the operation of the 'Swedish derogation' provided for in Regulation 10 of the 2010 Regulations was published in December 2012, and contains a detailed discussion of arrangements purporting to take advantage of the arrangements provided for in Article 5(2) of the Directive.[82] However, these are early days, and one awaits a more substantial flow of reported judgments before any view can be formed as to the manner in which the 2010 provisions are working in practice.

Nevertheless, it may be mentioned that the issue of the utilization and operation of the 'Swedish derogation' is clearly becoming a matter of high profile concern, with industrial action having recently been taken in the 'call centre' sector, where the Communication Workers Union (CWU) has been protesting against the Regulation 10 'loophole', in relation to which, in the reported words of the CWU General Secretary:[83]

> Both agencies and hirers [employers] are at fault for choosing to use these contracts which sign away workers' rights to equal pay, rather than sticking to the spirit of the new legislation which had equal pay at its heart. Agency staff earning less than the living wage are losing out to the tune of £500 or more a month. They're entitled to equal pay but are being exploited. This loophole should be closed.

---

80. See, for example, some of the challenges mentioned *supra*, at footnote 65 – particularly, *per* Mummery LJ in *James v. London Borough of Greenwich*.
81. Case Number 3302128/2012, *Unison v. (1) London Borough of Barnet and (2) NSL Ltd*, in which the judgment of the Employment Tribunal was sent to the parties on 4 Feb. 2013.
82. Case Numbers: 1801581/2012, 1801582/2012, 1801584/2012, 1801586/2012, 1801587/2012 and 1801588/2012, *Bray, Gardner, Hanley, Smith, Tunley and Woolnough v. Monarch Personnel Refuelling (UK) Limited*, in which the judgment of the Employment Tribunal was sent to the parties on 19 December 2012. See also *ACAS*, 'Workplace Snippets, February 2013: Understanding Swedish derogation', posted at http://www.acas.org.uk/index.aspx?articleid=4162 (February 2013).
83. See 'Protests Begin over Agency Workers "Cheated on Pay"', *The Daily Telegraph*, 16 Jan. 2013.

Given that there have been reports of widespread resort by employers in the UK to arrangements reflecting the 'Swedish derogation', this appears to constitute the first significant 'battleground' in relation to the post-Directive regulatory regime to deal with temporary agency work. If it is, indeed, correct that '… thousands of temporary staff working for supermarkets, manufacturers and services firms nationwide have been urged to waive their rights to the new rules, or risk losing their job',[84] one may anticipate a steady flow of challenges before the Employment Tribunals to test the limits of permissible flexibility bestowed by the Regulation 10 provisions.

§10.07 TEMPORARY AGENCY WORKING IN TIMES OF ECONOMIC CRISIS

The developments discussed above make clear that the UK labour market continues to face a period of change and turbulence. At a time when post-financial crisis pressure upon public funds has been driving budget cuts, public sector downsizing, and an increasingly 'cut-throat' environment for business, the tensions between the 'economic dimension' and the 'social dimension' of the world of work have arguably never been so marked. Meanwhile, a shift in government ideology towards increasing sympathy for 'the business case' to deregulate the labour market – a case which all too often finds its justification in anecdotal opinion-based propositions,[85] rather than on the basis of evidence-based research – means that arrangements such as those to provide for temporary agency work are under increasing scrutiny.

Yet, the (to some distasteful) reality remains that pressures for reform, in the name of 'growth, competitiveness and employment',[86] are, if anything, becoming ever more intense. The UK may not be subject to the democratically deficient and sovereign-autonomy-sucking interventions of the euphemistically labelled 'Memoranda of Understanding' imposed upon Greece, Ireland, Portugal, or (in all but name) Italy,[87] but there can be no doubt that – even for a country whose active labour force continues to grow, and where the rate of unemployment stands at a relatively low 7.7%[88] – there is no 'safe haven' in the tempestuous seas of 'austerity policies' for those who would hark back to 'the golden years' of social policy and employment protections.

---

84. *Ibid.*
85. See, for example, the manner in which the United Kingdom government's 'Red Tape Challenge' is conducted – *supra* n. 40.
86. *Supra* n. 25.
87. See Greece: *Memorandum of Understanding on Specific Economic Policy Conditionality, May 2, 2010*; Ireland: *Memorandum of Understanding on Specific Economic Policy Conditionality, November 28, 2010*; Portugal: *Memorandum of Understanding on Specific Economic Policy Conditionality, 3 May 2011*; and the Letter of 5 August 2011, from Mario Draghi (at that time the Governor of the Bank of Italy) and Jean-Claude Trichet (the then President of the European Central Bank) to the (then) Italian Prime Minister, Silvio Berlusconi.
88. Office for National Statistics, *Labour Market Statistics, January 2013* (published 23 Jan. 2013). These show that the employment rate for those aged from 16 to 64 was 71.4%, up 0.1 on June to August 2012 and up 1.1 on a year earlier. There were 29.68 million people in employment aged 16 and over, up 90,000 on June to August 2012 and up 552,000 on a year earlier. Meanwhile, the unemployment rate was 7.7% of the economically active population, down 0.1 on June to August 2012 and down 0.7 on a year earlier. There were 2.49 million unemployed people, down 37,000 on June to August 2012 and down 185,000 on a year earlier.

A decade ago, the *Financial Times* noted that 'sub-contracting as many non-core activities as possible is a central element of the new economy'.[89] That trend has been seen with increasing intensity during the early years of the twenty-first century, and is clearly facilitated in some instances by a move in the direction of utilizing greater number of workers provided through arrangements entered into with temporary work agencies.

So, too, in the wake of the global financial crisis post-2008, pressures upon business make even survival in globalized markets a struggle, while the adoption of measures to achieve an ever-'leaner' labour force constitutes one of the more tempting paths towards financial salvation and some measure of 'profitability'. Calls for the promotion of management methods, or human resource policies, which can promote that 'new, fit for purpose regulatory framework with minimum regulation' to which the UK government aspires ring ever louder,[90] and arrangements such as the provision of temporary agency work, with the 'flexibility' premiums which that is perceived to be capable of delivering, present themselves as ever more attractive.

Yet, there remains a balance to be struck. There are self-evident dangers in a wholehearted commitment to a 'deregulatory' agenda, just as there are problems with the attempt to maintain the protective 'floor of rights' for workers at historic levels. The challenge is whether the short-term price to be paid for long-term economic growth, greater competitiveness and improved prospects for employment is one which is not only 'a price worth paying', but whether it is possible to implement the scale of structural and regulatory reforms which are required for that task, without fatally undermining the social fabric of the very societies in which the world of work plays such an important role.

Writing in 2012, Bryson's research concluded that 'the use of [temporary agency workers] is positively associated with financial performance in the British private sector' and, furthermore, that the effects are 'quantitatively quite substantial'. At the same time, it was observed that the presence of such workers at the workplace 'is negatively associated with employees' well-being' – something which, it was suggested, could potentially be explicable by the presence of temporary agency workers giving rise to 'a labour intensification effect which operates at the level of the whole workplace'. When the impact on wages was taken into account, Bryson further postulated that his findings were consistent with temporary agency workers having 'an adverse effect on employees' experiences at work, perhaps due to a more labour intensive regime, one which is only partly compensated for with higher wages' – all of which, he noted, could be viewed as 'profitable from an employer perspective'.[91]

'Economic survival' *versus* 'employee well-being' is hardly a comfortable choice with which to be presented. As reform of the regulatory framework for employment agencies and businesses moves ahead under the current Coalition government's plans

---

89. *Financial Times*, 31 Jul. 2001, 10.
90. 'Ministerial Foreword' in Department for Business Innovation & Skills, *Implementation of the Agency Workers Directive: Response to Consultation on Draft Regulations* (January 2010), *supra* n. 45.
91. See A. Bryson, *supra* n. 10, at Part 5 (Conclusions).

for 'lighter touch' and more 'deregulated' arrangements, the hope has to be that those charged with the task of striking the appropriate balance between the 'economic' and the 'social' dimensions of the world of work will ensure that, as the government itself puts it, the UK labour market continues to display the fundamental characteristics of being 'flexible, efficient and fair'.

BCLR - BULLETIN OF COMPARATIVE LABOUR RELATIONS

Vol. Title/Author/Year/ISBN

1. Roger Blanpain, *Individual Employment Contracts: Collective Agreements*, 1970.
2. Roger Blanpain, *Social Planning*, 1971 (ISBN 90-312-0018-2).
3. Roger Blanpain, *Guaranteed Income Funds*, 1972 (ISBN 90-312-0019-0).
4. Roger Blanpain, *Employee Participation at the Level of the Enterprise*, 1973 (ISBN 90-312-0020-4).
5. Roger Blanpain, *Vastheid van Betrekking: Staking en Bezetting*, 1974.
6. Roger Blanpain, *Labour Law and Industrial Relations (International Bibliography)*, 1975 (ISBN 90-312-0023-9).
7. Roger Blanpain, *Multinational Enterprises*, 1976 (ISBN 90-312-0024-7).
8. Roger Blanpain, *Worker's Participation in the European Company*, 1977 (ISBN 90-312-0044-1).
9. Roger Blanpain, *Women and Labour*, 1978 (ISBN 90-312-0077-8).
10. Roger Blanpain, *European Conference on Labour Law and Industrial Relations: Multinational Enterprises*, 1979 (ISBN 90-312-0091-3).
11. Roger Blanpain, *Job Security and Industrial Relations*, 1980 (ISBN 90-312-0147-2).
12. Roger Blanpain, Greg Bamber & Russell Lansbury, *Technological Change and Industrial Relations: An International Symposium*, 1983 (ISBN 90-312-0205-3).
13. Roger Blanpain, James Janssen van Raay & A. Moulty, *Worker's Participation in the European Community: The Fifth Directive*, 1984 (ISBN 90-654-4187-5).
14. Roger Blanpain, *Equality and Prohibition of Discrimination in Employment*, 1985 (ISBN 90-654-4215-4).
15. Roger Blanpain, *Restructuring Labour in the Enterprise: Law and Practice in France, F.R. of Germany, Italy, Sweden and the United Kingdom*, 1986 (ISBN 90-654-4283-9).
16. Roger Blanpain & E. Kassalow, *Unions and Industrial Relations: Recent Trends and Prospect: A Comparative Treatment*, 1987 (ISBN 90-654-4294-4).
17. Roger Blanpain & Marco Biagi, *Trade Union Democracy and Industrial Relations*, 1988 (ISBN 90-654-4394-0).
18. Roger Blanpain & Jelle Visser, *In Search of Inclusive Unionism*, 1990 (ISBN 90-654-4439-4).
19. Roger Blanpain, *Flexibility and Wages: A Comparative Treatment*, 1990 (ISBN 90-654-4461-0).

20. Roger Blanpain, Stephen Frenkel & Oliver Clarke, *Economic Restructuring and Industrial Relations in Industrialised Countries,* 1990 (ISBN 90-654-4488-2).
21. Roger Blanpain & Friedrich Fürstenberg, *Structure and Strategy in Industrial Relations,* 1991 (ISBN 90-654-4559-5).
22. Roger Blanpain, Amira Galin & Ozer Carmi, *Flexible Work Patterns and Their Impact on Industrial Relations,* 1991 (ISBN 90-654-4572-2).
23. Roger Blanpain, *Workers' Participation: Influence on Management Decision-Making by Labour in the Private Sector,* 1992 (ISBN 90-654-4600-1).
24. Roger Blanpain, Brian Brooks & Chris Engels, *Employed or Self-Employed,* 1992 (ISBN 90-654-4613-3).
25. Roger Blanpain Tiziano Treu, *Industrial Relations Developments in the Telecommunications Industry,* 1993 (ISBN 90-654-4642-7).
26. Roger Blanpain & Marco Biagi, *Industrial Relations in Small and Medium Sized Enterprises,* 1993 (ISBN 90-654-4696-6).
27. Roger Blanpain & Marco Biagi, *Participative Management and Industrial Relations in a Worldwide Perspective,* 1993 (ISBN 90-654-4769-5).
28. Roger Blanpain, Jacques Rojot & Hoyt N. Wheeler, *Employee Rights and Industrial Justice,* 1994 (ISBN 90-654-4804-7).
29. Roger Blanpain & Ruth Ben-Israel, *Strikes and Lock-Outs in Industrialized Market Economies,* 1994 (ISBN 90-654-4841-1).
30. Roger Blanpain, Kazuo Sugeno & Yasuo Suwa, *The Harmonization of Working Life and Family Life,* 1995 (ISBN 90-411-0064-4).
31. Roger Blanpain & Laszio Nagy, *Labour Law and Industrial Relations in Central and Eastern Europe,* 1996 (ISBN 90-411-0298-1).
32. Roger Blanpain, *Labour Law and Industrial Relations in the European Union,* 1997 (ISBN 90-411-0527-1).
33. Taco Van Peijpe, *Employment Protection under Strain,* 1998 (ISBN 90-411-0528-8).
34. Roger Blanpain, Takashi Araki & Ryuichi Yamakawa, *The Process of Industrialization and the Role of Labour Law in Asia,* 1999 (ISBN 9-041-1104-7-X).
35. Roger Blanpain & Marco Biagi, *Non-standard Work and Industrial Relations,* 1999 (ISBN 90-411-1117-4).
36. Roger Blanpain, *Private Employment Agencies: The Impact of ILO Convention 181 (1997) and the Judgment of the European Court of Justice of 11 December 1997,* 1999 (ISBN 90-411-1118-2).
37. Roger Blanpain, *Multinational Enterprises and the Social Challenges of the XXIst Century: The ILO Declaration on Fundamental* Principles *at Work, Public and Private Corporate Codes of Conduct,* 2000 (ISBN 90-411-1280-4).
38. Roger Blanpain, Ryuichi Yamakawa & Takashi Araki, *Deregulation and Labour Law: In Search of a Labour Concept for the 21st Century,* 2000 (ISBN 90-411-1370-3).
39. Roger Blanpain, *The Council of Europe and the Social Challenges of the XXIst Century,* 2001 (ISBN 90-411-1543-9).

40. Roger Blanpain, *On-Line Rights for Employees in the Information Society, Use & Monitoring of E-Mail & Internet at Work*, 2002 (ISBN 90-411-1626-5).
41. Roger Blanpain, *The Evolving Employment Relationship and the New Economy: The Role of Labour Law & Industrial Relations*, 2001 (ISBN 90-411-1691-5).
42. Roger Blanpain, *Involvement of Employees in the European Union, Works Councils, Company Statute, Information and Consultation Rights*, 2002 (ISBN 90-411-1760-1).
43. Michele Colucci, *The Impact of the Internet and New Technologies on the Workplace: A Legal Analysis from a Comparative Point of View*, 2002 (ISBN 90-411-1824-1).
44. Roger Blanpain, *White Paper on the Labour Market in Italy: The Quality of European Industrial Relations and Changing Industrial Relations*, 2002 (ISBN 90-411-1841-1).
45. Roger Blanpain, Russell D. Lansbury & Young-Bum Park, *Impact of Globalisation on Employment Relations: A Comparison of the Automobile and Banking Industries in Australia and Korea*, 2002 (ISBN 90-411-1850-0).
46. Roger Blanpain & Antoine Jacobs, *Employee Rights in Bankruptcy: A Comparative-Law Assessment*, 2002 (ISBN 90-411-1942-6).
47. Roger Blanpain, Takashi Araki & Shinya Ouchi, *Corporate Restructuring and the Role of Labour Law*, 2003 (ISBN 90-411-1949-3).
48. Roger Blanpain, *Collective Bargaining, Discrimination, Social Security and European Integration*, 2003 (ISBN 90-411-2010-6).
49. Roger Blanpain & Luis Aparicio-Valdez, *Labour Relations in the Asia- Pacific Countries*, 2004 (ISBN 90-411-2239-7).
50. Roger Blanpain & Ronnie Graham, *Temporary Agency Work and the Information Society*, 2004 (ISBN 90-411-2252-4).
51. Roger Blanpain, *The Actors of Collective Bargaining: A World Report*, 2004 (ISBN 90-411-2253-2).
52. Roger Blanpain & Michele Colucci, *The Globalisation of Labour Standards: The Soft Law Track*, 2004 (ISBN 90-411-2303-2).
53. Roger Blanpain, Takashi Araki & Shinya Ouchi, *Labour Law in Motion: Diversification of the Labour Force & Terms and Conditions of Employment*, 2005 (ISBN 90-411-2315-6).
54. Roger Blanpain, *Smoking and the Workplace*, 2005 (ISBN 90-411-2325-3).
55. Roger Blanpain, *Confronting Globalization: The Quest for a Social Agenda*, 2005 (ISBN 90-411-2381-4).
56. Roger Blanpain, Thomas Blanke & Edgar Rose, *Collective Bargaining Wages in Comparative Perspective: Germany, France, the Netherlands, Sweden and the United Kingdom*, 2005 (ISBN 90-411-2388-1).
57. Roger Blanpain & Anne Numhauser-Henning, *Women in Academia & Equality Law: Aiming High - Falling Short?*, 2006 (ISBN 978-90-411-2427-6).
58. Roger Blanpain, *Freedom of Services in the European Union: Labour and Social Security Law: The Bolkestein Initiative*, 2006 (ISBN 978-90-411-2453-5).
59. Roger Blanpain, Frans Pennings & Nurhan Sural, *Flexibilisation and Modernisation of the Turkish Labour Market*, 2006 (ISBN 978-90-411-2490-X).

60. Roger Blanpain & Boel Flodgren, *Corporate and Employment Perspectives in a Global Business Environment* 2006 (ISBN 978-90-411-2537-X).
61. Roger Blanpain, Shinya Ouchi & Takashi Araki, *Decentralizing Industrial Relations and The Role of Labor Unions and Employee Representatives*, 2007 (ISBN 978-90-411-2583-3).
62. Roger Blanpain, *European Framework Agreements and Telework: Law and Practice: A European and Comparative Study*, 2007 (ISBN 978-90-411-2560-4).
63. Roger Blanpain, Jim Kitay, Leanne Cutcher & Nick Wailes, *Globalization and Employment Relations in Retail Banking*, 2007 (ISBN 978-90-411-2620-1).
64. Roger Blanpain, Russell Lansbury, Jim Kitay, Nick Wailes & Anja Kirsch, *Globalization and Employment Relations in the Auto Assembly Industry*: A *Study of Seven Countries*, 2008 (ISBN 978-90-411-2698-6).
65. Roger Blanpain & Michele Tiraboschi, *The Global Labour Market: From Globalization to Flexicurity*, 2008 (ISBN 978-90-411-2722-8).
66. Roger Blanpain, Michele Colucci & Frank Hendrickx, *The Future of Sport in the European Union: Beyond the EU Reform Treaty and the White Paper*, 2008 (ISBN 978-90-411-2761-7).
67. Roger Blanpain, Linda Dickens, *Challenges in European Employment Relations: Employment Regulation, Trade Union Organization, Equality, Flexicurity, Training and New Approaches to Pay*, 2008 (ISBN 978-90-411-2771-6).
68. Roger Blanpain, Hiroya Nakakubo & Takashi Araki, *New Developments in Employment Discrimination Law*, 2008 (ISBN 978-90-411-2782-2).
69. Roger Blanpain, Andrzej Marian Świątkowski, *The Laval and Viking Cases: Freedom of Services and Establishment v. Industrial Conflict in the European Economic Area and Russia*, 2009 (ISBN 978-90-411-2850-8).
70. Roger Blanpain, William Bromwich, Olga Rymkevich, Silvia Spattini, *The Modernization of Labour Law and Industrial Relations in a Comparative Perspective*, 2009 (ISBN 978-90-411-2865-2).
71. Roger Blanpain, Juan Pablo Landa & Brian Langille, *Employment Policies and Multilevel Governance*, 2009 (ISBN 978-90-411-2866-9).
72. Roger Blanpain, European Works Councils; *The European Directive 2009/ 38/EC of 6 May 2009*, 2009 (ISBN 978-90-411-3208-6).
73. Roger Blanpain, William Bromwich, Olga Rymkevich & Silvia Spattini, *Labour Productivity, Investment in Human Capital and Youth Employment: Comparative Developments and Global Responses*, 2010 (ISBN 978-90-411-3249-9).
74. Greg J. Bamber & Philippe Pochet, *Regulating Employment Relations, Work and Labour Laws: International Comparisons between Key Countries*, 2010 (ISBN 978-90-411-3199-7). General Editor: Roger Blanpain.
75. Roger Blanpain, Desislava Nikolaeva Dimitrova, *Seafarers' Rights in the Globalized Maritime Industry*, 2010 (ISBN 978-90-411-3349-6).
76. Roger Blanpain, Hiroya Nakakubo & Takashi Araki, *Regulation of Fixed- Term Employment Contracts*, 2010 (ISBN 978-90-411-3356-4).
77. Roger Blanpain, William Bromwich, Olga Rymkevich & Iacopo Senatori, *Rethinking Corporate Governance*, 2011 (ISBN 978-90-411-3450-9).

78. Roger Blanpain & Frank Hendrickx, *Labour Law between Change and Tradition: Liber Amicorum Antoine Jacobs,* 2011 (ISBN 978-90-411-3424-0).
79. Roger Blanpain, Thomas Klebe, Marlene Schmidt & Bernd Waas, *Trade Union Rights at the Workplace,* 2012 (ISBN 978-90-411-3460-8).
80. Roger Blanpain, William Bromwich, Olga Rymkevich & Iacopo Senatori, *Labour Markets, Industrial Relations and Human Resources Management: From Recession to Recovery,* 2012 (ISBN 978-90-411-4004-3).
81. Roger Blanpain, Hiroya Nakakubo & Takashi Araki, *Systems of Employee Representation at the Enterprise: A Comparative Study,* 2012 (ISBN 978-90-411-4080-7).
82. Roger Blanpain & Frank Hendrickx, *Temporary Agency Work in the European Union and the United States*, 2013 (ISBN 978-90-411-4769-1).